Exercises in Sociology
A Lab Manual for the Study of Social Behavior

Kelly McGeever
State University of New York at Albany

and

Charles Faupel
Auburn University

Upper Saddle River, New Jersey 07458

Dedicated to
sociology undergraduate students everywhere,
and especially to our students at
SUNY-Albany and Auburn University

Editorial Director: Leah Jewell
AVP, Publisher: Nancy Roberts
Director of Marketing: Brandy Dawson
Marketing Manager: Lindsey Prudhomme
Marketing Assistant: Jessica Muraviov
Editiorial Assistant: Lee Peterson
Prepress and Manufacturing Buyer: Christina Amato
Full-Service Project Management: Bruce Hobart/Pine Tree Composition, Inc.
Production Liaison: Cheryl Keenan
Cover Art Director: Jayne Conte
Cover Designer: Bruce Kenselaar
Composition: Laserwords Private Limited
Printer/Binder: Bind-Rite Graphics
Type Font/Style: 10/12 Baskerville

For permission to use copyrighted material, grateful acknowledgment is made to the copyright holders listed on the appropriate page within the text.

10 9 8 7 6 5 4 3 2 1

ISBN-13: 978-0-13-194661-3
ISBN-10: 0-13-194661-7

Contents

Introduction

We are pleased to make this collection of exercises and readings available to our colleagues. This project began a number of years ago as a response to a need at our school, Auburn University, for what we called a "lab component" to our introductory sociology courses. We were not comfortable with many of the materials available. It was not so much the fact that there were not good outside-of-class exercises available; there were. Some of them were even included as part of student and instructor manuals or in the end-of-chapter materials in textbooks. The problem, rather, was a lack of consistency in quality and availability across textbooks. Hence, the purpose of this manual is to bring together a variety of materials with different levels of difficulty in a single volume.

There are several features that we would like to highlight in this volume of *Exercises in Sociology*. First, each chapter begins with a short reading to introduce the topic with substantive material that will be meaningful to the student. Some of these readings are classical materials, such as an excerpt from C. Wright Mills, *The Promise* (excerpted from *The Sociological Imagination*), that in our opinion, every student of sociology should be exposed to if only in abbreviated form. There are also several excerpts from some of the more readable but nevertheless scholarly materials produced by sociologists, such as the colorful *Banana Time* by Donald Roy. Finally, we have included several articles published in the popular press and written for lay audiences, which have a strong sociological message. *Millions for Viagra, Pennies for Diseases of the Poor*, authored by Ken Silverstein and published in *The Nation* is one such article.

Each chapter includes three major exercises that require distinct types of research. First, there are *internet exercises* which require students to search the internet for information, and, in many cases, to reflect on that information. Some of these exercises provide the necessary URL addresses, while others require the students to conduct their own search. The second type of exercises we have titled *individual writing exercises*. Responses to these exercises are varied and may involve outside reading, interviews with individuals, or observations of social life. In all cases, students are asked to synthesize a written response to these assignments. Finally, there are *group exercises*, which typically involve group discussions with group or individual written summaries of these discussions.

Finally, in addition to the exercises themselves, each exercise comes with a discussion of the issue at hand, and an *idea in use* that highlights some research on this particular issue, all relevant to the exercise to be completed. These discussions provide students with the necessary background material to complete the exercise if this information is not covered by the text or lecture. While we do not intend this volume to be used as a sole text for this course, these discussions should provide sufficient background for the student to complete the exercise effectively if a professor decides not to use another text. We do want to emphasize, however, that these discussions do not address all of the issues and topics that are necessary to provide a comprehensive overview of the general topic in question.

We urge professors to use this volume in ways that will enhance the course. The quantity of exercises contained here are much too numerous to use completely. Faculty who are prone to have a heavy load of exercises may find that they can use one exercise per chapter. Some courses will allow less. The purpose here is to provide enough material so that faculty can have an ample selection of meaningful out-of-class assignments for their students. Indeed, individual faculty may decide to require certain exercises, but eliminate one or more of the questions or research activities associated with that exercise. *This is the way that this volume should be used.* Our hope is that careful and strategic use of these materials will provide the student with the basis for a much richer experience and a more compelling introduction to the world through the lens of sociology.

Kelly McGeever
State University of New York at Albany

Charles Faupel
Auburn University

The Sociological Perspective

The Promise
C. Wright Mills

Labs
Internet Exercise: Sociology on the Internet
Individual Writing Exercise: Marginal Voices in Sociology
Group Exercise: The Sociological Imagination

The Promise

Nowadays men often feel that their private lives are a series of traps. They sense that within their everyday worlds, they cannot overcome their troubles, and in this feeling, they are often quite correct: What ordinary men are directly aware of and what they try to do are bounded by the private orbits in which they live; their visions and their powers are limited to the close-up scenes of job, family, neighborhood; in other milieux, they move vicariously and remain spectators. And the more aware they become, however vaguely, of ambitions and of threats which transcend their immediate locales, the more trapped they seem to feel.

Underlying this sense of being trapped are seemingly impersonal changes in the very structure of continent-wide societies. The facts of contemporary history are also facts about the success and the failure of individual men and women. When a society is industrialized, a peasant becomes a worker; a feudal lord is liquidated or becomes a businessman. When classes rise or fall, a man is employed or unemployed; when the rate of investment goes up or down, a man takes new heart or goes broke. When wars happen, an insurance salesman becomes a rocket launcher; a store clerk, a radar man; a wife lives alone; a child grows up without a father. Neither the life of an individual nor the history of a society can be understood without understanding both.

Yet men do not usually define the troubles they endure in terms of historical change and institutional contradiction. The well-being they enjoy, they do not usually impute to the big ups and downs of the societies in which they live. Seldom aware of the intricate connection between the patterns of their own lives and the course of world history, ordinary men do not usually know what this connection means for the kinds of men they are becoming and for the kinds of history-making in which they might take part. They do not possess the quality of mind essential to grasp the interplay of man and society, of biography and history, of self and world. They cannot cope with their personal troubles in such ways as to control the structural transformations that usually lie behind them....

...What they need, and what they feel they need, is a quality of mind that will help them to use information and to develop reason in order to achieve lucid summations of what is going on in the world and of what may be happening within themselves. It is this quality, I am going to contend, that journalists and scholars, artists and publics, scientists and editors are coming to expect of what may be called the sociological imagination.

1

The sociological imagination enables its possessor to understand the larger historical scene in terms of its meaning for the inner life and the external career of a variety of individuals. It enables him to take into account how individuals, in the welter of their daily experience, often become falsely conscious of their social positions. Within that welter, the framework of modern society is sought, and within that framework the psychologies of a variety of men and women are formulated. By such means the personal uneasiness of individuals is focused upon explicit troubles and the indifference of publics is transformed into involvement with public issues.

The first fruit of this imagination—and the first lesson of the social science that embodies it—is the idea that the individual can understand his own experience and gauge his own fate only by locating himself within his period, that he can know his own chances in life only by becoming aware of those of all individuals in his circumstances. In many ways it is a terrible lesson; in many ways a magnificent one. We do not know the limits of man's capacities for supreme effort or willing degradation, for agony or glee, for pleasurable brutality or the sweetness of reason. But in our time we have come to know that the limits of 'human nature' are frighteningly broad. We have come to know that every individual lives, from one generation to the next, in some society; that he lives out a biography, and that he lives it out within some historical sequence. By the fact of his living he contributes, however minutely, to the shaping of this society and to the course of its history, even as he is made by society and by its historical push and shove.

The sociological imagination enables us to grasp history and biography and the relations between the two within society. That is its task and its promise. To recognize this task and this promise is the mark of the classic social analyst. It is characteristic of Herbert Spencer—turgid, polysyllabic, comprehensive; of E. A. Ross—graceful, muckraking, upright; of Auguste Comte and Emile Durkheim; of the intricate and subtle Karl Mannheim. It is the quality of all that is intellectually excellent in Karl Marx; it is the clue to Thorstein Veblen's brilliant and ironic insight, to Joseph Schumpeter's many-sided constructions of reality; it is the basis of the psychological sweep of W.E.H. Lecky no less than of the profundity and clarity of Max Weber. And it is the signal of what is best in contemporary studies of man and society.

No social study that does not come back to the problems of biography, of history, and of their intersections within a society has completed its intellectual journey. Whatever the specific problems of the classic social analysts, however limited or however broad the features of social reality they have examined, those who have been imaginatively aware of the promise of their work have consistently asked three sorts of questions:

1.   What is the structure of this particular society as a whole? What are its essential components, and how are they related to one another? How does it differ from other varieties of social order? Within it, what is the meaning of any particular feature for its continuance and for its change?

2.   Where does this society stand in human history? What are the mechanics by which it is changing? What is its place within and its meaning for the development of humanity as a whole? How does any particular feature we are examining affect, and how is it affected by, the historical period in which it moves? And this period— what are its essential features? How does it differ from other periods? What are its characteristic ways of history-making?

3.   What varieties of men and women now prevail in this society and in this period? And what varieties are coming to prevail? In what ways are they selected and formed, liberated and repressed, made sensitive and blunted? What kinds of 'human nature' are revealed in the conduct and character we observe in this society in this period? And what is the meaning for 'human nature' of each and every feature of the society we are examining?

Whether the point of interest is a great power state or a minor literary mood, a family, a prison, a creed—these are the kinds of questions the best social analysts have asked. They are the intellectual pivots of classic studies of man in society—and they are the questions inevitably raised by any mind possessing the sociological imagination. For that imagination is the capacity to shift from one perspective to another—from the political to the psychological; from examination of a single family to comparative assessment of the national budgets of the world; from the theological school to the military establishment; from considerations of an oil industry to studies of contemporary poetry. It is the capacity to range from the most impersonal and remote transformations to the most intimate features of the human self— and to see the relations between the two. Back of its use there is always the urge to know the social and historical meaning of the individual in the society and in the period in which he has his quality and his being.

That, in brief, is why it is by means of the sociological imagination that men now hope to grasp what is going on in the world, and to understand what is happening in themselves as minute points of the intersections of biography and history within society. In large part, contemporary man's self-conscious view of himself as at least an outsider, if not a permanent stranger, rests upon an absorbed realization of social relativity and of the transformative power of history. The sociological imagination is the most fruitful form of this self-consciousness. By its use men whose mentalities have swept only a series of limited orbits often come to feel as if suddenly awakened in a house with which they had only supposed themselves to be familiar. Correctly or incorrectly, they often come to feel that they can now provide themselves with adequate summations, cohesive assessments, comprehensive orientations. Older decisions that once appeared sound now seem to them products of a mind unaccountably dense. Their capacity for astonishment is made lively again. They acquire a new way of thinking, they experience a transvaluation of values: in a word, by their reflection and by their sensibility, they realize the cultural meaning of the social sciences.

2

Perhaps the most fruitful distinction with which the sociological imagination works is between 'the personal troubles of milieu' and 'the public issues of social structure.'

This distinction is an essential tool of the sociological imagination and a feature of all classic work in social science.

Troubles occur within the character of the individual and within the range of his immediate relations with others; they have to do with his self and with those limited areas of social life of which he is directly and personally aware. Accordingly, the statement and the resolution of troubles properly lie within the individual as a biographical entity and within the scope of his immediate milieu—the social setting that is directly open to his personal experience and to some extent his willful activity. A trouble is a private matter: values cherished by an individual are felt by him to be threatened.

Issues have to do with matters that transcend these local environments of the individual and the range of his inner life. They have to do with the organization of many such milieu into the institutions of an historical society as a whole, with the ways in which various milieux overlap and interpenetrate to form the larger structure of social and historical life. An issue is a public matter: some value cherished by publics is felt to be threatened. Often there is a debate about what that value really is and about what it is that really threatens it. This debate is often without focus if only because it is the very nature of an issue, unlike even widespread trouble, that it cannot very well be defined in terms of the immediate and everyday environments of ordinary men. An issue, in fact, often involves a crisis in institutional arrangements, and often too it involves what Marxists call 'contradictions' or 'antagonisms.'

In these terms, consider unemployment. When, in a city of 100,000, only one man is unemployed, that is his personal trouble and for its relief we properly look to the character of the man, his skills, and his immediate opportunities. But when in a nation of 50 million employees, 15 million men are unemployed, that is an issue, and we may not hope to find its solution within the range of opportunities open to any one individual. The very structure of opportunities has collapsed. Both the correct statement of the problem and the range of possible solutions require us to consider the economic and political institutions of the society, and not merely the personal situation and character of a scatter of individuals.

Consider war. The personal problem of war, when it occurs may be how to survive it or how to die in it with honor; how to make money out of it; how to climb into the higher safety of the military apparatus; or how to contribute to the war's termination. In short, according to one's values, to find a set of milieu and within it to survive the war or make one's death in it meaningful. But the structural issues of war have to do with its causes; with what types of men it throws up into command, with its effects upon economic and political, family and religious institutions, with the unorganized irresponsibility of a world of nation-states.

Consider marriage. Inside a marriage a man and a woman may experience personal troubles, but when the divorce rate during the first four years of marriage is 250 out of every 1,000 attempts this is an indication of a structural issue having to do with the institutions of marriage and the family and other institutions that bear upon them.

Or consider the metropolis—the horrible, beautiful, ugly, magnificent sprawl of the great city. For many upper-class people, the personal solution to 'the problem of the city' is to have an apartment with private garage under it in the heart of the city, and forty miles out, a house by Henry Hill, garden by Garrett Eckbo, on a hundred acres of private land. In these two controlled environments—with a small staff at each end and a private helicopter connection—most people could solve many of the problems of personal milieu caused by the facts of the city. But all this, however splendid, does not solve the public issues that the structural fact of the city poses. What should be done with this wonderful monstrosity? Break it all up into scattered units, combining residence and work? Refurbish it as it stands? Or, after evacuation, dynamite it and build new cities according to new plans in new places?

What should those plans be? And who is to decide and to accomplish whatever choice is made? These are structural issues; to confront them and to solve them requires us to consider political and economic issues that affect innumerable milieu.

In so far as an economy is so arranged that slumps occur, the problem of unemployment becomes incapable of personal solution. In so far as war is inherent in the nation-state system and in the uneven industrialization of the world, the ordinary individual in his restricted milieu will be powerless—with or without psychiatric aid—to solve the troubles this system or lack of system imposes upon him. In so far as the family as an institution turns women into darling little slaves and men into their chief providers and unweaned dependents, the problem of a satisfactory marriage remains incapable of purely private solution. In so far as the overdeveloped megalopolis and the overdeveloped automobile are built-in features of the overdeveloped society, the issues of urban living will not be solved by personal ingenuity and private wealth.

What we experience in various and specific milieu, I have noted, is often caused by structural changes. Accordingly, to understand the changes of many personal milieu we are required to look beyond them. And the number and variety of such structural changes increase as the institutions within which we live become more embracing and more intricately connected with one another. To be aware of the idea of social structure and to use it with sensibility is to be capable of tracing such linkages among a great variety of milieu. To be able to do that is to possess the sociological imagination.

LABS

Internet Exercise

Sociology on the Internet

Introduction

The cyberspace community provides a wide variety of informational and recreational sites that are quickly accessible. According to the United States Census Department, in 2001, 56 percent of households owned one or more home computers and 50 percent had internet access at the home. Of households containing children ages 6–17, over 70 percent had a computer and 64 percent had the internet at home. Clearly, technology and communication has infiltrated households and spawned a global generation. The internet allows for the global transfer of ideas and has greatly affected economics and globalization.

Sociology websites are available on the internet that allow both the professional sociologist and the novice student to learn more about the discipline, explore the social world, and make available research findings. Professional associations utilize the net to easily inform their global and national membership of meetings, exciting findings, and to offer networking opportunities. Sociology departments in colleges and universities create webpages to inform prospective students about their programs and to allow current students to be informed about requirements and classes. Other sociology websites are created by individuals and supply a general overview of what sociology is (or what they think it should be!) and its many uses. Oftentimes, sociology websites will provide links to other websites that may prove useful.

Idea in Use

The creation of a global internet community has spawned a new sociology sub-field, oftentimes called cybersociology or sociology of the internet. This new field encompasses many of the other sub-fields in sociology. For instance, one can look at the culture of internet usage; investigate the socialization process and interaction of such usage; and identify dimensions of stratification and identity, globalization, and even deviance.

However, there are unintended consequences of immediate access to a multitude of informative sites on the web. Academic cheating, plagiarism, and copyright infringements are some of the most central issues for students. The Center for Academic Integrity (CAI) at Rutgers University has found a considerable increase in the number of college students who admit to internet plagiarism. In 1999, only 10 percent of those surveyed admitted to lifting internet material and using it as their own. However, just two years later, 41 percent admitted to such behavior. In a comparative survey using high school students, more than half admitted to plagiarizing term papers and essays they found on the internet. Various websites now offer term papers for a price, but the quality and price can vary with each click of the mouse. Teachers and educational administrators have tried to counteract the cheating with their own websites that will review suspect papers.

Colleges and universities take academic integrity very seriously and will enact disciplinary measures on students and prospective students who have been dishonest. For instance, in Spring 2005, hackers posted instructions on a *Business Week Online* forum for applicants to find out school admissions decisions before the school released such information. Harvard University, the Massachusetts Institute of Technology, and Stanford University's Graduate School of Business uniformly rejected all applicants who tried to access the records before their scheduled release dates.

Activity Instructions

You will be visiting and exploring various sociology-related websites and evaluating them by their appearance, content provided, and relevance to a non-academic. There is much information that can be learned from these websites and it may be useful to revisit them throughout this course and any other sociology class you may take.

1. Go to two websites from the general sociology website category.

   General Sociology Websites:
   www2.pfeiffer.edu/~lridener/dss/deadsoc.html
   www.trinity.edu/~mkearl/index.html
   www.pscw.uva.nl/sociosite/
   www.socioweb. com/~markbl/socioweb

   a. What are the titles of the websites (the names are generally found on the top bar running across the page)?
   b. Explore each website and give a general description of the focus of the site.
   c. Compare and contrast the websites. Which one is more useful for you? Is the information provided fact-based or are they opinion? Are there problems with either site? If so, what are they?

2. Now evaluate two of the websites from the professional associations category and complete parts a through c as you did in question 1.

   Professional Associations:
   www.alpha-kappa-delta.org
   www.asanet.org
   www.socwomen.org
   www.blacksociologists.org
   www.sssp1.org

3. Finally, you are to pick two colleges or universities (other than your own) and find their sociology department websites. Evaluate these sites for content and appearance. Which one appeals to you more? Is the site focused more on prospective or current students? Do they have links to other sociology homepages? Any other interesting observations?

4. Turn in your completed assignment to your instructor. Make sure that you indicate which websites you visited to get full credit.

Individual Writing Exercise

Marginal Voices in Sociology

Introduction

While often overlooked in their lifetime, racial minorities, and women contributed to the science of sociology. Recent attention to the marginal voices has uncovered a wealth of knowledge and insight to social problems. Many of the sociologists who were ignored at the time made specific strides in identifying and describing social structures that affected their very own marginalized group. Unfortunately, because of the political and social climate of the times, their contributions were largely ignored.

The first woman pioneer in the sociological discipline was Harriet Martineau (1802–1876). Martineau first translated Comte's work before concentrating on her own research. She then turned her attention to the customs of her native Britain and the United States. Her most recognized work is the book *Society in America* which examined social institutions with respect to race and gender. Jane Addams (1860–1935), from the sociology department at the University of Chicago, developed the field of applied sociology. Her work with the underprivileged, political activism, and urban studies earned her recognition as a winner of the Nobel Peace Prize in 1931. While these are certainly not the only marginalized female voices, they are two of the first female pioneers in the field.

Racial minorities have also contributed to the field although their voices were initially muted due to societal conditions. African American, Hispanic, Native American, and Asian sociologists continually contribute to sociological advancements. One of the first black sociologists recognized as a contributor was W.E.B. DuBois. He was the first black man to earn his doctorate in sociology (from Harvard) and used his position to challenge the status quo. He advocated for more political freedom for blacks, wrote about the condition of black Americans in urban society and was outspoken about racial inequalities. He went on to serve as a founding member of the National Association for the Advancement of Colored People.

Idea in Use

While it is easy to see and believe that in the past marginal voices were not as loud, some people still may be hesitant to believe that minorities are silenced in the present day. A 2004 article in *Teaching Sociology* suggests that the work of women sociologists is still not fully integrated into sociology curriculum. Jan Thomas and Annis Kukulan contend in their article "Why Don't I Know about These Women?: The Integration of Early Women Sociologists in Classical Theory Courses," contend that the training of graduate students perpetuates the silencing since graduate students may not be exposed to the influential work of women sociologists. They reviewed graduate school syllabi and found that the work of women sociologists comprise only 17 percent of the overall material assigned. Rather than being pessimistic, the authors feel that this 17 percent is an improvement on the past and push for more inclusion of the writings of women sociologists at all academic levels.

Activity Instructions

In this exercise, you will be learning more about marginal sociologists by writing a biography of a minority social scientist.

1. From the list below choose one of the sociologists to investigate. If you have a special preference to learn more about another minority sociologist not listed,

you may do so but be sure to clear your choice with your instructor before you proceed. Some of the sociologists listed below are historical figures, while others are currently working in the field.

Ruth Benedict	Patricia Hill Collins
Jessie Bernard	Charles Johnson
Nancy Chodorow	Ramiro Martinez
Oliver Cox	Alejandro Portes
W.E.B. DuBois	Ruben Rumbaut
E. Franklin Frazier	Julian Samora
Martha Gimenez	William Julius Wilson

2. Using library and internet resources, briefly sketch their biography. Identify important dates, their education, major themes of their work, their important contributions to the field and any pertinent personal details. Also discuss why you chose to profile them and provide a list of their books or major articles.

3. Your write-up should provide a good overview of your chosen's life in about two typed, double-spaced pages. In your final paragraph, summarize the difficulty level for finding information about your selected person.

4. Turn in your exercise as directed by your instructor.

Group Exercise

The Sociological Imagination

Introduction

There are several social sciences that attempt to explain the human condition. Cultural anthropology, economics, history, political science, psychology, social work, and sociology are scientific disciplines that often overlap in subject matter, but approach social problems with different perspectives.

Most simply, sociology is the study of human social behavior. Among other things, sociologists are interested in learning about the relationship between the individual and society. They look for societal influences on individual experiences and how social networks create social change. They also search for general patterns of behavior.

One unique aspect of the sociological perspective is a term coined by sociologist C. Wright Mills in 1959 to describe a way of thinking. The *sociological imagination* is a way of thinking creatively about ourselves, society, and the relationship between self and society. The sociological imagination is a tool that people can use to observe and analyze society as an outsider, without the biases of experience and socialization. It allows one to be able to discuss faraway nations and cultures, to see connections between social problems and individual problems, and provides the ability to sense the connections between our own private lives and the larger social world. Sociological imagination is shaped by the history of social structures and their unending effects on a person's life history.

For example, when one is investigating the plight of the homeless, it is necessary to look at the social structures that created the situation, rather than blaming a personal defect as the cause of their status. Perhaps the person received little or poor education and faced limited work opportunities as a result, economic downturns may have caused layoffs, addiction problems may have consumed all monies, an abusive relationship may have forced a family onto the street, etc. There are a myriad of possible scenarios that could have contributed to the situation and each scenario must be investigated to benefit the individual.

Idea in Use

The sociological imagination is an important tool to be used by an effective and creative interviewer. Studs Terkel, a Pulitzer Prize-winning author and interviewer specializing in oral history, uses the sociological imagination to conduct numerous interviews of celebrities and everyday American people. His book, *American Dreams: Lost and Found,* features interviews from across the country with people of diverse socioeconomic backgrounds. Terkel has a talent for delving into an individual's private world and relating the individual experience to a collective American life. Other books focus on the oral histories of the Depression era, World War II, race relations, labor and working, and aging. He is a prolific interviewer and has been awarded the Presidential National Humanities Award (1999) and the National Medal of Humanities (1997) among numerous book awards. For more information about the life and work of Studs Terkel, visit www.studsterkel.org.

Activity Instructions

In small groups, you will discuss your own biography and the personal experiences that have shaped your identity. Then, you will relate your individual experiences to those in your small group, and then to the larger social world that surrounds you. Using sociological imagination, you will relate the personal to the communal and then to social structures and processes. One person should record the main findings.

1. In groups of 3–5 people, take turns talking about your own biography. The prompts below should guide your history but feel free to discuss more.

   - Discuss your family. Were you raised by both your parents, or was your primary caregiver someone else? Any siblings? What was the household division of labor . . . who had full-time jobs, cooked, cleaned, and was responsible for childcare, etc.?
   - Describe your economic history. What social class would you characterize your family? What kind of occupations and education did your parent(s) have? What kind of school did you attend? How are money matters different now that you are in college?
   - Discuss any significant events that you feel shaped your life. Did you move across the country, have you been the victim of a mugging, been a part of a championship athletic team, etc.? What special events were memorable? What impact do these experiences and events have on your life now?

2. When everyone in your group has gone through their biographies, identify threads that have been repeated by more than one group member. For instance, how many people experienced a divorce within the family while growing up?

3. For one of the most popular threads, discuss how it relates to social institutions and processes. For example, how is society different when divorce is prevalent than when it is more rare? Does divorce create changes in economy, education, family life, culture, crime levels, and so on? On the other hand, do you think changes in the economy, education, family life, culture, and crime levels have an effect on divorce?

4. In your group write up, list the items that your biographies had in common and briefly summarize the links your group found between individual experiences and social structures.

Research Methods

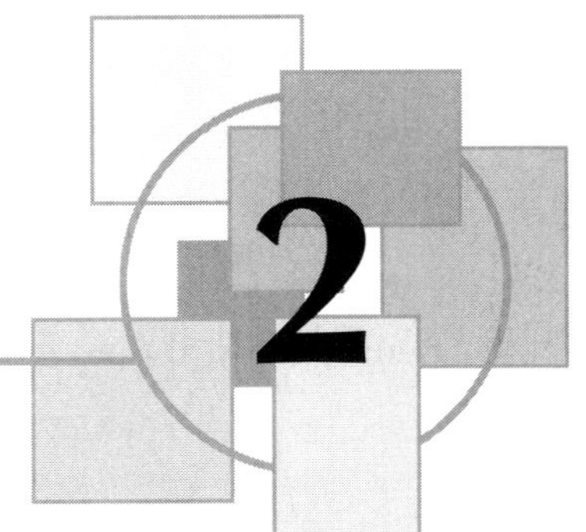

Say What You Mean
G. Evans Witt

Labs
Internet Exercise: Survey Design
Individual Writing Exercise: Participant and Non-Participant Observation
Group Exercise: Choosing a Research Approach

Say What You Mean

Sometimes, just a word or two makes all the difference. Take "as a person." Add that phrase to a question about Bill Clinton and the President's favorability scores drop 20 points.

Or take the emotion-laden issue of abortion. Do 57 percent of Americans think abortion is wrong? Or do 69 percent think a woman should be able to get an abortion? In fact, both are valid poll results. The difference is all in the way the questions are worded.

Critics often dismiss survey results, saying that people's opinions are being forced into neat little boxes of Yes/No or Favor/Oppose on questions that overlook the complexity of many issues in these complicated times. What the critics fail to appreciate is how carefully people listen to poll questions when they are asked for their opinion, and how precisely they are trying to respond.

For example, pollsters trying to gauge the public's reaction to various well-known people often use a "favorability" question that is meant to tap into attitudes toward the person overall, not just his or her job performance. The question is usually asked about a list of people, using wording such as: "I'd like to get your overall opinion of some people in the news. As I read each name, please say if you have a favorable or unfavorable opinion of this person...or if you have never heard of him or her. First..."

But last August, the Gallup Organization conducted a poll for CNN and *USA Today* after President Clinton's grand jury testimony on August 17. With a shorter questionnaire, Gallup simply asked: "Now, thinking about Bill Clinton as a person, do you have a favorable or unfavorable opinion of him?"

That wording—with the magic phrase "as a person"—found a favorability rating for Clinton that was 20 percentage points below that which was found using the longer question the previous week. Gallup did a follow-up survey that showed the change in the wording was responsible for perhaps half of the plunge.

Polls on issues that evoke strong reactions are particularly vulnerable to small changes in wording. At first blush, the poll results regarding gun control and abortion seem to indicate that the American public holds wildly varying views simultaneously.

As part of a regular *Newsweek* poll, Princeton Survey Research Associates asked a series of questions about abortion in late 1998. The response to one question— "Do you personally believe that abortion is wrong?"—seemed to indicate strong support for the pro-life view. A total of 57 percent of the public answered that abortion is wrong. Thirty-six percent said abortion is not wrong. That is solid majority support for the pro-life side. Or so it would appear.

But the very next question found results that the pro-choice side couldn't help but like: "Whatever your own personal view of abortion, do you favor or oppose a woman in this country having the choice to have an abortion with the advice of her doctor?" On this question, 69 percent said they favor a woman having the choice to have an abortion. Only 24 percent said no.

How can these two sets of numbers be reconciled? Isn't the public taking two opposing views on abortion at the same time?

The answer is that the public is listening to the exact questions and giving a nuanced set of answers. It is one thing to be asked if abortion is wrong. But that is not necessarily the same thing as saying a woman should never have the choice to have an abortion under any and all circumstances. For some people, abortion is so wrong that it should never be allowed. For others, their personal opinion on the morality of abortion does not extend to limiting the actions of others.

What's clear is that abortion is a complex and difficult question for many Americans, and they hold complex views on it; no single question can adequately portray those views. The questions that probe into this area must be carefully phrased to pick up these subtleries. Poorly stated or slanted questions simply generate confusing and often meaningless results.

The wording of poll questions is important, whether the issue is abortion, Bill Clinton, what brand of gasoline you buy or what TV show you like. It's impossible to understand a poll's findings without knowing the exact wording of the questions.

The next time someone quotes a poll to you, make sure you ask: "What was the question?"

LABS

Internet Exercise

Survey Design

Introduction

A survey is a research method that sociologists often employ. Surveys are useful in gathering information that is not readily observable, such as people's opinions, attitudes and beliefs. The information collected in surveys can be quantitative (reduced to numbers) and/or qualitative in nature.

The first consideration in using a survey is the *sample*. The sample must be representative of the population in question. A *population* is the collection of people that the researcher wants to study. However, in most cases it would be impossible to survey the entire population. For instance, if one wanted to examine the religious views of Hispanics, it would be nearly impossible and very impractical to attempt to survey every individual. Therefore, a research draws a representative sample from the population. There are various sampling methods that the researcher can use, but oftentimes, *random sampling* is preferred. Random sampling ensures that every member of the population has an equal chance of being included in the study sample.

There are two main forms of surveys: interview and questionnaire. Researchers using an interview form of survey ask individuals a series of open-ended questions, usually in a face-to-face format. An advantage of this form of survey is that the researcher may want to ask follow-up questions to clarify the subject's responses. Also, the subject is likely to complete the interview, which raises the response rate for the study. However, the interviewing process may be extremely time-consuming depending on sample size and study topic. The questionnaire is a written survey that can utilize both open-ended and forced choice responses. Questionnaires are advantageous when the research is studying a large sample that is geographically dispersed. However, it must be properly created to limit any confusion over what the question is intended to ask and avoid any biased phrasing. Questionnaires are notoriously known for low response rates, which can be problematic in generating a sample that is representative of the population.

Idea in Use

It would seem that some questions in surveys are easy to obtain and reliable. A respondent's self-reported racial identification is one that would seem to be consistently reported. However, David Harris and Jeremiah Joseph Sim, sociologists from the University of Michigan, found that about 12 percent of surveyed adolescents provided inconsistent responses to four practically identical questions about their racial identification. In the *American Sociological Review* 2002 article "Who is Multiracial? Assessing the Complexity of Lived Race" the authors found that racial identification can depend on context and that self-classification of race is fluid.

Activity Instructions

In this exercise, you will be using the internet to learn more about sociological surveys.

1. From the list below, select one survey that is commonly used in sociological research to investigate, locate it through search tools on the internet, and then follow the instructions below.

   American Community Survey
   General Social Survey
   National Crime Victimization Survey
   National Election Studies
   National Longitudinal Survey of Youth
   National Survey of Families and Households
   Panel Study of Income Dynamics

2. What is the purpose of the survey? What part of the social world does the survey attempt to evaluate? When did the survey start and how often are people polled?

3. For your selected survey, identify the agency or organization that designs and completes the survey. In addition, determine what population the survey intends to study and how the population is sampled.

4. What types of questions are asked? Are they open-ended or multiple choice? Give examples of the categories of questions asked and specific questions that are asked.

5. Based on your knowledge of the survey, provide a unique research question that the survey may help to answer.

6. Write-up your findings in a brief paper (1–2 double spaced pages) and turn in to your instructor as directed.

Individual Writing Exercise

Participant and Non-Participant Observation

Introduction

Participant observation is a research method in which the researcher interacts and is involved with the society or group that they are studying. This technique is more popular in anthropology but has valid applications in sociology. This *qualitative method* is exploratory and is useful in helping the researcher determine what future research may be needed. The level of participation by the researcher in the group often varies on a continuum of complete immersion in the group at one and a strict observation role on the other. For instance, the researcher may gain access to the group by participating fully with the other group members. They may even try to develop the same thinking patterns, feelings, and behaviors as those they are studying. Other researchers may take a *non-participation* approach and merely observe the behaviors of the group without attempting to present themselves as members of the group. There are often practical and ethical questions about the methodology employed and the level of participation needed for studies. For instance, studying and trying to gain access to and the trust of street gang members might be problematic for some researchers, and could cause ethical problems if the researcher was expected to participate in certain illegal activities.

One of the benefits of using a participation observation design is that the research can provide intimate observations of the behaviors that may not be visible to an outsider. For instance, certain rites of passage that members complete to increase their status may now be detailed and used in understanding the group. By interacting with the subjects, the researcher is able to achieve more insight to the groups' activities than a questionnaire or experimental design might provide. Benefits of taking a non-participatory approach are that it often eliminates the ethical dilemma of deceiving and abusing the trust of true group members and it allows the researcher to study the subjects in their natural setting. Also, when the researcher is concealed to the group and subjects are unaware that they are being watched, the likelihood of the group members acting naturally is greater, generating more quality data.

There are downsides to both the participation observation and non-participation observation methods. Gaining access to the group that the researcher wants to study may be difficult. For example, a researcher may have difficulties obtaining access to the leaders of the Ku Klux Klan. There may be observer effects. This means that group members may project certain attitudes, behaviors, or activities that are favorable to their image, rather than the reality of the group construct. Data collected are subject to researcher bias and rely on the subjective measurement of the researcher. Non-participant observers may not learn all the secretive and detailed activities and may make wrong assumptions about the mindset, beliefs, and values of the group. In addition, time may be a factor for both participant and non-participant observers, as it may take more time to learn the more detailed aspects of the group.

Idea in Use

The studies of race, stratification, poverty, and urban life intersect in Mary Patillo-McCoy's award winning book *Black Picket Fences: Privilege and Peril Among the Black Middle Class* (1999). The book is based on Patillo-McCoy's experience in a middle class neighborhood on the south side of Chicago. She lived in Groveland for three years and participated in community events and organizations. She also completed in-depth interviews with black, middle class residents of Groveland. Through her research, she concluded that the black middle class is in a precarious state, where slight changes to economic and social positions will result in their decline to the poor neighborhoods that surround them. In addition, members of the black middle class have to negotiate and "code switch" between being "street" and being "decent" depending on their interaction partners and environment. Patillo-McCoy richly and truthfully describes the black middle class in a manner that is appealing to academics and people interested in social life. In an appendix of her book, Patillo-McCoy describes her research method as well as problems and limitations of her work.

Activity Instructions

For this exercise, you will complete a non-participant observation study. Choose a public arena—party, shopping mall, athletic event, etc.—and observe as much detail as possible for about an hour. Before you do your fieldwork, jot down some hypotheses (expectations) regarding what you think you will see.

1. Take notes on what you observe. Include how people interact, if the interactions change over time, if there seems to be certain norms or rules to the interaction, what occurs if the norms are violated, etc.?

2. From observing the interactions, what can you tell about the people? Are there differences of ages, genders, ethnicities, and social classes or do the people with the same apparent demographics only interact with each other?

3. When you have completed your observations, organize them into meaningful categories. For example, you might have a category entitled "Non-verbal communication" and another category called "Rules for interaction," etc. Your category topics should emerge out of your notes as you review them.

4. Write up your observations in a meaningful narrative or story of about 2–3 double-spaced pages. You will probably not use all of your observations, but you should include a good number. Be sure to indicate whether (and how) your observations support your hypotheses. Make sure that you also include the details of when and where you completed your study.

5. Submit both your organized fieldwork notes and your summary paper to your instructor as directed.

Group Exercise

Choosing a Research Approach

Introduction

Choosing how one is going to approach the investigation of a problem is a crucial decision. If one chooses a faulty design, the entire research and work will be inconclusive and invalid, as well as a major waste of time. There are roughly four different areas of research design: the survey, observation, experiment, and secondary analysis.

The survey is a study that generally takes the form of a questionnaire or interview and asks about people's opinions, feelings, or actions regarding a particular issue. Survey formulation must take into account wording and question structure so that misunderstandings are limited. The questions should be precise and direct to avoid confusion. Also of importance in an effective survey design is the role of sampling. The researcher must try to find a sample that is representative of the population in question. One disadvantage of surveys is that they usually have low return rates. Interviews can be costly, both monetarily and in terms of time expended.

Observation is a research technique that is often used when one wants to do exploratory research on a population. The researcher joins the population that he or she wants to study and observes the subjects in the natural environment. The amount of involvement that the researcher takes within the study group's environment falls along a continuum. For instance, a researcher wanting to study gang initiations may have to slowly gain the trust of the gang members and participate in their social world. Insofar as the researcher also takes an active role in the life of the group or community he or she is studying, he or she is playing the role of a participant observer. If the researcher merely observes and is not considered another participant, he or she is a non-participant observer. Participant observation is especially demanding as the research must balance the roles of unbiased observer and also participate enough to gain access to the social world of the population. Such a research design is often hard to duplicate and is time-consuming to complete.

Experimentation is another type of research design. It is highly controlled and evaluates cause and effect relationships. The researcher manipulates the variables to test the hypotheses that were specified before beginning the project. Data are collected and analyzed for any links between variables. Experiments are often completed in laboratory settings, which contribute an artificial quality to the study. Another drawback of the experiment design is that the researcher may contribute biasness to the results and might affect how subjects participate.

The existence of previous sources of data is the foundation of secondary analysis. Datasets from agencies like the United States Census Bureau or from past surveys such as the General Social Survey are often utilized. It is easier, less expensive, and more timesaving to use already collected data than to create their own samples and surveys. It also allows the researcher to evaluate how opinions, actions, or feelings have changed over time. However, the researcher has no control over how the data were collected and therefore may have to alter their specific topic to correspond with what is available.

Idea in Use

Not only is the initial choice of research method vital to a researcher's credibility, the implementation and execution of the research plan must also be carefully designed. Extreme findings can receive a lot of attention throughout academia and in the media. For instance, in the book *The Divorce Revolution* (1985), author Lenore Weitzman claimed that women experienced a 73 percent decline in their standard of living after divorce and the standard of living for men in the year following a divorce actually improved by 42 percent. This gender gap garnered attention from the media, policy makers, the public, and of course other sociologists. Some sociologists were skeptical of such a high differential and decided to investigate the claim further. After a decade of debate about the accuracy of the figure and a threat by the National Science Foundation to deny her any chance of future funding, Weitzman finally granted sociologist Richard Peterson access to the data. Using the same methodology as Weitzman, Peterson found that about half of the sample was missing information on a key variable, large discrepancies between the original paper files and those reported electronically, and concluded there were more moderate effects of divorce on standard of living. Specifically, Peterson quantified the standard of living in the one year after a divorce for women to be a 27 percent decrease and a 10 percent increase for men. A single statistical claim erupted a decade long controversy and debate that highlights the importance of not only selecting an appropriate research design, but also giving consideration to the selection of appropriate variables and measures, the value of good record keeping, and the importance of maintaining a critical and analytical approach to evaluating extreme findings. Your reputation may be put on the line if you don't!

Activity Instructions

This group exercise will test your ability to choose the best possible research design to gather information to address specific questions. Your group is asked to identify the most appropriate research design and provide the rationale for the selection.

1. For each of the following scenarios, identify the research design that you feel best investigates the problem. Indicate your reasons for selecting the model and also explain any drawbacks or problems that you may encounter because of your selection.

   Scenario 1: The local city government wants to know whether the local police department has been participating in racial profiling during traffic stops.

   Scenario 2: The college administration wants to know what kinds of classes liberal arts majors enjoy the most, what they plan to do after graduation, and which teachers have most influenced them.

   Scenario 3: You are interested in learning how opinions about homosexuals have changed in the United States, and the differences in approval by men and women.

   Scenario 4: A national parenting group is concerned about violence in the media and the effect on children, so they lobby for a study. Your main objective in the research study is to determine whether watching movies and television shows that contain gratuitous violence increases the aggressiveness level of the viewers more than watching non-violent movies and television shows does.

2. For one of the scenarios, brainstorm with your group about possible variables that you will need to include and problems that you may encounter in trying to complete your research.

3. Turn in the completed assignment to your instructor as directed.

Culture

Body Ritual Among the Nacirema
Horace Miner

Labs
Internet Exercise: Cultural Diversity
Individual Writing Exercise: Cultural Universals and Rites of Passage
Group Exercise: Subcultures

Body Ritual Among the Nacirema

The anthropologist has become so familiar with the diversity of ways in which different peoples behave in similar situations that he is not apt to be surprised by even the most exotic customs. In fact, if all of the logically possible combinations of behavior have not been found somewhere in the world, he is apt to suspect that they must be present in some yet undescribed tribe. This point has, in fact, been expressed with respect to clan organization by Murdock (1949:71). In this light, the magical beliefs and practices of the Nacirema present such unusual aspects that it seems desirable to describe them as an example of the extremes to which human behavior can go.

Professor Linton first brought the ritual of the Nacirema to the attention of anthropologists twenty years ago (1936:326), but the culture of this people is still very poorly understood. They are a North American group living in the territory between the Canadian Cree, the Yaqui and Tarahumare of Mexico, and the Carib and Arawak of the Antilles. Little is known of their origin, although tradition states that they came from the east. According to Nacirema mythology, their nation was originated by a culture hero, Notgnihsaw, who is otherwise known for two great feats of strength—the throwing of a piece of wampum across the river Po-To-Mac and the chopping down of a cherry tree in which the Spirit of Truth resided.

Reprinted from *American Anthropologist*, vol. 58, no. 3, June, 1956, pp. 503–507.

Nacirema culture is characterized by a highly developed market economy which has evolved in a rich natural habitat. While much of the people's time is devoted to economic pursuits, a large part of the fruits of these labors and a considerable portion of the day are spent in ritual activity. The focus of this activity is the human body, the appearance and health of which loom as a dominant concern in the ethos of the people. While such a concern is certainly not unusual, its ceremonial aspects and associated philosophy are unique.

The fundamental belief underlying the whole system appears to be that the human body is ugly and that its natural tendency is to debility and disease. Incarcerated in such a body, man's only hope is to avert these characteristics through the use of the powerful influences of ritual and ceremony. Every household has one or more shrines devoted to this purpose. The more powerful individuals in the society have several shrines in their houses and, in fact, the opulence of a house is often referred to in terms of the number of such ritual centers it possesses. Most houses are of wattle and daub construction, but the shrine rooms of the more wealthy are walled with stone. Poorer families imitate the rich by applying pottery plaques to their shrine walls.

While each family has at least one such shrine, the rituals associated with it are not family ceremonies but are private and secret. The rites are normally only discussed with children, and then only during the period when they are being initiated into these mysteries. I was able, however, to establish sufficient rapport with the natives to examine these shrines and to have the rituals described to me.

The focal point of the shrine is a box or chest which is built into the wall. In this chest are kept the many charms and magical potions without which no native believes he could live. These preparations are secured from a variety of specialized practitioners. The most powerful of these are the medicine men, whose assistance must be rewarded with substantial gifts. However, the medicine men do not provide the curative potions for their clients, but decide what the ingredients should be and then write them down in an ancient and secret language. This writing is understood only by the medicine men and by the herbalists who, for another gift, provide the required charm.

The charm is not disposed of after it has served its purpose, but is placed in the charm-box of the household shrine. As these magical materials are specific for certain ills, and the real or imagined maladies of the people are many, the charm-box is usually full to overflowing. The magical packets are so numerous that people forget what their purposes were and fear to use them again. While the natives are very vague on this point, we can only assume that the idea in retaining all the old magical materials is that their presence in the charm-box, before which the body rituals are conducted, will in some way protect the worshipper.

Beneath the charm-box is a small font. Each day every member of the family, in succession, enters the shrine room, bows his head before the charm-box, mingles different sorts of holy water in the font, and proceeds with a brief rite of ablution. The holy waters are secured from the Water Temple of the community, where the priests conduct elaborate ceremonies to make the liquid ritually pure.

In the hierarchy of magical practitioners, and below the medicine men in prestige, are specialists whose designation is best translated "holy-mouth-men." The Nacirema have an almost pathological horror of and fascination with the mouth, the condition of which is believed to have a supernatural influence on all social relationships. Were it not for the rituals of the mouth, they believe that their teeth would fall out, their gums bleed, their jaws shrink, their friends desert them, and their lovers reject them. They also believe that a strong relationship exists between oral and moral characteristics. For example, there is a ritual ablution of the mouth for children which is supposed to improve their moral fiber.

The daily body ritual performed by everyone includes a mouth-rite. Despite the fact that these people are so punctilious about care of the mouth, this rite involves a practice which strikes the uninitiated stranger as revolting. It was reported to me that the ritual consists of inserting a small bundle of hog hairs into the mouth, along with certain magical powders and then moving the bundle in a highly formalized series of gestures.

In addition to the private mouth-rite, the people seek out a holy-mouth-man once or twice a year. These practitioners have an impressive set of paraphernalia, consisting of a variety of augers, awls, probes, and prods. The use of these objects in the exorcism of the evils of the mouth involves almost unbelievable ritual torture of the client. The holy-mouth-man opens the client's mouth and, using the above-mentioned tools, enlarges any holes which decay may have created in the teeth. Magical materials are put into these holes. If there are no naturally occurring holes in the teeth, large sections of one or more teeth are gouged out so that the supernatural substance can be applied. In the client's view, the purpose of these ministrations is to arrest decay and to draw friends. The extremely sacred and traditional character of the rite is evident in the fact that the natives return to the holy-mouth-men year after year, despite the fact that their teeth continue to decay.

It is to be hoped that, when a thorough study of the Nacirema is made, there will be careful inquiry into the personality structure of these people. One has but to watch the gleam in the eye of a holy-mouth-man, as he jabs an awl into an exposed nerve, to suspect that a certain amount of sadism is involved. If this can be established, a very interesting pattern emerges, for most of the population shows definite masochistic tendencies. It was to these that Professor Linton referred in discussing a distinctive part of the daily body ritual which is performed only by men. This part of the rite involves scraping and lacerating the surface of the face with a sharp instrument. Special women's rites are performed only four times during each lunar month, but what they lack in frequency is made up in barbarity. As part of this ceremony, women bake their heads in small ovens for about an hour. The theoretically interesting point is that what seems to be a preponderantly masochistic people have developed sadistic specialists.

The medicine men have an imposing temple, or *latipso*, in every community of any size. The more elaborate ceremonies required to treat very sick patients can only be performed at this temple. These ceremonies involve not only the thaumaturge but a permanent group of vestal maidens who move sedately about the temple chambers in distinctive costume and headdress.

The *latipso* ceremonies are so harsh that it is phenomenal that a fair proportion of the really sick natives who enter the temple ever recover. Small children whose indoctrination is still incomplete have been known to resist attempts to take them to the temple because "that is where you go to die." Despite this fact, sick adults are not only willing but eager to undergo the protracted ritual purification, if they can afford to do so. No matter how ill the supplicant or how grave the emergency, the guardians of many temples will not admit a client if he cannot give a rich gift to the custodian. Even after one has gained admission and survived the ceremonies, the guardians will not permit the neophyte to leave until he makes still another gift.

The supplicant entering the temple is first stripped of all his or her clothes. In everyday life the Nacirema avoids exposure of his body and its natural functions. Bathing and excretory acts are performed only in the secrecy of the household shrine, where they are ritualized as part of the body-rites. Psychological shock results from the fact that body secrecy is suddenly lost upon entry into the *latipso*. A man, whose own wife has never seen him in an excretory act, suddenly finds himself naked and assisted by a vestal maiden while he performs his natural functions into a sacred vessel. This sort of ceremonial treatment is necessitated by the fact that the excreta are used by a diviner to ascertain the course and nature of the client's sickness. Female clients, on the other hand, find their naked bodies are subjected to the scrutiny, manipulation and prodding of the medicine men.

Few supplicants in the temple are well enough to do anything but lie on their hard beds. The daily ceremonies, like the rites of the holy-mouth-men, involve discomfort and torture. With ritual precision, the vestals awaken their miserable charges each dawn and roll them about on their beds of pain while performing ablutions, in the formal movements of which the maidens are highly trained. At other times they insert magic wands in the supplicant's mouth or force him to eat substances which are supposed to be healing. From time to time the medicine men come to their clients and jab magically treated needles into their flesh. The fact that these temple ceremonies may not cure, and may even kill the neophyte, in no way decreases the people's faith in the medicine men.

There remains one other kind of practitioner, known as a "listener." This witch-doctor has the power to exorcise the devils that lodge in the heads of people who have been bewitched. The Nacirema believe that parents bewitch their own children. Mothers are particularly suspected of putting a curse on children while teaching them the secret body rituals. The counter-magic of the witch-doctor is unusual in its lack of ritual. The patient simply tells the "listener" all his troubles and fears, beginning with the earliest difficulties he can remember. The memory displayed by the Nacirema in these exorcism sessions is truly remarkable. It is not uncommon for the patient to bemoan the rejection he felt upon being weaned as a babe, and a few individuals even see their troubles going back to the traumatic effects of their own birth.

In conclusion, mention must be made of certain practices which have their base in native esthetics but which depend upon the pervasive aversion to the natural body and its functions. There are ritual fasts to make fat people thin and ceremonial feasts to make thin people fat. Still other rites are used to make women's breasts larger if they are small, and smaller if they are large. General dissatisfaction with breast shape is symbolized in the fact that the ideal form is virtually outside the range of human variation. A few women afflicted with almost inhuman hypermammary development are so idolized that they make a handsome living by simply going from village to village and permitting the natives to stare at them for a fee.

Reference has already been made to the fact that excretory functions are ritualized, routinized, and relegated to secrecy. Natural reproductive functions are similarly distorted. Intercourse is taboo as a topic and scheduled as an act. Efforts are made to avoid pregnancy by the use of magical materials or by limiting intercourse to certain phases of the moon. Conception is actually very infrequent. When pregnant, women dress so as to hide their condition. Parturition takes place in secret, without friends or relatives to assist, and the majority of women do not nurse their infants.

Our review of the ritual life of the Nacirema has certainly shown them to be a magic-ridden people. It is hard to understand how they have managed to exist so long under the burdens which they have imposed upon themselves. But even such exotic customs as these take on real meaning when they are viewed with the insight provided by Malinowski when he wrote (1948:70):

> Looking from far and above, from our high places of safety in the developed civilization, it is easy to see all the crudity and irrelevance of magic. But without its power and guidance early man could not have mastered his practical difficulties as he has done, nor could man have advanced to the higher stages of civilization.

References

Linton, R. (1936). *The study of man.* New York: D. Appleton-Century Co.
Malinowski, B. (1948). *Magic, science, and religion.* Glencoe, IL: The Free Press.
Murdock, G. P. (1949). *Social structure.* New York: The Macmillan Co.

LABS

Internet Exercise

Cultural Diversity

Introduction

The sheer number of diverse cultures within the United States and across the world is astounding. *Multiculturalism* refers to the acknowledgment and awareness of, and respect for, the diversity of cultural groups that coexist in one larger culture. In the United States, Native American, African, Hispanic, Asian, Anglo, and numerous other ethnic groups share most American values and norms while also celebrating differences. Multiculturalism programs have been the source of discussion and debate. Critics believe that by emphasizing multiculturalism, the country will become divided and the unity of the United States might be jeopardized. Multiculturalism is not contained solely within the United States, but can be evidenced throughout the world.

Ethnocentrism is the tendency that people in any given culture have to evaluate cultural content of other cultures from the perspective of one's own culture. This tendency often is a result of believing that one's own culture, beliefs, and values are superior to all others. The problem with ethnocentric judgment is that it can severely limit understanding and can be offensive and disrespectful to other cultures. For instance, Americans who question why people from Australia or the United Kingdom drive on "the wrong side of the street" are displaying ethnocentric judgment. This is a rather benign example, more is at stake when core values of the culture are questioned or deemed inferior.

Cultural relativism is an objective practice employed by sociologists and other social scientists. There are two ways in which cultural relativism is understood and employed. Some social scientists are committed to a *philosophical* or *ideological* cultural relativism, which is the philosophical premise that there are no absolute values, that all ways of life are equally valid, confirmed as good or bad only by the cultural context in which they occur. This was once a very popular position among social scientists. Increasingly, however, as we are considering cultural practices such as clitorectomies of young girls in some parts of the world (see *Idea in Use*) and other practices which inflict pain or dehumanizing conditions on people, social scientists are seriously rethinking their *philosophical* commitment to cultural relativism. There is a second understanding of cultural relativism, however, which we term *methodological relativism*, which simply demands that as we interpret cultural content we be cognizant of the cultural context within which the behaviors and beliefs we are observing occur. For example, we might not agree that stealing from others is acceptable behavior from a philosophical point of view, but if we are going to understand why heroin addicts commit acts of theft, we cannot fully understand this behavior unless we recognize that they are part of a culture that highly rewards successful criminal enterprise. It is this understanding of cultural relativism, as *methodological relativism*, that is important to the enterprise of social science, and indeed to a multicultural agenda.

Idea in Use

Female genital mutilation has received considerable attention in the media and in academia. Disputes over whether the rite of passage in some African and Middle Eastern societies is justified abound and many argue by referencing cultural relativity and ethnocentrism. Female genital mutilation is a custom and tradition that has been practiced for centuries and generally recognizes a female's transition to adulthood. There are many reasons why groups believe it is necessary: tradition, group conformity, gender identity, the control of a woman's sexual and reproductive powers, to improve hygiene, and as a religious symbol. In the westernized world, however, the surgical removal of the female's labia and clitoris is often considered unnecessary and barbaric. While female genital mutilation has gained worldwide attention and several groups have formed to protest the process, families within the United States continue to practice male circumcision without protest. Since Europeans don't practice male circumcision at nearly the high levels of Americans, they oftentimes view the practice as needless and horrifying. For a review of female genital mutilation and cultural relativism see John Caldwell, J.O. Orubuloye, and Pat Caldwell's article "Female Genital Mutilation: Conditions of Decline" in a 2000 volume of *Population Research and Policy Review.*

Activity Instructions

You will be using the internet to investigate more about cultural diversity.

1. Multiculturalism debates often center on the issue of language. Within the United States there has been much debate about the official language of the country and of each state. First, go to the Census Bureau website and click on your state within the American FactFinder Page. For the latest year available, report on what percentage of state residents speak a language other than English at home (population 5 years and over). Also, report the overall percentage of US residents who speak a language other than English at home, your state's ranking within this category, and the three states that have the highest and lowest ranking. Now go to www.proenglish.org, a website that advocates English as the official language of the United States. Go to the state profiles and find out whether your state has a law that claims English as the official language. Explore the "Official English" section under the "Our Issues" heading and find out what the common languages, other than English, are in your state. Finally, go to the National Council of Teachers of English website at www .ncte.org. Explore the Press Section and find out what their positions are regarding the language and diversity freedoms. Specifically, what is their position on English as the "Official Language" and when did they make a formal stance? Record your answers in a brief narrative.

2. Language is a cue to culture and can differ by region. Go to http://www.uwm .edu/~vaux/ and click on 'Maps of Results' on the left side menu. Click again on 'Maps and Results' and you will see a listing of over 100 different dialectical probes. Write down the city, state, and region where you were primarily raised and, without looking at the results, answer the following questions yourself: 58, 73, 75, 103, 104, 105, and 106. Once you have written down your answers, check the results of the survey. How do your answers fit in with the results presented? What patterns do you see for each indicator?

3. Choose a country that you have never visited and want to learn more about. Searching on the internet, find out about different customs that are very common in your choice country but differ markedly from United States culture (or your country of origin). For instance, in Thailand, it is very common for people to blow and pick noses in public, but very offensive to touch a person's head or hair as the top part of the body is the highest and most respected part of the body. Good sites to check out first would be the country's tourism website, and use search engines with search terms such as culture, customs, gestures, and taboos (along with your country of choice). Write up what you found and indicate the websites where you found the information.

4. Be sure to read Horace Miner's "Body Ritual Among the Nacirema" and "The Sacred Rac" by Pat Hughes. You can find Miner's article in this book as well as on the web at: http://www.msu.edu/~jdowell/miner.html. "The Sacred Rac"

can be found at: http://www.drabruzzi.com/sacred_rac.html. What does the tribe Nacirema represent and what does Rac mean/symbolize? How does this relate to ethnocentrism and cultural relativism?

5. Record your responses to each of these four areas in narrative form, signifying each response by its appropriate number, and submit the completed narrative to your instructor.

Individual Writing Exercise

Subcultures

Introduction

Culture refers to the beliefs, customs, values, and all of those human creations, material and nonmaterial, that society has incorporated into its way of life. The study of culture is a predominant and important part of sociological study. Sociologists often compare and contrast distinct cultures in cross-cultural research. Another important area within cultural studies is the investigation of subcultures and countercultures within a more general culture. A researcher must understand the overall culture to evaluate the norms of human behavior. Then, by studying subcultures and/or countercultures the researcher has a broader context from which to evaluate behaviors.

A *subculture* is a "culture within a culture." It is part of the larger culture, but yet distinct from that culture and the behaviors, beliefs, customs, norms, values, or other cultural content that it promotes. Subcultures maintain their distinctiveness by creating boundaries that demarcate them from the larger culture. *Boundary maintenance mechanisms* include unique symbols, often worn as part of one's clothing, specialized vocabulary, called *argot*, use of special gestures, and even special nicknames that denote one's membership in the subculture.

There are numerous types of subcultures: religious, political, deviant, recreational, occupational, musical, and sexual, just to name a few. A person can be a member of various subcultures at one time and can accumulate several subcultural memberships throughout his or her lifetime. The level and degree of membership can also vary, from a fringe member who identifies with a few ideas of the subculture to a zealot who passionately espouses all the values and beliefs of the subculture. For example, motorcycle riders can vary greatly on their level of immersion within the "biker subculture." Perhaps they participate in an annual event such as Daytona Bike Week or the Sturgis Rally. Others may take it more seriously, donning black leather jackets and other biker apparel, getting a tattoo, or even joining a biker gang such as the Hell's Angels.

Idea in Use

Sarah Thornton uses a sociological perspective in analyzing youth club culture in her 1996 book *Club Cultures: Music, Media and Subcultural Capital.* Her research focuses on raves and clubs that became popular in the late 1980s and early 1990s. Thornton identifies three main elements within the subculture that help to define the members. First, she distinguishes between the 'authentic vs. the phony.' She elaborates further on distinctions such as the 'hip vs. the mainstream' and the 'underground vs. the media.' Thornton's research also describes several types of mini-subcultures within the club subculture. Occupations such as DJs or spinners, taking part in ecstasy and other drug use, club specialization (gay, straight, techno, house, etc.) and socialization into the subculture are also addressed by Thornton. While the premise of club culture may at first seem elementary, Thornton clearly explains the multitudes of nuances that define club subculture. Through the use of a topical trend of raves and clubs, Thornton demonstrates the sociological relevance of subculture and the effects on the distinctions between members and non-members.

Activity Instructions

As a college student, you have likely been exposed to several subcultures. Think about what you have experienced and observed and what areas you may want to investigate in the future. You can choose any type of subculture to report on (categories include deviance, recreational, occupational, lifestyle, political, ideological, etc.; examples include goth, heroin users, trekkies, anime, professional wrestlers, nudists, extreme environmentalists, skinheads, new agers).

1. Identify and list the subcultures of which you have been a member or which you have observed. Briefly describe some of the unique features of each and indicate your level of immersion. For instance, you may occasionally surf, but don't identify fully with the "surfer" subculture. Be sure to discuss the nuances of the subculture; that is, does the subculture have a different language or terminology, are there important symbols that represent the subculture, is the clothing different, etc.?

2. Compare the subculture that you most identify with or know about to the larger culture from which it stems. Be sure to describe how your subculture is similar to the large culture, as well as the areas in which they diverge. Focus specifically on the following: 1) values, 2) norms, 3) prominent symbols, 4) language or terminology, and 5) distinctive dress.

3. Submit your list and write-up to your teacher as instructed.

Group Exercise

Cultural Universals and Rites of Passage

Introduction

Sociologists and anthropologists often focus their studies on traits that are shared by cultures, as well as traits that are unique to certain cultures. There are several ways in which everyon [...] *cultural universal* is a characteristic [...] in every culture. The cultural univ [...] es and may evolve over time and ch [...] a cultural universal, but differs in [...] ineal families are found among etl [...] e found in Swaziland, and family v [...] past few decades, the United State [...] orms such as single parent and e [...] itation. Whatever the particular ex [...] all cultures.

Another cultu [...] is a public event that marks major [...] s to another. Rites of passage incluc [...] es have life transitions that are a [...] characters of the ritual may differ. [...] a transition from childhood to ol [...] This rite involves taking driver ed [...] taking a written and driving test. [...] er gets his or her picture taken for display on the driver's license, which serves as the physical symbol of this rite.

Idea in Use

A recent article suggests that inventive individuals can create rites of passage especially if traditional rites and rituals are limiting. The 2002 article, "Intoxication and Rite of Passage to Adulthood in Norway," found in *Contemporary Drug Problems* focuses on prolonged graduation ceremonies that occur from May 1st to May 17th each year. The rite of passage from adolescence to adulthood is celebrated during this time, with participants wearing special clothes, taking part in events and parades, and of course, drinking beer and liquor. A year before graduation, committees of students form to plan their parties and events. The majority of graduating youths take part in this celebration, and parents, police officers, and other adults typically accept the rite of passage with little interference.

Activity Instructions

In small groups, you will be evaluating rites of passage, the nature of the ritual/s, their importance, and how they mark life transitions.

1. List as many rites of passage that your group can come up with. If these are not rites of passage that are used in the United States, be sure to specify to what culture they are integral.

2. Identify the life transition that the rite of passage celebrates. What statuses is one moving from? To?

3. Identify the rites of passage that you and at least one other member from your group have already experienced. For these rites of passage, how did your

experience and rituals used differ from others in your group? How were they alike? Make sure to discuss at what age you experienced the rite of passage, and important clothing or other symbolic gestures that were used.

4. For the rites of passage that you have listed but that no one in the group has yet to experience, discuss how you envision marking the rite of passage and identify the ways the different group members differ and agree on how to observe the rite of passage.

5. Discuss whether group members believe that certain rites of passage are more important than others. Which ones are most agreed upon as important, and what are the ones that are deemed more trivial?

6. Select one of the rites of passage and describe how it has changed over time.

7. Turn in your lists, descriptions, and discussion notes to your instructor. To receive full credit, your write-up should be thorough, thoughtful, and descriptive.

Socialization

Identity Transformation in a Maximum Security Prison
Thomas J. Schmid and Richard S. Jones

Labs
Internet Exercise: Social-Psychological Theories
Individual Writing Exercise: Television as a Socializing Agent
Group Exercise: Life Course Socialization and Crisis

Identity Transformation in a Maximum Security Prison

The extent to which people hide behind the masks of impression management in everyday life is a point of theoretical controversy. A variety of problematic circumstances can be identified, however, in which individuals find it necessary to accommodate a sudden but encompassing shift in social situations by establishing temporary identities. These circumstances, which can range from meteoric fame (Adler and Adler 1989) to confinement in total institutions, place new identity demands on the individual, while seriously challenging his or her prior identity bases.

A prison sentence constitutes a "massive assault" on the identity of those imprisoned (Berger 1963: 100–101). This assault is especially severe on first-time inmates, and we might expect radical identity changes to ensue from their imprisonment. At the same time, a prisoner's awareness of the challenge to his identity affords some measure of protection against it. As part of an ethnographic analysis of the prison experiences of first-time, short-term inmates, this article presents an identity transformation model that differs both from the gradual transformation processes that characterize most adult identity changes and from such radical transformation processes as brainwashing or conversion.

Data for the study are derived principally from ten months of participant observation at a maximum security prison for men in the upper midwest of the United States. One of the authors was an inmate serving a felony sentence for one year and one day, while the other participated in the study as an outside observer. Relying on traditional ethnographic data collection and analysis techniques, this approach offered us general observations of hundreds of prisoners, and extensive fieldnotes that were based on repeated, often daily, contacts with about fifty inmates, as well as on personal relationships established with a smaller number of inmates. We subsequently returned to the prison to conduct focused interviews with other prisoners; using information provided by prison officials, we were able to identify and interview twenty additional first-time inmates who were serving sentences of two years or less.

Three interrelated research questions guided our analysis: How do first-time, short-term inmates define the prison world, and how do their definitions change during their prison careers? How do these inmates adapt to the prison world, and how do their adaptation strategies change during their prison careers? How do their self-definitions change during their prison careers?

Preprison Identity

Our data suggest that the inmates we studied have little in common before their arrival at prison, except their conventionality. Although convicted of felonies, most do not possess "criminal" identities. They begin their sentences with only a vague, incomplete image of what prison is like, but an image that nonetheless stands in contrast to how they view their own social worlds. Their prison image is dominated by the theme of violence: they see prison inmates as violent, hostile, alien human beings, with whom they have nothing in common. They have several specific fears about what will happen to them in prison, including fears of assault, rape, and death. They are also concerned about their identities, fearing that—if they survive prison at all—they are in danger of changing in prison, either through the intentional efforts of rehabilitation personnel or through the unavoidable hardening effects of the prison environment. Acting on this imagery—or, more precisely, on the inconsonance of their self-images with this prison image—they develop an anticipatory survival strategy that consists primarily of protective resolutions: a resolve to avoid all hostilities; a resolve to avoid all nonessential contacts with inmates and guards; a resolve to defend themselves in any way possible; and a resolve not to change, or to be changed, in prison.

Managing a Dualistic Self

An inmate is able to express both directions of his ambivalence (and to address his need for more information about the prison) by drawing a distinction between his "true" identity (i.e., his outside, preprison identity) and a "false" identity he creates for the prison world. For most of a new inmate's prison career, his preprison identity remains a "subjective" or "personal" identity while his prison identity serves as his "objective" or "social" basis for interaction in prison. This bifurcation of his self is not a conscious decision made at a single point in time, but it does represent two conscious and interdependent identity-preservation tactics, formulated through self-dialogue and refined through tentative interaction with others.

First, after coming to believe that he cannot "be himself" in prison because he would be too vulnerable, he decides to "suspend" his preprison identity for the duration of his sentence. He retains his resolve not to let prison change him, protecting himself by choosing not to reveal himself (his "true" self) to others. Expressions of a suspension of identity emerged repeatedly and consistently in both the fieldwork and interview phases of our research through such statements as

> I was reserved.…I wouldn't be very communicative, you know. I'd try to keep conversation to a minimum.…I wasn't interested in getting close to anybody … or asking a lot of questions. You know, try to cut the conversation short …go my own way back to my cell or go to the library or do something.

* * *

> I didn't want nobody to know too much about me. That was part of the act.

An inmate's decision to suspend his preprison identity emanates directly from his feelings of vulnerability, discontinuity and differentiation from other inmates. These emotions foster something like a "proto-sociological attitude" (Weigert 1986: 173) in which new inmates find it necessary to step outside their taken-for-granted preprison identities. Rather than viewing these identities and the everyday life experience in which they are grounded as social constructions, however, inmates see the *prison* world as an artificial construction, and judge their "naturally occurring" preprison identities to be out of place within this construction. By attempting to suspend his preprison identity for the time that he spends in prison an inmate believes that he will again "be his old self" after his release.

While he is in confinement, an inmate's decision to suspend his identity leaves him with little or no basis for interaction. His second identity tactic, then, is the creation of an identity that allows him to interact, however cautiously, with others. This tactic consists of his increasingly sophisticated impression management skills (Goffman 1959) which are initially designed simply to hide his vulnerability, but which gradually evolve into an alternative identity felt to be more suitable to the prison world. The character of the presented identity is remarkably similar from inmate to inmate:

> Well, I learned that you can't act like—you can't get the attitude where you are better than they are. Even where you might be better than them, you can't strut around like you are. Basically, you can't stick out. You don't stare at people and things like that. I knew a lot of these things from talking to people and I figured them out by myself. I sat down and figured out just what kind of attitude I'm going to have to take.

* * *

> Most people out here learn to be tough, whether they can back it up or not. If you don't learn to be tough, you will definitely pay for it. This toughness can be demonstrated through a mean look, tough language, or an extremely big build.…One important thing is never to let your guard down.

An inmate's prison identity, as an inauthentic presentation of self, is not in itself a form of identity transformation but is rather a form of identity construction. His prison identity is simply who he must pretend to be while he is in prison. It is a false identity created for survival in an artificial world. But this identity nonetheless emerges in the same manner as any other identity: it is learned from others, and it must be presented to, negotiated with, and validated by others. A new inmate arrives at prison with a general image of what prisoners are like, and he begins to flesh out this image from the day of his arrival, warily observing others just as they are observing him. Through watching others, through eavesdropping, through cautious conversation and selective interaction, a new inmate refines his understanding of what maximum security prisoners look like, how they talk, how they move, how they act. Despite his belief that he is different from these other prisoners, he knows that he cannot appear to be too different from them, if he is to hide his vulnerability. His initial image of other prisoners, his early observations, and his concern over how he appears to others thus provide a foundation for the identity he gradually creates through impression management.

Impression management skills, of course, are not exclusive to the prison world; a new inmate, like anyone else, has had experience in presenting a "front" to others, and he draws upon his experience in the creation of his prison identity. He has undoubtedly even had experience in projecting the very attributes—strength, stoicism, aplomb—required by his prison identity. Impression management in prison differs, however, in the totality with which it governs interactions and in the perceived costs of failure: humiliation, assault, or death. For these reasons the entire impression management process becomes a more highly conscious endeavor. When presenting himself before others, a new inmate pays close attention to such minute details of his front as eye contact, posture, and manner of walking:

> I finally got out of orientation. I was going out with the main population, going down to get my meals and things. The main thing is not to stare at a bunch of people, you know. I tried to just look ahead, you know, not stare at people. 'Cause I didn't really know; I just had to learn a little at a time.

* * *

> The way you look seems to be very important. The feeling is you shouldn't smile, that a frown is much more appropriate. The eyes are very important. You should never look away; it is considered a sign of weakness. Either stare straight ahead, look around, or look the person dead in the eyes. The way you walk is important. You shouldn't walk too fast; they might think you were scared and in a hurry to get away.

To create an appropriate embodiment (Weigert 1986) of their prison identities, some new inmates devote long hours to weightlifting or other body-building exercises, and virtually all of them relinquish their civilian clothes—which might express their preprison identities—in favor of the standard issue clothing that most inmates wear. Whenever a new inmate is open to the view of other inmates, in fact, he is likely to relinquish most overt symbols of his individuality, in favor of a standard issue "prison inmate" appearance.

By acting self-consciously, of course, a new inmate runs the risk of exposing the fact that he is acting. But he sees no alternative to playing his part better; he cannot "not act" because that too would expose the vulnerability of his "true" identity. He thus sees every new prison experience, every new territory that he is allowed to explore, as a test of his impression management skills. Every nonconfrontive encounter with another inmate symbolizes his success at these skills, but it is also a social validation of his prison identity. Eventually he comes to see that many, perhaps most, inmates are engaging in the same kind of inauthentic presentations of self. Their identities are as "false" as his, and their validations of his identity may be equally false. But he realizes that he is powerless to change this state of affairs, and that he must continue to present his prison identity for as long as he remains in prison.

A first-time inmate enters prison as an outsider, and it is from an outsider's perspective that he initially creates his prison identity. In contrast to his suspended preprison identity, his prison identity is a *shared* identity, because it is modeled on his observations of other inmates. Like those of more experienced prisoners, his prison identity is tied directly to the social role of "prison inmate" because he is an outsider, however, his prison identity is also severely limited by his narrow understanding of that role. It is based on an outsider's stereotype of who a maximum security inmate is and what he acts like. It is, nonetheless, a *structural* identity (Weigert

1986), created to address his outsider's institutional problems of social isolation and inadequate information about the prison world.

By the middle of his sentence, a new inmate comes to adopt what is essentially an insider's perspective on the prison world. His prison image has evolved to the point where it is dominated by the theme of boredom rather than violence. His survival strategy, although still extant, has been supplemented by such general adaptation techniques as legal and illegal diversionary activities and conscious efforts to suppress his thoughts about the outside world. His impression management tactics have become second nature rather than self-conscious, as he routinely interacts with others in terms of his prison identity.

References

Adler, Patricia A. and Peter Adler. 1989. "The Gloried Self: The Aggrandizement and the Constriction of Self." *Social Psychology Quarterly* 52:299–310.

Berger, Peter L. 1963. *Invitation to Sociology: A Humanistic Perspective.* Garden City, NY: Doubleday Anchor Books.

Goffman, 1959. *The Presentation of Self in Everyday Life.* Garden City, NY: Doubleday Anchor Books.

Irwin, John. 1970. *The Felon.* Englewood Cliffs, NJ: Prentice-Hall, 1977——. *Scenes.* Beverly Hills: Sage.

Weigert, Andrew J. 1986. "The Social Production of Identity: Metatheoretical Foundations." *Sociological Quarterly* 27:165–183.

LABS

Internet Exercise

Social-Psychological Theories

Introduction

Several social scientists have formulated theories about the process of socialization and personality development. Socialization theories recognize the importance of self and society, and thus draw from both psychology and sociology.

Sigmund Freud developed a theory about the structure of the personality and advanced a hypothesis about the stages of personality development. Freud believed that the personality was made of three parts: the id, the ego, and the superego. Suggesting that most development takes place in childhood, the stages of personality development fittingly are centered in the early years. Freud asserted that everyone passes through the oral stage, anal stage, phallic stage, latency stage, and the genital stage. At each stage, conflicts may emerge and if not appropriately managed, could result in personality problems throughout the life course.

George Herbert Mead's main theme is that the *self* and *mind* develop as a result of social interaction. Exchanging gestures, symbols, and language is instrumental in our social experience. Importantly, individuals must ascertain the meaning of such gestures, symbols, and words. This is possible because these meanings are shared within the context of a given culture. Another important aspect in developing the self is the idea of *taking the role of the other*. This means that we can anticipate how others see us and thus see ourselves as others do. The social philosopher Charles Horton Cooley referred to this dynamic as the *looking glass self*. Mead also developed a theory of socialization that is rooted in childhood and adolescence. It is a three-stage model:

- *imitation stage*—does not involve taking the role of the other, but simply mimics the behavior of others
- *play stage*—involves taking the role of a single person, called a "particular other," at a time, and is not capable of internalizing how others *generally* might respond
- *game stage*—involves taking the role of others generally, called the "generalized other"

Jean Piaget focused his work on how people think, reason, and understand themselves as well as the world around them. Piaget also centered his *cognitive development theory* in childhood. The sensorimotor stage, preoperational stage, concrete operational stage, and the formal operational stage are the steps in a process that begins at birth and ends in the early teens.

Lawrence Kohlberg drew from Piaget's cognitive development, but centered his own work on *moral development*. The process of learning right from wrong, appropriate from unacceptable, and moral from immoral occurs after an individual has a rudimentary level of cognitive development. The three stages of moral development according to Kohlberg are: preconventional, conventional, and post-conventional levels.

Idea in Use

The flirtations of men and women illustrate Mead's idea of a conversation of gestures and symbolized language. A 1995 study entitled "Courtship Signaling and Adolescents: "Girls Just Wanna have Fun?" in the *Journal of Sex Research* evaluated 100 girls' nonverbal techniques toward men. Researcher Monica Moore indicated that several gestures are employed including three types of glances (the all encompassing glance, the short darting glance, and the extended gaze), hair-tossing, primping of clothes, and a variety of smiles. Moore concluded that younger girls use more pronounced and dominant gestures than older adolescent girls. There were no concrete conclusions about the effectiveness of the flirting gestures in acquiring a significant other.

Activity Instructions

In this exercise, you will be using the internet to learn more about the theories of socialization and the people associated with the theory.

1. In the following section, you will be going on an internet scavenger hunt to find the answers. All the following refer to either: Freud, Mead, Piaget, or Kohlberg.

   a. What social scientists did Time magazine name as two of the most important people of the twentieth century?
   b. Who wrote extensively about "I" and "Me?"
   c. What social scientist wrote about dreams and the unconscious?
   d. Who has won Europe's Erasmus Prize for exceptionally contributing to the culture, and society of social science?
   e. Who popularized the Heinz dilemma and what is it?

2. Choose one of the social scientists discussed in this exercise. Using the internet (please note which websites you referred to) briefly write a description of the stages that they developed. To what ages does each stage correspond? Do you think that the stages accurately describe personality development and socialization?

3. Finally, many other social scientists have contributed to the field of socialization and development. Write a brief biography of such a person based on information you find on the internet (you may write about anyone other than those discussed in this exercise). Be sure to discuss what they contribute to the psychosocial development field and include the citations for the internet sites used. Some possible options: Charles Horton Cooley, Erik Erikson, and Carol Gilligan.

4. Please submit your write-ups to your instructor as directed.

Individual Writing Exercise

Television as a Socializing Agent

Introduction

The process in which people learn appropriate behaviors, values, and norms specific to a culture is called *socialization.* There are various socializing agents such as the family, school, and peers. Mass media, and television in particular, have increasingly been recognized as socializing agents. There has been considerable debate about the advantages and limitations that television offers as a socializing agent, especially for young children.

Television programming can be creative, informative, and stimulating. It does not have to be factual and represent reality. In fact, part of the enjoyment of watching television is to *escape* from reality. Without proper supervision and direction from adults, however, children may believe all that they see on television is reality. Certain types of programming may be especially problematic, as is an excessive amount of time spent watching television. Violent, sexual, or sensationalist content on television, for instance, are probably not the best shows for children to be watching on a daily basis. The average daily amount of time the television is on in a U.S. home is seven hours and 40 minutes (Nielsen Media Research 2000). Over a quarter of all children under the age of 6 have a television in their bedroom and overall, children of this age watch about two hours of television a day (Kaiser Family Foundation 2003). Television has also been thought to promote a sedentary lifestyle and obesity, violence among children, overconsumption, and desensitization to sexual behavior. In addition, the images that are displayed in the mass media often present a distorted view of the world, provide little recognition of the diversity that exists, and sometimes perpetuate antiquated gender roles that are not real representations of society.

Not all television is bad however. Children's programming can spark the imagination and encourage creativity. There has been some proliferation of educational programming and shows that represent more diversity (e.g., *Dora the Explorer, Liberty's Kids*, etc). Cable has provided multitudes of channels that can be quickly accessed for news, educational opportunities focused on history, music and the arts, and the entertainment options are endless.

Idea in Use

Researchers Daniel Anderson and Tiffany Pempek from the University of Massachusetts Amherst, reviewed the plentiful literature pertaining to television viewing by very young children in their 2005 article "Television and Very Young Children" published in the *American Behavioral Scientist.* They found that very young children are exposed to more television viewing than ever before and there are implications of such contact. Children are less likely to learn from educational television than from personal contact with educators, and television viewing is almost always negatively associated with cognitive, language, and social development. In addition, they concluded that television in the background, that is, on but not necessarily on for children to watch, also is negatively related to positive child development.

Activity Instructions

In this assignment you will be analyzing the content of television programming for children. Take special care to note the powerful effects that television potentially has for socializing children.

1. Spend one hour watching television programming that specifically targets young children. You can watch a one-hour show or two half-hour shows. You may want to select your shows from channels such as PBS, Disney, the Cartoon Network, and Nickelodeon, which provide a lot of programs created for children.

2. During the show, take notes about what themes are presented. What (if any) is the moral message of the show? Educational content? What themes are explored (e.g., violence, adventure, family problems, boy-girl relationships)? What is the type of show that you watched (cartoon, family sitcom, etc.)? What is the plot? Who are the main characters and how are they displayed (male, female, animal, black, white, etc.)?

3. Be sure to keep track of the commercials that are broadcast between the show segments. Do they tend to be gender specific or gender neutral?

4. After you are finished viewing the shows, carefully analyze your notes and develop lists of themes. Below each list, write out behaviors and conversations that are illustrative of the theme. Also, make a "methodological note" on the first page of your list about where and when you watched as well as the name of the show. When you are finished, you will want the following information:

   - Name of show
   - Channel on which the show airs
   - Day of week watched
   - Time of day watched
   - Themes identified (there are likely to be several)
   - (Under each theme) Behaviors and conversations that convey the theme

5. From your list of themes, prioritize the three that dominated the show(s).

6. Turn in your list with commentary, and your detailed notes as directed by your instructor.

Group Exercise

Life Course Socialization and Crisis

Introduction

Many think of the socialization process as occurring primarily in the early years of life, when one learns language and other basic skills. However, the socialization process is a continual development that people experience throughout their lives, during which they continue to develop an identity, learn new skills, and adapt to changing conditions.

Crises can occur at any point in one's life and certain stages of the *life course* can incite a crisis. New experiences can bring new expectations, different roles and statuses, as well as dilemmas about work and family. These experiences often come during transitions in the life course.

The media often links crisis with the onset of middle-age. Commonly between the ages of forty and sixty, individuals may reflect back on their life and anticipate the future, waning years of their life yet to come. Children may be moving out of the house, retirement may be looming, and the physical aging process may set in with wrinkles and hair loss. Adult socialization must deal with these realizations and may require that the individual hold new statuses and perform more, less, or different roles as they age. This may contribute to what is commonly called a "mid-life crisis."

Early adulthood can also present problems and obstacles in the socialization process. The idea of a "quarterlife crisis" has gained popularity in our culture. Generally located in the mid-20s, young adults can experience difficult transitions. After graduating from college, the ordeal of finding a stable and rewarding job, being financially independent and on your own for the first time, and weeding through possible lifetime mates, can be a stress-filled, anxiety-ridden time. Finding a direction in life can bring turmoil to a once carefree individual. For instance, the typical middle class college graduate has led a relatively sheltered existence for 20-plus years. Finding a suitable entry-level job is difficult when most corporations and businesses indicate that experience is necessary. When one finally does find a job, the beginning salary may be lower than expected and a tight budget needs to be created so that present and future bills and loans can be paid. The constant comparing of oneself to friends who have settled down and "made it" contributes much anxiety about your own future direction. Being in the "Real World" is not all that MTV has made it appear.

Idea in Use

The term "midlife crisis" conjures up many images for people of all ages. From a red sports car to face lifts, the media depiction of what a midlife crisis looks like can be vastly different from actual experience. Psycho-sociological research has often debunked the notion that a midlife crisis is inevitable and universal, with some estimating that only about 10 percent experience such a crisis. Elaine Wetherton, a researcher at Cornell University, qualitatively examined American ideas and beliefs about midlife crises. In *Motivation and Emotion* (2000), she reports that Americans can indeed provide a definition for the phenomenon, and that their definitions generally coincide with the ones researchers use in the field. Only about a quarter of the participants reported that they had experienced a midlife crisis, however, and they credit the crisis not to aging, but rather due to stressful life events. For more information about research on the research presented here, see "Expecting Stress: Americans" and the "Midlife Crisis" in volume 24 of *Motivation and Emotion.*

Activity Instructions

In this assignment, you will work in small groups to discuss the answers.

1. Terms such as adult, old, and midlife are often used but have varying definitions. For instance, the age to be tried as an adult in a criminal justice system may be vastly different than the age you associate as "adult." For the following terms, write down the age or ages you associate as fitting in the category.

   Infant _____________   Child _____________

   Adult _____________   Midlife _____________

   Old _____________   Elderly _____________

2. In your small groups, compare your answers with others. How do they compare? Does everyone have the same ideas about what the terms refer to?

3. There is often a dispute about whether nature (biologically wired) or nurture (socialization) spurs the socialization process. For the following concepts, assign a value between 1 and 10 (nature = 0, nurture = 10) that indicates how much you think nature or nurture is the driving force.

   Sexual Identity _____________   Sports Ability _____________

   Intelligence _____________   Violent Tendencies _____________

4. In your small groups, compare your answers. Discuss the reasons behind your answers and respectfully debate. Identify the common reasons why people associated the concepts as nature or nurture.

5. With your small group, identify what you believe a midlife crisis would look like. Do the images differ for men and women? What are some of the experiences or circumstances your group thinks would instigate a midlife crisis? What age do you think that a midlife crisis is likely to occur? What are some of the ramifications for the individual who experiences the crisis, and the people close to the individual?

6. Within your group, discuss whether you think a quarterlife crisis is a valid social problem. Do you expect to experience such a crisis when you graduate? What would buffer such an experience?

7. Turn in your individual answers and designate one person to record the main themes of your discussions.

Social Interaction

Pathology of Imprisonment
Philip G. Zimbardo

Labs
Internet Exercise: The Social Construction of Reality
Individual Writing Exercise: Social Interaction
Group Exercise: Status and Role

Pathology of Imprisonment

*I was recently released from solitary confinement after being held therein for 37 months [months!].
A silent system was imposed upon me and to even whisper to the man in the next cell resulted in
being beaten by guards, sprayed with chemical mace, blackjacked, stomped and thrown into a
strip-cell naked to sleep on a concrete floor without bedding, covering, wash basin or even a toilet. The floor served as toilet and bed, and even there the silent system was enforced. To let a
moan escape your lips because of the pain and discomfort . . . resulted in another beating. I spent
not days, but months there during my 37 months in solitary. . . . I have filed every writ possible
against the administrative acts of brutality. The state courts have all denied the petitions. Because
of my refusal to let the things die down and forget all that happened during my 37 months in
solitary. . . I am the most hated prisoner in [this] penitentiary, and called a "hard-core incorrigible."*

*Maybe I am an incorrigible, but if true, it's because I would rather die than to accept being
treated as less than a human being. I have never complained of my prison sentence as being
unjustified except through legal means of appeals. I have never put a knife on a guard's throat
and demanded my release. I know that thieves must be punished and I don't justify stealing,
even though I am a thief myself. But now I don't think I will be a thief when I am released. No,
I'm not rehabilitated. It's just that I no longer think of becoming wealthy by stealing. I now
only think of killing–killing those who have beaten me and treated me as if I were a dog. I hope
and pray for the sake of my own soul and future life of freedom that I am able to overcome the
bitterness and hatred which eats daily at my soul, but I know to overcome it will not be easy.*

"Pathology of Imprisonment," by Philip G. Zimbardo. Reprinted with permission from *Society*, 1972, pp.
4, 6, 8. Copyright © by Transaction.

This eloquent plea for prison reform–for humane treatment of human beings, for the basic dignity that is the right of every American–came to me secretly in a letter from a prisoner who cannot be identified because he is still in a state correctional institution. He sent it to me because he read of an experiment I recently conducted at Stanford University. In an attempt to understand just what it means psychologically to be a prisoner or a prison guard, Craig Haney, Curt Banks, Dave Jaffe and I created our own prison. We carefully screened over 70 volunteers who answered an ad in a Palo Alto city newspaper and ended up with about two dozen young men who were selected to be part of this study. They were mature, emotionally stable, normal, intelligent college students from middle-class homes throughout the United States and Canada. They appeared to represent the cream of the crop of this generation. None had any criminal record and all were relatively homogeneous on many dimensions initially.

Half were arbitrarily designated as prisoners by a flip of a coin, the others as guards. These were the roles they were to play in our simulated prison. The guards were made aware of the potential seriousness and danger of the situation and their own vulnerability. They made up their own formal rules for maintaining law, order and respect, and were generally free to improvise new ones during their eight-hour, three-man shifts. The prisoners were unexpectedly picked up at their homes by a city policeman in a squad car, searched, handcuffed, fingerprinted, booked at the Palo Alto station house and taken blindfolded to our jail. There they were stripped, deloused, put into a uniform, given a number and put into a cell with two other prisoners where they expected to live for the next two weeks. The pay was good ($15 a day) and their motivation was to make money.

We observed and recorded on videotape the events that occurred in the prison, and we interviewed and tested the prisoners and guards at various points throughout the study. Some of the videotapes of the actual encounters between the prisoners and guards were seen on the *NBC News* feature "Chronolog" on November 26, 1971.

At the end of only six days we had to close down our mock prison because what we saw was frightening. It was no longer apparent to most of the subjects (or to us) where reality ended and their roles began. The majority had indeed become prisoners or guards, no longer able to clearly differentiate between role playing and self. There were dramatic changes in virtually every aspect of their behavior, thinking and feeling. In less than a week the experience of imprisonment undid (temporarily) a lifetime of learning; human values were suspended, self-concepts were challenged and the ugliest, most base, pathological side of human nature surfaced. We were horrified because we saw some boys (guards) treat others as if they were despicable animals, taking pleasure in cruelty, while other boys (prisoners) became servile, dehumanized robots who thought only of escape, of their own individual survival and of their mounting hatred for the guards.

We had to release three prisoners in the first four days because they had such acute situational traumatic reactions as hysterical crying, confusion in thinking and severe depression. Others begged to be paroled, and all but three were willing to forfeit all the money they had earned if they could be paroled. By then (the fifth day) they had been so programmed to think of themselves as prisoners that when their request for parole was denied, they returned docilely to their cells. Now, had they been thinking as college students acting in an oppressive experiment, they would have quit once they no longer wanted the $15 a day we used as our only incentive. However, the reality was not quitting an experiment but "being paroled by the parole board from the Stanford County Jail." By the last days, the earlier solidarity among the prisoners (systematically broken by the guards) dissolved into "each man for himself." Finally, when one of their fellows was put in solitary confinement (a small closet) for refusing to eat, the prisoners were given a choice by one of the guards: give up their blankets and the incorrigible prisoner would be let out, or keep their blankets and he would be kept in all night. They voted to keep their blankets and to abandon their brother.

About a third of the guards became tyrannical in their arbitrary use of power, in enjoying their control over other people. They were corrupted by the power of their roles and became quite inventive in their techniques of breaking the spirit of the prisoners and making them feel they were worthless. Some of the guards merely did their jobs as tough but fair correctional officers, and several were good guards from the prisoners' point of view since they did them small favors and were friendly. However, no good guard ever interfered with a command by any of the bad guards; they never intervened on the side of the prisoners, they never told the others to ease off because it was only an experiment, and they never even came to me as prison superintendent or experimenter in charge to complain. In part, they were good because the others, were bad; they needed the others to help establish their own egos in a positive light. In a sense, the good guards perpetuated the prison more than the other guards because their own needs to be liked prevented them from disobeying or violating the implicit guards' code. At the same time, the act of befriending the prisoners created a social reality which made the prisoners less likely to rebel.

By the end of the week the experiment had become a reality, as if it were a Pirandello play directed by Kafka that just keeps going after the audience has left. The consultant for our prison, Carlo Prescott, an ex-convict with 16 years of imprisonment in California's jails, would get so depressed and furious each time he visited our prison, because of its psychological similarity to his experiences, that he would have to leave. A Catholic priest who was a former prison chaplain in Washington, D. C. talked to our prisoners after four days and said they were just like the other first-timers he had seen.

But in the end, I called off the experiment not because of the horror I saw out there in the prison yard, but because of the horror of realizing that *I* could have easily traded places with the most brutal guard or become the weakest prisoner full of hatred at being so powerless that I could not eat, sleep or go to the toilet without permission of the authorities. *I* could have become Calley at My Lai, George Jackson at San Quentin, one of the men at Attica or the prisoner quoted at the beginning of this article.

Individual behavior is largely under the control of social forces and environmental contingencies rather than personality traits, character, will power or other empirically unvalidated constructs. Thus we create an illusion of freedom by attributing more internal control to ourselves, to the individual, than actually exists. We thus underestimate the power and pervasiveness of situational controls over behavior because: a) they are often non-obvious and subtle, b) we can often avoid entering situations where we might be so controlled, c) we label as "weak" or "deviant" people in those situations who do behave differently from how we believe we would.

Each of us carries around in our heads a favorable self-image in which we are essentially just, fair, humane and understanding. For example, we could not imagine inflicting pain on others without much provocation or hurting people who had done nothing to us, who in fact were even liked by us. However, there is a growing body of social psychological research which underscores the conclusion derived from this prison study. Many people, perhaps the majority, can be made to do almost anything when put into psychologically compelling situations–regardless of their morals, ethics, values, attitudes, beliefs or personal convictions. My colleague, Stanley Milgram, has shown that more than 60 percent of the population will deliver what they think is a series of painful electric shocks to another person even after the victim cries for mercy, begs them to stop and then apparently passes out. The subjects complained that they did not want to inflict more pain but blindly obeyed the command of the authority figure (the experimenter) who said that they must go on. In my own research on violence, I have seen mild-mannered co-eds repeatedly give shocks (which they thought were causing pain) to another girl, a stranger whom they had rated very favorably, simply by being made to feel anonymous and put in a situation where they were expected to engage in this activity.

Observers of these and similar experimental situations never predict their outcomes and estimate that it is unlikely that they themselves would behave similarly. They could be so confident only when they were outside the situation. However, since the majority of people in these studies do act in non-rational, non-obvious ways, it follows that the majority of observers would also succumb to the social psychological forces in the situation.

With regard to prisons, we can state that the mere act of assigning labels to people and putting them into a situation where those labels acquire validity and meaning is sufficient to elicit pathological behavior. This pathology is not predictable from any available diagnostic indicators we have in the social sciences, and is extreme enough to modify in very significant ways fundamental attitudes and behavior. The prison situation, as presently arranged, is guaranteed to generate severe enough pathological reactions in both guards and prisoners as to debase their humanity, lower their feelings of self-worth and make it difficult for them to be part of a society outside of their prison.

For years our national leaders have been pointing to the enemies of freedom, to the fascist or communist threat to the American way of life. In so doing they have overlooked the threat of social anarchy that is building within our own country without any outside agitation. As soon as a person comes to the realization that he is being imprisoned by his society or individuals in it, then, in the best American tradition, he demands liberty and rebels, accepting death as an alternative. The third alternative, however, is to allow oneself to become a good prisoner–docile, cooperative, uncomplaining, conforming in thought and complying in deed.

Our prison authorities now point to the militant agitators who are still vaguely referred to as part of some communist plot, as the irresponsible, incorrigible troublemakers. They imply that there would be no trouble, riots, hostages or deaths if it weren't for this small band of bad prisoners. In other words, then, everything would return to "normal" again in the life of our nation's prisons if they could break these men.

The riots in prison are coming from within–from within every man and woman who refuses to let the system turn them into an object, a number, a thing or a nothing. It is not communist inspired, but inspired by the spirit of American freedom. No man wants to be enslaved. To be powerless, to be subject to the arbitrary exercise of power, to not be recognized as a human being is to be a slave.

To be a militant prisoner is to become aware that the physical jails are but more blatant extensions of the forms of social and psychological oppression experienced daily in the nation's ghettos. They are trying to awaken the conscience of the nation to the ways in which the American ideals are being perverted, apparently in the name of justice but actually under the banner of apathy, fear and hatred. If we do not listen to the pleas of the prisoners at Attica to be treated like human beings, then we have all become brutalized by our priorities for property rights over human rights. The consequence will not only be more prison riots but a loss of all those ideals on which this country was founded.

The public should be aware that they own the prisons and that their business is failing. The 70 percent recidivism rate and the escalation in severity of crimes committed by graduates of our prisons are evidence that current prisons fail to rehabilitate the inmates in any positive way. Rather, they are breeding grounds for hatred of the establishment, a hatred that makes every citizen a target of violent assault. Prisons are a bad investment for us taxpayers. Until now we have not cared, we have turned over to wardens and prison authorities the unpleasant job of keeping people who threaten us out of our sight. Now we are shocked to learn that their management practices have failed to improve the product and instead turn petty thieves into murderers. We must insist upon new management or improved operating procedures.

The cloak of secrecy should be removed from the prisons. Prisoners claim they are brutalized by the guards, guards say it is a lie. Where is the impartial test of the truth in such a situation? Prison officials have forgotten that they work for us, that they are only public servants whose salaries are paid by our taxes. They act as if it is their prison, like a child with a toy he won't share. Neither lawyers, judges, the legislature nor the public is allowed into prisons to ascertain the truth unless the visit is sanctioned by authorities and until all is prepared for their visit. I was shocked to learn that my request to join a congressional investigating committee's tour of San Quentin and Soledad was refused, as was that of the news media.

There should be an ombudsman in every prison, not under the pay or control of the prison authority, and responsible only to the courts, state legislature and the public. Such a person could report on violations of constitutional and human rights.

Guards must be given better training than they now receive for the difficult job society imposes upon them. To be a prison guard as now constituted is to be put in a situation of constant threat from within the prison, with no social recognition from the society at large. As was shown graphically at Attica, prison guards are also prisoners of the system who can be sacrificed to the demands of the public to be punitive and the needs of politicians to preserve an image. Social scientists and business administrators should be called upon to design and help carry out this training.

The relationship between the individual (who is sentenced by the courts to a prison term) and his community must be maintained. How can a prisoner return to a dynamically changing society that most of us cannot cope with after being out of it for a number of years? There should be more community involvement in these rehabilitation centers, more ties encouraged and promoted between the trainees and family and friends, more educational opportunities to prepare them for returning to their communities as more valuable members of it than they were before they left.

Finally, the main ingredient necessary to effect any change at all in prison reform, in the rehabilitation of a single prisoner or even in the optimal development of a child is caring. Reform must start with people—especially people with power—caring about the well-being of others. Underneath the toughest, society-hating convict, rebel or anarchist is a human being who wants his existence to be recognized by his fellows and who wants someone else to care about whether he lives or dies and to grieve if he lives imprisoned rather than lives free.

LABS

Internet Exercise

The Social Construction of Reality

Introduction

The phrase "social construction of reality" relies on the belief that events are open to interpretation and reality is shaped by individual perceptions, definitions, and subjective assessments presented in social interactions. Through social interactions, people are able to assign meaning to the actions of others and shape a personal reality. The meaning we assign is often based on our past experiences and cultural background. By continually linking the interpretations of social interactions to culture and society we construct social reality.

Different societies and groups within societies can have different interpretations of the same social interaction because each group brings a unique cultural context as a reference point. Giving someone a "thumbs up" in the United States is commonly understood as "OK" or "right on!," but in parts of the Middle East the gesture is obscene. Language can also be interpreted in various ways, with the inflection and tone changing the context of conversation and interpretation. Also putting a "spin" on events by choosing or creating specialized phrases can help create a different reality. Finally, text is clearly interpretable. An e-mail can be construed as rude, flirty, or curt without the sender meaning any of these things. However, the interpretation is reality for the reader even when it is not the same reality for the sender.

Clearly, not everyone determines reality in the same way. The response to Hurricane Katrina that devastated the Gulf region is one contemporary example. In a September 2005 CNN/*US Today*/Gallup poll there was an obvious racial split on the recovery efforts. About 60 percent of blacks interviewed thought that race was a contributing factor to a slow federal response but only about 12 percent of whites interviewed thought the same. Additionally, about 63 percent of blacks and 21 percent of whites agreed that poverty was a factor in the slow response in New Orleans.

Idea in Use

In the July 2001 publication of *The Journal of Urban Affairs*, research by Danilo Yanich evaluated how television news programs help viewers shape their views on crime locations. Yanich reported that "newscasts played a pre-eminent role in the social construction of reality and, by extension, in forming the cognitive maps that citizens use to understand their communities." Yanich analyzed Baltimore and Philadelphia local television news for location biases in their reporting of crime. Both Baltimore and Philadelphia markets reported more on crime in cities than in suburban areas, and in general reported on the most violent crimes rather than those crimes that occur with far more regularity but are less sensational. This generates a message that cities are more dangerous places than suburban locales. More time was spent on the coverage of violent crime, the specific street location was often reported, interviews with local residents occurred, and the crime news was presented with both packaged and live location remotes. The emphasis that the newscasts placed on the city crimes often exaggerates the idea that crimes are more important and influential in the city than in the suburbs. Using the information obtained from local newscasts, it is easy to see how local citizens may socially construct a sense of reality that cities are crime-ridden and less safe than other locations within a viewing area, which may not necessarily be accurate.

Activity Instructions

This internet exercise will illustrate how individuals can perceive situations, objects, and conditions differently. Senses, intuition, and experience will guide you through this exercise. Hopefully, you will conclude after viewing the websites that objective things can be perceived and interpreted in subjective ways. This is even more complicated when it is social interactions between two or more social beings!

1. Go to Michael Bach's website featuring optical illusions and visual phenomena. It is located at http://www.michaelbach.de/ot/

   a. View one optical illusion/phenomena from each of the seven categories.
   b. Which ones did you complete?
   c. Write a brief note about whether it was easy for you to see or took some time for you to identify.

2. Now head to http://www.puzzle.dse.nl/tests/index_us.html

   a. Complete the following tests/puzzles

      i. Color Reading Test
      ii. Black Dots
      iii. Quick Eye Exam
      iv. Mental Arithmetic Test

   b. Report on your success (or failure!)

3. Doublespeak is a term that refers to language that is used to intentionally conceal or distort actual meaning. Oftentimes, it is used by people and institutions of power, such as those associated with the government, the military, or corporations. Search the internet for instances of doublespeak in speeches, statements, or in the news. Good places to start your search would be http://www.historychannel.com/speeches/archive1.html or by searching news outlets such as www.cnn.com, www.foxnews.com, or www. msnbc .com for contemporary quotes, press statement transcripts, etc. You may also want to venture to the National Council of Teachers of English Doublespeak Awards at http://www.ncte.org/about/awards/council/jrnl/106868.htm or http://www. stim.com/Stim-x/8.2/doublespeak/doublespeak.html for examples of doublespeak.

   a. In the speech, statement, or story, indicate how many instances of doublespeak you found. What were the exact phrases/words used and why were these words used rather than more precise language (e.g., was the subject matter controversial, etc.)?
   b. Write a brief paragraph about whether you feel doublespeak is a vindictive or negative concept or whether it is just political correctness to the extreme.

4. Turn in your assignment to your instructor as directed.

Individual Writing Exercise

Social Interaction

Introduction

Social interaction takes various forms. Sometimes interaction is very conscious and intentional, such as when we communicate verbally with someone. We also interact in less conscious ways, such as with voice inflection, non-verbal gestures, and body language. Sociologists distinguish between the following types of social interactions:

- Exchange—interaction with the expectation of a material or non-material reward
- Cooperation—interaction with others to achieve a shared goal
- Conflict—interaction with another to achieve a goal at the other's expense
- Competition—conflict interaction based on shared rules

Erving Goffman was a sociologist who concentrated his work on identifying social interactions in everyday life. He concluded that people interact with one another as if they were performing on a stage. He called this phenomenon *dramaturgy*. When we interact, we attempt to project our best image, concealing flaws and minimizing embarrassing situations. We also try to lessen any uneasiness of the other 'actor' in the interaction by maintaining eye contact, avoiding invasion of their personal space, and appropriately responding to the other participant. The dramaturgical event comprises a number of components:

- *Costumes*—dress
- *Props*—any material object used in the interaction
- *Stages*—contexts for interaction, which can be either *backstage* (out of view of a critically observing public); or *frontstage* (in the presence, and for the benefit, of a public)
- *Scripts*—typical responses, use of titles, dialogue, etc.)

An example of all of these dramaturgical components might be illustrated with an interaction ritual that many Americans participate in on Sunday mornings, going to church. The individual dresses appropriately and arrives promptly. The "worship service" is one of the stages on which interaction takes place, which includes responding to prayers, singing of hymns (with the use of a hymnal as a prop), and avoiding irreverent behavior so as to avoid a stigma.

Idea in Use

David John Erikson and Richard Tewksbury report in a 2000 edition of *Deviant Behavior: An Interdisciplinary Journal* on their dramaturgical analysis of social interactions that occur in gentlemen's clubs between patrons and workers. Based on their qualitative research, they created a six-category typology of male strip club patrons. This classification scheme was generated based on the observations of the male's actions in the club as well as the interactions males had with dancers. The authors contend that research within gentlemen's clubs provides insight into men's backstage area where they can reveal all their "latent sexual desires" and "male privilege." Also discussed extensively in the article is the role of impression management.

Activity Instructions

You will be observing everyday behaviors and identifying the types of interaction as well as completing a dramaturgical analysis of people's behaviors.

1. For an entire day, take time to observe the behaviors of the people around you. Make sure to note where you are at the time of your observations—in the dorm, in class, at work, at practice, etc.

2. Jot down the interactions that you see and classify them as non-verbal, exchange, cooperation, conflict, or competition. Make sure to indicate who was involved in the interaction, what you think the interaction was about, where it took place, and your reaction. Analyze the interactions based on type of interaction (exchange, competition, etc.). Which type did you encounter the most? Where did each type typically take place?

3. Now select one social interaction that you were a part of and complete a dramaturgical analysis on that interaction. Indicate what the interaction was about, what the actors wore, what props were used, and what measures were taken to maintain good impression management. What other factors of the dramaturgical experience can you describe?

4. You will be graded on the extensiveness of your lists of interactions, as well as the thoughtfulness and thoroughness of analysis.

5. Turn in to your instructor as directed.

Group Exercise

Status and Role

Introduction

Two core concepts of social interaction are *status* and *role*. Status refers to the social position that one holds. Individuals can hold many different statuses at once, and can gain or lose a status throughout a lifetime. The collection of statuses that an individual occupies at any given time is called their *status set*. Moreover, there are two categories of statuses: *ascribed* and *achieved*. Ascribed statuses are those positions that a person has no control of and no ability to change. For instance, the status of "daughter" is an ascribed status. An achieved status is a social position that one voluntarily attains through their ability, hard work, or natural skill. For example, being a "Democrat" or a "graduate student" is an achieved status. A *master status* refers to the overriding status that is most influential in shaping an individual's identity at a given time. A master status could be either ascribed or achieved. An ascribed master status might be one's race or gender classification, especially when this is a minority status. For example, when a woman joins a construction crew her coworkers may only see her gender, which then takes on the character of a master status. Achieved master statuses often relate to one's occupation since this often communicates clues regarding education, income, and prestige. Occupation is not the only type of master status, however. Any status that supersedes all others can be classified as a master status.

Each status has one or more roles attached to it. A role refers to the behavior that is expected of an individual who occupies a status A *role set* comprises the multiple roles attached to a single status. For instance, a person's status as student could have a role set that involves studying for exams, writing papers, making presentations, going to parties, and participating in study groups.

With many different statuses and all the accompanying role expectations, it is inevitable that individuals will encounter difficulty meeting all of the demands that will be imposed. When confronted with potentially contradictory demands from the various role expectations attached to their statuses, individuals will likely encounter *role strain* and *role conflict*. *Role strain* occurs when two or more roles *within a single status* compete and are incompatible. Role strain might occur when a social worker wants to have a friendly relationship with his or her client, but at the same time must remain at a professional distance to insure that needs are met and decisions are made without a personal bias. *Role conflict* occurs when two or more roles *attached to different statuses* compete and are incompatible. A young college student may feel role conflict when they would like to celebrate a friends' 21st birthday but has a final exam at 8 a.m. the next morning. The role conflict between being a good, supportive *friend* and a successful *student* can be stressful.

Idea in Use

There is a considerable amount of literature related to work-family role conflicts. One such article, "Work and Family Role Strain among University Employees" published in 2003 in the *Journal of Family and Economic Issues,* used results from a survey of faculty and staff from a Midwestern University. The goal of the project was to determine whether the indicators of role conflict and role strain differ by position (faculty or staff) or by gender. Researcher Marta Elliot found that the main sources of stress for all surveyed within the family sphere are related to the difficulties with caregiving. Regardless of position and gender, Elliot found that in the work domain, stress was related to frustration with provided resources and unwarranted, negatively perceived reviews related to their work. The only clear division on how men and women felt the effects of role strain related to competing work and family responsibilities was that women who reported having a supportive partner found that strain was much reduced. Men did not report lower levels of role strain even when they indicated they had a supportive partner.

Figure 5.1   Role Strain/Conflict

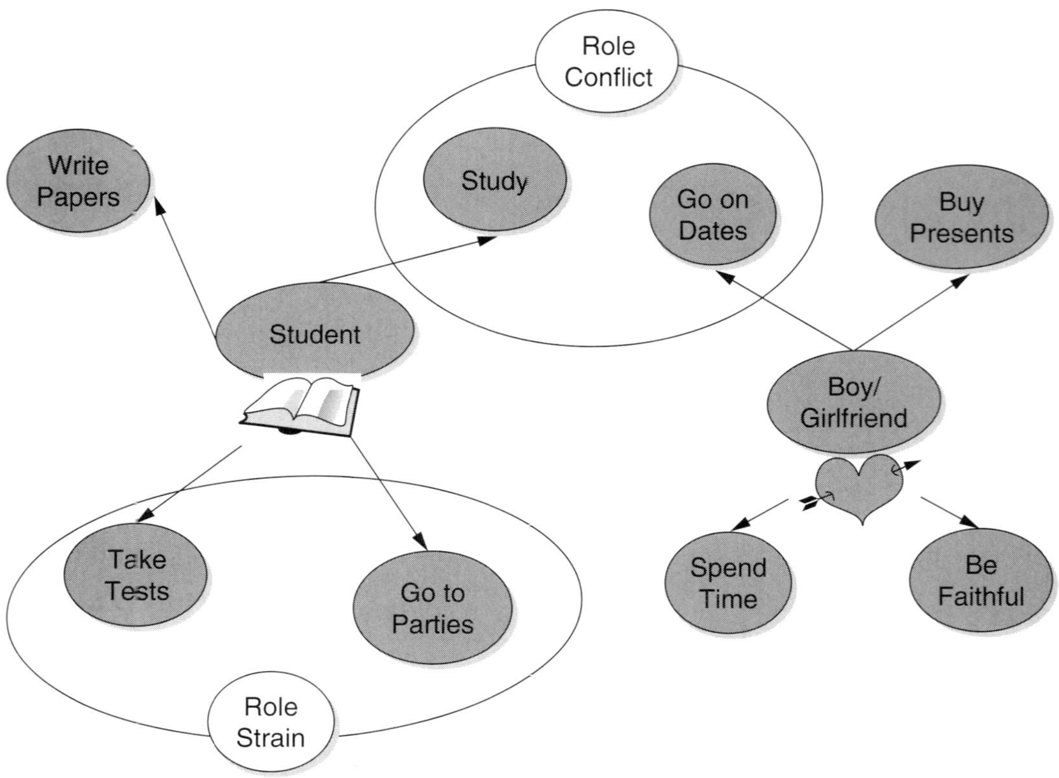

Activity Instructions

In small groups, you will evaluate the statuses that you hold and the roles that you perform in each status and compare to other people's statuses and associated roles. For each of your statuses, you will create a role set and evaluate it for role strain. Then you will compare the statuses and roles, and assess areas of role conflict.

1. Identify the three primary statuses that you occupy that are most important to your identity. You will be creating a free form figure like the example from above.

   a. Determine the roles that these statuses require you to perform to maintain the status. Indicate which roles you play for each status.
   b. Now circle the roles that have caused, or are likely to cause, role strain.
   c. Circle the role conflicts that you most experience.

2. Identify what you consider to be your master status. Do you occupy more than one status that might be possible contenders for your master status?

3. In small groups, create a list of everyone's statuses and the roles they identified for each status. How many statuses and roles overlapped among group members? Where did most people indicate that they had role strain and role

conflicts? Was there much diversity in the individual figures or did people bring similar drawings?

4. Create a list of master statuses identified by your group members. Indicate whether these master statuses are ascribed or achieved.

5. Turn in your individual drawings of role strain/conflict. Also submit one copy of your group lists and answers. You will be graded on your extensiveness of lists and thoughtfulness.

Groups and Organizations

"Banana Time"
Donald F. Roy

Labs
Internet Exercise: Social Groups
Individual Writing Exercise: McDonaldization of Society
Group Exercise: Bureaucracy

"Banana Time"

My account of how one group of machine operators kept from "going nuts" in a situation of monotonous work activity attempts to lay bare the tissues of interaction which made up the content of their adjustment. The talking, fun, and fooling which provided solution to the elemental problem of "psychological survival" will be described according to their embodiment in intra-group relations. In addition, an unusual opportunity for close observation of behavior involved in the maintenance of group equilibrium was afforded by the fortuitous introduction of a "natural experiment." My unwitting injection of explosive materials into the stream of interaction resulted in sudden, but temporary, loss of group interaction.

My fellow operatives and I spent our long days of simple, repetitive work in relative isolation from other employees of the factory. Our line of machines was sealed off from other work areas of the plant by the four walls of the clicking room. The one door of this room was usually closed. Even when it was kept open, during periods of hot weather, the consequences were not social; it opened on an uninhabited storage room of the shipping department. Not even the sounds of work activity going on elsewhere in the factory carried to this isolated work place. There were occasional contacts with "outside" employees, usually on matters connected with the work; but, with the exception of the daily calls of one fellow who came to pick up finished materials for the next step in processing, such visits were sporadic and infrequent.

Reprinted with permission from "Banana Time: Job Satisfaction and Informal Interaction" by Donald F. Roy in *Human Organization*, 1960, vol. 18, pp. 158–168. Copyright © Society for Applied Anthropology.

Moreover, face-to-face contact with members of the managerial hierarchy were few and far between. No one bearing the title of foreman ever came around. The only company official who showed himself more than once during the two-month observation period was the plant superintendent. Evidently overloaded with supervisory duties and production problems which kept him busy elsewhere, he managed to pay his respects every week or two. His visits were in the nature of short, businesslike, but friendly exchanges. Otherwise he confined his observable communications with the group to occasional utilization of a public address system. During the two-month period, the company president and the chief chemist paid one friendly call apiece. One man, who may or may not have been of managerial status, was seen on various occasions lurking about in a manner which excited suspicion. Although no observable consequences accrued from the peculiar visitations of this silent fellow, it was assumed that he was some sort of efficiency expert, and he was referred to as "The Snooper."

As far as our work group was concerned, this was truly a situation of laissez-faire management. There was no interference from staff experts, no hounding by time-study engineers or personnel men hot on the scent of efficiency or good human relations. Nor were there any signs of industrial democracy in the form of safety, recreational, or production committees. There was an international union, and there was a highly publicized union-management cooperation program; but actual interactional processes of cooperation were carried on somewhere beyond my range of observation and without participation of members of my work group. Furthermore, these union-management get-togethers had no determinable connection with the problem of "toughing out" a twelve-hour day at monotonous work.

Our work group was thus not only abandoned to its own resources for creating job satisfaction, but left without that basic reservoir of ill-will toward management which can sometimes be counted on to stimulate the development of interesting activities to occupy hand and brain. Lacking was the challenge of intergroup conflict, that perennial source of creative experience to fill the otherwise empty hours of meaningless work routine.[1]

The clicking machines were housed in a room approximately thirty by twenty-four feet. They were four in number, set in a row, and so arranged along one wall that the busy operator could, merely by raising his head from his work, freshen his reveries with a glance through one of three large harred windows. To the rear of one of the end machines sat a long cutting table; here the operators cut up rolls of plastic materials into small sheets manageable for further processing at the clickers. Behind the machine at the opposite end of the line sat another table which was intermittently the work station of a female employee who performed sundry scissors operations of a more intricate nature on raincoat parts. Boxed in on all sides by shelves and stocks of materials, this latter locus of work appeared a cell within a cell.

The clickers were of the genus punching machines; of mechanical construction similar to that of the better-known punch presses, their leading features were hammer and block. The hammer, or punching head, was approximately eight inches by twelve inches at its flat striking surface. The descent upon the block was initially forced by the operator, who exerted pressure on a handle attached to the side of the hammer head. A few inches of travel downward established electrical connection for a sharp, power-driven blow. The hammer also traveled, by manual guidance, in a horizontal plane to and from, and in an arc around, the central column of the machine. Thus the operator, up to the point of establishing electrical connections for the sudden and irrevocable downward thrust, had flexibility in maneuvering his instrument over the larger surface of the block. The latter, approximately twenty-four inches wide, eighteen inches deep, and ten inches thick, was made, like a butcher's block, of inlaid hardwood; it was set in the machine at a convenient waist height. On it the operator placed his materials, one sheet at a time if leather, stacks of sheets if plastic, to be cut with steel dies of assorted sizes and shapes. The particular die in use would be moved, by hand, from spot to spot over the materials each time a cut was made; less frequently, materials would be shifted on the block as the operator saw need for such adjustment.

Introduction to the new job, with its relatively simple machine skills and work routines, was accomplished with what proved to be, in my experience, an all-time minimum of job training. The clicking machine assigned to me was situated at one end of the row. Here the superintendent and one of the operators gave a few brief demonstrations, accompanied by bits of advice which included a warning to keep hands clear of the descending hammer. After a short practice period, at the end of which the superintendent expressed satisfaction with progress and potentialities, I was left to develop my learning curve with no other supervision than that afforded by members of the work group. Further advice and assistance did come, from time to time, from my fellow operatives, sometimes upon request, sometimes unsolicited.

The Work Group

Absorbed at first in three related goals of improving my clicking skill, increasing my rate of output, and keeping my left hand unclicked, I paid little attention to my fellow operatives save to observe that they were friendly, middle-aged, foreign-born, full of advice, and very talkative. Their names, according to the way they addressed each other, were George, Ike, and Sammy.[2] George, a stocky fellow in his late fifties, operated the machine at the opposite end of the line; he, I later discovered, had emigrated in early youth from a country in Southeastern Europe. Ike, stationed at George's left, was tall, slender, in his early fifties, and Jewish; he had come from Eastern Europe in his youth. Sammy, number three man in the line, and my neighbor, was heavy set, in his late fifties, and Jewish; he had escaped from a country in Eastern Europe just before Hitler's legions had moved in. All three men had been downwardly mobile as to occupation in recent years. George and Sammy had been proprietors of small businesses; the former had been "wiped out" when his uninsured establishment burned down; the latter had been entrepreneuring on a small scale before he left all behind him to flee the Germans. According to his account, Ike had left a highly skilled trade which he had practiced for years in Chicago.

I discovered also that the clicker line represented a ranking system in descending order from George to myself. George not only had top seniority for the group, but functioned as a sort of leadman. His superior status was marked in the fact that he received five cents more per hour than the other clickermen, put in the longest workday, made daily contact, outside the workroom, with the superintendent on work matters which concerned the entire line, and communicated to the rest of us the directives which he received. The narrow margin of superordination was seen in the fact that directives were always relayed in the superintendent's name; they were on the order of, "You'd better let that go now, and get on the green. Joe says they're running low on the fifth floor," or, "Joe says he wants two boxes of the 3-die today." The narrow margin was also seen in the fact that the superintendent would communicate directly with his operatives over the public address system; and, on occasion, Ike or Sammy would leave the workroom to confer with him for decisions or advice in regard to work orders.

Ike was next to George in seniority, then Sammy. I was, of course, low man on the totem pole. Other indices to status differentiation lay in informal interaction, to be described later.

With one exception, job status tended to be matched by length of workday. George worked a thirteen-hour day, from 7 a.m. to 8:30 p.m. Ike worked eleven hours, from 7 a.m. to 6:30 p.m.; occasionally he worked until 7 or 7:30 for an eleven and a half- or a twelve-hour day. Sammy put in a nine-hour day, from 8 a.m. to 5:30 p.m. My twelve hours spanned from 8 a.m. to 8:30 p.m. We had a half hour for lunch, from 12 to 12:30.

The female who worked at the secluded table behind George's machine put in a regular plant-wide eight-hour shift from 8 to 4:30. Two women held this job during the period of my employment; Mable was succeeded by Baby. Both were Negroes, and in their late twenties.

A fifth clicker operator, an Arabian *emigré* called Boo, worked a night shift by himself. He usually arrived about 7 p.m. to take over Ike's machine.

The Work

It was evident to me, before my first workday drew to a weary close, that my clicking career was going to be a grim process of fighting the clock, the particular timepiece in this situation being an old-fashioned alarm clock which ticked away on a shelf near George's machine. I had struggled through many dreary rounds with the minutes and hours during the various phases of my industrial experience, but never had I been confronted with such a dismal combination of working conditions as the extra-long workday, the infinitesimal cerebral excitation, and the extreme limitation of physical movement. The contrast with a recent stint in the California oil fields was striking. This was no eight-hour day of racing hither and yon over desert and foothills with a rollicking crew of "roustabouts" on a variety of repair missions at oil wells, pipe lines, and storage tanks. Here there were no afternoon dallyings to search the sands for horned toads, tarantulas, and rattlesnakes, or to climb old wooden derricks for raven's nests, with an eye out, of course, for the tell-tale streak of dust in the distance which gave ample warning of the approach of the boss. This was standing all day in one spot beside three old codgers in a dingy room looking out through barred windows at the bare walls of a brick warehouse, leg movements largely restricted to the shifting of body weight from one foot to the other, hand and arm movements confined, for the most part, to a simple repetitive sequence of place the die,—punch the clicker,—place the die,—punch the clicker, and intellectual activity reduced to computing the hours to quitting time. It is true that from time to time a fresh stack of sheets would have to be substituted for the clicked-out old one; but the stack would have been prepared by someone else, and the exchange would be only a minute or two in the making. Now and then a box of finished work would have to be moved back out of the way, and an empty box brought up; but the moving back and the bringing up involved only a step or two. And there was the half hour for lunch, and occasional trips to the lavatory or the drinking fountain to break up the day into digestible parts. But after each momentary respite, hammer and die were moving again: click,—move die,—click,—move die.

Before the end of the first day, Monotony was joined by his twin brother, Fatigue. I got tired. My legs ached, and my feet hurt. Early in the afternoon I discovered a tall stool and moved it up to my machine to "take the load off my feet." But the superintendent dropped in to see how I was "doing" and promptly informed me that "we don't sit down on this job." My reverie toyed with the idea of quitting the job and looking for other work.

The next day was the same: the monotony of the work, the tired legs and sore feet and thoughts of quitting.

The Game of Work

The game developed was quite simple, so elementary, in fact, that its playing was reminiscent of rainy-day preoccupations in childhood, when attention could be centered by the hour on colored bits of things of assorted sizes and shapes. But this adult activity was not mere pottering and piddling; what it lacked in the earlier imaginative content, it made up for in clean-cut structure. Fundamentally involved were:

a) variation in color of the materials cut, b) variation in shapes of the dies used, and c) a process called "scraping the block." The basic procedure which ordered the particular combination of components employed could be stated in the form: "As soon as I do so many of these, I'll get to do those." If, for example, production scheduled for the day featured small, rectangular strips in three colors, the game might go: "As soon as I finish a thousand of the green ones, I'll click some brown ones." And, with success in attaining the objective of working with brown materials, a new goal of "I'll get to do the white ones" might be set. Or the new goal might involve switching dies.

Scraping the block made the game more interesting by adding to the number of possible variations in its playing; and, what was perhaps more important, provided the only substantial reward, save for going to the lavatory or getting a drink of water, on days when work with one die and one color of material was scheduled. As a physical operation, scraping the block was fairly simple; it involved application of a coarse file to the upper surface of the block to remove roughness and unevenness resulting from the wear and tear of die penetration. But, as part of the intellectual and emotional content of the game of work, it could be in itself a source of variation in activity. The upper left-hand corner of the block could be chewed up in the clicking of 1,000 white trapezoid pieces, then scraped. Next, the upper right-hand corner, and so on until the entire block had been worked over. Then, on the next round of scraping by quadrants, there was the possibility of a change of color or die to green trapezoid or white oval pieces.

Thus the game of work might be described as a continuous sequence of short-range production goals with achievement rewards in the form of activity change. The superiority of this relatively complex and self-determined system over the technically simple and outside-controlled job satisfaction injections experienced by Milner at the beginner's table in a shop of the feather industry should be immediately apparent:

> Twice a day our work was completely changed to break the monotony. First Jennie would give us feathers of a brilliant green, then bright orange or a light blue or black. The "ohs" and "ahs" that came from the girls at each change was proof enough that this was an effective way of breaking the monotony of the tedious work.[3]

But a hasty conclusion that I was having lots of fun playing my clicking game should be avoided. These games were not as interesting in the experiencing as they might seem to be from the telling. Emotional tone of the activity was low, and intellectual currents weak. Such rewards as scraping the block or "getting to do the blue ones" were not very exciting, and the stretches of repetitive movement involved in achieving them were long enough to permit lapses into obsessive reverie. Henri de Man speaks of "clinging to the remnants of joy in work," and this situation represented just that. How tenacious the clinging was, how long I could have "stuck it out" with my remnants, was never determined. Before the first week was out this adjustment to the work situation was complicated by other developments. The game of work continued, but in a different context. Its influence became decidedly subordinated to, if not completely overshadowed by, another source of job satisfaction.

Informal Social Activity of the Work Group: Times and Themes

The change came about when I began to take serious note of the social activity going on around me; my attentiveness to this activity came with growing involvement in it. What I heard at first, before I started to listen, was a stream of disconnected bits of communication which did not make much sense. Foreign accents were strong and referents were not joined to coherent contexts of meaning. It was just "jabbering." What I saw at first, before I began to observe, was occasional flurries of horseplay so simple and unvarying in pattern and so childish in quality that they made no strong bid for attention. For example, Ike would regularly switch off the power at Sammy's machine whenever Sammy made a trip to the lavatory or the drinking fountain. Correlatively, Sammy invariably fell victim to the plot by making an attempt to operate his clicking hammer after returning to the shop. And, as the simple pattern went, this blind stumbling into the trap was always followed by indignation and reproach from Sammy, smirking satisfaction from Ike, and mild paternal scolding from George. My interest in this procedure was at first confined to wondering when Ike would weary of his tedious joke or when Sammy would learn to check his power switch before trying the hammer.

But, as I began to pay closer attention, as I began to develop familiarity with the communication system, the disconnected became connected, the nonsense made sense, the obscure became clear, and the silly actually funny. And, as the content of the interaction took on more and more meaning, the interaction began to reveal structure. There were "times" and "themes," and roles to serve their enaction. The interaction had subtleties, and I began to savor and appreciate them. I started to record what hitherto had seemed unimportant.

Times

This emerging awareness of structure and meaning included recognition that the long day's grind was broken by interruptions of a kind other than the formally instituted or idiosyncratically developed disjunctions in work routine previously described. These additional interruptions appeared in daily repetition in an ordered series of informal interactions.

Most of the breaks in the daily series were designated as "times" in the parlance of the clicker operators, and they featured the consumption of food or drink of one sort or another. There was coffee time, peach time, banana time, fish time, coke time, and, of course, lunch time. Other interruptions, which formed part of the series but were not verbally recognized as times, were window time, pickup time, and the staggered quitting times of Sammy and Ike. These latter unnamed times did not involve the partaking of refreshments.

My attention was first drawn to this times business during my first week of employment when I was encouraged to join in the sharing of two peaches. It was Sammy who provided the peaches; he drew them from his lunch box after making the announcement, "Peach time!" On this first occasion I refused the proffered fruit, but thereafter regularly consumed my half peach. Sammy continued to provide the peaches and to make the "Peach time!" announcement, although there were days when Ike would remind him that it was peach time, urging him to hurry up with the mid-morning snack. Ike invariably complained about the quality of the fruit, and his complaints fed the fires of continued banter between peach donor and critical recipient. I did find the fruit a bit on the scrubby side but felt, before I achieved insight into the function of peach time, that Ike was showing poor manners by looking a gift horse in the mouth. I wondered why Sammy continued to share his peaches with such an ingrate.

Banana time followed peach time by approximately an hour. Sammy again provided the refreshments, namely, one banana. There was, however, no four-way sharing of Sammy's banana. Ike would gulp it down by himself after surreptitiously extracting it from Sammy's lunch box, kept on a shelf behind Sammy's work station. Each morning, after making the snatch, Ike would call out, "Banana time!" and proceed to down his prize while Sammy made futile protests and denunciations. George would join in with mild remonstrances, sometimes scolding Sammy for making so much fuss. The banana was one which Sammy brought for his own consumption at lunch time; he never did get to eat his banana, but kept bringing one for his lunch. At first this daily theft startled and amazed me. Then I grew to look forward to the daily seizure and the verbal interaction which followed.

Window time came next. It followed banana time as a regular consequence of Ike's castigation by the indignant Sammy. After "taking" repeated references to himself as a person badly lacking in morality and character, Ike would "finally" retaliate by opening the window which faced Sammy's machine, to let the "cold air" blow in on Sammy. The slandering which would, in its echolalic repetition, wear down Ike's patience and forbearance usually took the form of the invidious comparison: "George is a good daddy! Ike is a bad man! A very bad man!" Opening the window would take a little time to accomplish and would involve a great deal of verbal interplay between Ike and Sammy, both before and after the event. Ike would threaten, make feints toward the window, then finally open it. Sammy would protest, argue, and make claims that the air blowing in on him would give him a cold; he would eventually have to leave his machine to close the window. Sometimes the weather was slightly chilly, and the draft from the window unpleasant; but cool or hot, windy or still, window time arrived each day. (I assume that it was originally a cold season development.) George's part in this interplay, in spite of the "good daddy" laudations, was to encourage Ike in his window work. He would stress the tonic values of fresh air and chide Sammy for his unappreciativeness.

Following window time came lunch time, a formally designated half-hour for the midday repast and rest break. At this time, informal interaction would feature exchanges between Ike and George. The former would start eating his lunch a few minutes before noon, and the latter, in his role as straw boss, would censure him for malobservance of the rules. Ike's off-beat luncheon usually involved a previous tampering with George's alarm clock. Ike would set the clock ahead a few minutes in order to maintain his eating schedule without detection, and George would discover these small daylight saving changes.

The first "time" interruption of the day I did not share. It occurred soon after I arrived on the job, at eight o'clock. George and Ike would share a small pot of coffee brewed on George's hot plate.

Pickup time, fish time, and coke time came in the afternoon. I name it pickup time to represent the official visit of the man who made daily calls to cart away boxes of clicked materials. The arrival of the pickup man, a Negro, was always a noisy one, like the arrival of a daily passenger train in an isolated small town. Interaction attained a quick peak of intensity to crowd into a few minutes all communications, necessary and otherwise. Exchanges invariably included loud depreciations by the pickup man of the amount of work accomplished in the clicking department during the preceding twenty-four hours. Such scoffing would be on the order of "Is that all you've got done? What do you boys do all day?" These devaluations would be countered with allusions to the "soft job" enjoyed by the pickup man. During the course of the exchanges news items would be dropped, some of serious import, such as reports of accomplished or impending layoffs in the various plants of the company, or of gains or losses in orders for company products. Most of the news items, however, involved bits of information on plant employees told in a light vein. Information relayed by the clicker operators was usually told about each other, mainly in the form of summaries of the most recent kidding sequences. Some of this material was repetitive, carried over from day to day. Sammy would be the butt of most of this newscasting, although he would make occasional counter-reports on Ike and George.

An invariable part of the interactional content of pickup time was Ike's introduction of the pickup man to George. "Meet Mr. Papeatis!" Ike would say in mock solemnity and dignity. Each day the pickup man "met" Mr. Papeatis, to the obvious irritation of the latter. Another pickup time invariably would bring Baby (or Mable) into the interaction. George would always issue the loud warning to the pickup man: "Now I want you to stay away from Baby! She's Henry's girl!" Henry was a burly Negro with a booming bass voice who made infrequent trips to the clicking room with lift-truck loads of materials. He was reputedly quite a ladies' man among the colored population of the factory. George's warning to "Stay away from Baby!" was issued to every Negro who entered the shop. Baby's only part in this was to laugh at the horseplay.

About mid-afternoon came fish time. George and Ike would stop work for a few minutes to consume some sort of pickled fish which Ike provided. Neither Sammy nor I partook of this nourishment, nor were we invited. For this omission I was grateful; the fish, brought in a newspaper and with head and tail intact, produced a reverse effect on my appetite. George and Ike seemed to share a great liking for fish. Each Friday night, as a regular ritual, they would enjoy a fish dinner together at a nearby restaurant. On these nights Ike would work until 8:30 and leave the plant with George.

Coke time came late in the afternoon, and was an occasion for total participation. The four of us took turns in buying the drinks and in making the trip for them to a fourth floor vending machine. Through George's manipulation of the situation, it eventually became my daily chore to go after the cokes; the straw boss had noted that I made a much faster trip to the fourth floor and back than Sammy or Ike.

Sammy left the plant at 5:30, and Ike ordinarily retired from the scene an hour and a half later. These quitting times were not marked by any distinctive interaction save the one regular exchange between Sammy and George over the former's "early washup." Sammy's tendency was to crowd his washing up toward five o'clock, and it was George's concern to keep it from further creeping advance. After Ike's departure came Boo's arrival. Boo's was a striking personality productive of a change in topics of conversation to fill in the last hour of the long workday.

Themes

To put flesh, so to speak, on this interactional frame of "times," my work group had developed various "themes" of verbal interplay which had become standardized in their repetition. These topics of conversation ranged in quality from an extreme of nonsensical chatter to another extreme of serious discourse. Unlike the times, these themes flowed one into the other in no particular sequence of predictability. Serious conversation could suddenly melt into horseplay, and vice versa. In the middle of a serious discussion on the high cost of living, Ike might drop a weight behind the easily startled Sammy, or hit him over the head with a dusty paper sack. Interaction would immediately drop to a low comedy exchange of slaps, threats, guffaws, and disapprobations which would invariably include a ten-minute echolalia of "Ike is a bad man, a very bad man! George is a good daddy, a very fine man!" Or, on the other hand, a stream of such invidious comparisons as followed a surreptitious switching-off of Sammy's machine by the playful Ike might merge suddenly into a discussion of the pros and cons of saving for one's funeral.

"Kidding themes" were usually started by George or Ike, and Sammy was usually the butt of the joke. Sometimes Ike would have to "take it," seldom George. One favorite kidding theme involved Sammy's alleged receipt of $100 a month from his son. The points stressed were that Sammy did not have to work long hours, or did not have to work at all, because he had a son to support him. George would always point out that he sent money to his daughter; she did not send money to him. Sammy received occasional calls from his wife, and his claim that these calls were requests to shop for groceries on the way home were greeted with feigned disbelief. Sammy was ribbed for being closely watched, bossed, and henpecked by his wife, and the expression "Are you man or mouse?" became an echolalic utterance, used both in and out of the original context.

Ike, who shared his machine and the work scheduled for it with Boo, the night operator, came in for constant invidious comparison on the subject of output. The socially isolated Boo, who chose work rather than sleep on his lonely night shift, kept up a high level of performance, and George never tired of pointing this out to Ike. It so happened that Boo, an Arabian Moslem from Palestine, had no use for Jews in general; and Ike, who was Jewish, had no use for Boo in particular. Whenever George would extol Boo's previous night's production, Ike would try to turn the conversation into a general discussion on the need for educating the Arabs. George, never permitting the development of serious discussion on this topic, would repeat a smirking warning, "You watch out for Boo! He's got a long knife!"

The "poom poom" theme was one that caused no sting. It would come up several times a day to be enjoyed as unbarbed fun by the three older clicker operators. Ike was usually the one to raise the question, "How many times you go poom poom last night?" The person questioned usually replied with claims of being "too old for poom poom." If this theme did develop a goat, it was I. When it was pointed out that I was a younger man, this provided further grist for the poom poom mill. I soon grew weary of this poom poom business, so dear to the hearts of the three old satyrs, and, knowing where the conversation would inevitably lead, winced whenever Ike brought up the subject.

Serious themes included the relating of major misfortunes suffered in the past by group members. George referred again and again to the loss, by fire, of his business establishment. Ike's chief complaints centered around a chronically ill wife who had undergone various operations and periods of hospital care. Ike spoke with discouragement of the expenses attendant upon hiring a housekeeper for himself and his children; he referred with disappointment and disgust to a teen-age son, an inept lad who "couldn't even fix his own lunch. He couldn't even make himself a sandwich!" Sammy's reminiscences centered on the loss of a flourishing business when he had to flee Europe ahead of Nazi invasion.

There was one theme of especially solemn import, the "professor theme." This theme might also be termed "George's daughter's marriage theme;" for the recent marriage of George's only child was inextricably bound up with George's connection with higher learning. The daughter had married the son of a professor who instructed in one of the local colleges. This professor theme was not in the strictest sense a conversation piece; when the subject came up, George did all the talking. The two Jewish operatives remained silent as they listened with deep respect, if not actual awe, to George's accounts of the Big Wedding which, including the wedding pictures, entailed an expense of $1,000. It was monologue, but there was listening, there was communication, the sacred communication of a temple, when George told of going for Sunday afternoon walks on the Midway with the professor, or of joining the professor for a Sunday dinner. Whenever he spoke of the professor, his daughter, the wedding, or even of the new son-in-law, who remained for the most part in the background, a sort of incidental like the wedding cake, George was complete master of the interaction. His manner, in speaking to the rank-and-file of clicker operators, was indeed that of master deigning to notice his underlings. I came to the conclusion that it was the professor connection, not the straw-boss-ship or the extra nickel an hour, which provided the fount of George's superior status in the group.

If the professor theme may be regarded as the cream of verbal interaction, the "chatter themes" should be classed as the dregs. The chatter themes were hardly themes at all; perhaps they should be labelled "verbal states," or "oral autisms." Some were of doubtful status as communication; they were like the howl or cry of an animal responding to its own physiological state. They were exclamations, ejaculations, snatches of song or doggerel, talkings-to-oneself, mutterings. Their classification as themes would rest on their repetitive character. They were echolalic utterances, repeated over and over. An already mentioned example would be Sammy's repetition of "George is a good daddy, a very fine man! Ike is a bad man, a very bad man!" Also, Sammy's repetition of "Don't bother me! Can't you see I'm busy? I'm a very busy man!" for ten minutes after Ike had dropped a weight behind him would fit the classification. Ike would shout "Mamariba!" at intervals between repetition of bits of verse, such as:

> Mama on the bed,
> Papa on the floor,
> Baby in the crib
> Says giver some more!

Sometimes the three operators would pick up one of these simple chatterings in a sort of chorus. "Are you man or mouse? I ask you, are you man or mouse?" was a favorite of this type.

So initial discouragement with the meagerness of social interaction I now recognized as due to lack of observation. The interaction was there, in constant flow. It captured attention and held interest to make the long day pass. The twelve hours of "click,—move die,—click,—move die" became as easy to endure as eight hours of varied activity in the oil fields or eight hours of playing the piecework game in a machine shop. The "beast of boredom" was gentled to the harmlessness of a kitten.

Black Friday: Disintegration of the Group

But all this was before "Black Friday." Events of that dark day shattered the edifice of interaction, its framework of times and mosaic of themes, and reduced the work situation to a state of social atomization and machine-tending drudgery. The explosive element was introduced deliberately, but without prevision of its consequences.

On Black Friday, Sammy was not present; he was on vacation. There was no peach time that morning, of course, and no banana time. But George and Ike held their coffee time, as usual, and a steady flow of themes was filling the morning quite adequately. It seemed like a normal day in the making, at least one which was going to meet the somewhat reduced expectations created by Sammy's absence.

Suddenly I was possessed of an inspiration for modification of the professor theme. When the idea struck, I was working at Sammy's machine, clicking out leather parts for billfolds. It was not difficult to get the attention of close neighbor Ike to suggest *sotto voce*, "Why don't you tell him you saw the professor teaching in a barber college on Madison Street?...Make it near Halsted Street."

Ike thought this one over for a few minutes, and caught the vision of its possibilities. After an interval of steady application to his clicking, he informed the unsuspecting George of his near West Side discovery; he had seen the professor busy at his instructing in a barber college in the lower reaches of Hobohemia.

George reacted to this announcement with stony silence. The burden of questioning Ike for further details on his discovery fell upon me. Ike had not elaborated his story very much before we realized that the show was not going over. George kept getting redder in the face, and more tight-lipped; he slammed into his clicking with increased vigor. I made one last weak attempt to keep the play on the road by remarking that barber colleges paid pretty well. George turned to hiss at me, "You'll have to go to Kankakee with Ike!" I dropped the subject. Ike whispered to me, "George is sore!"

George was indeed sore. He didn't say another word the rest of the morning. There was no conversation at lunchtime, nor was there any after lunch. A pall of silence had fallen over the clicker room. Fish time fell a casualty. George did not touch the coke I brought for him. A very long, very dreary afternoon dragged on. Finally, after Ike left for home, George broke the silence to reveal his feelings to me:

> Ike acts like a five-year-old, not a man! He doesn't even have the respect of the
> niggers. But he's got to act like a man around here! He's always fooling
> around! I'm going to stop that! I'm going to show him his place!

> …Jews will ruin you, if you let them. I don't care if he sings, but the first time he mentions my name, I'm going to shut him up! It's always "Meet Mr. Papeatis! George is a good daddy!" And all that. He's paid to work! If he doesn't work, I'm going to tell Joe! [The superintendent.]

Then came a succession of dismal workdays devoid of times and barren of themes. Ike did not sing, nor did he recite bawdy verse. The shop songbird was caught in the grip of icy winter. What meager communication there was took a sequence of patterns which proved interesting only in retrospect.

For three days, George would not speak to Ike. Ike made several weak attempts to break the wall of silence which George had put between them, but George did not respond; it was as if he did not hear. George would speak to me, on infrequent occasions, and so would Ike. They did not speak to each other.

On the third day George advised me of his new communication policy, designed for dealing with Ike, and for Sammy, too, when the latter returned to work. Interaction was now on a "strictly business" basis, with emphasis to be placed on raising the level of shop output. The effect of this new policy on production remained indeterminate. Before the fourth day had ended, George got carried away by his narrowed interests to the point of making sarcastic remarks about the poor work performances of the absent Sammy. Although addressed to me, these caustic depreciations were obviously for the benefit of Ike. Later in the day Ike spoke to me, for George's benefit, of Sammy's outstanding ability to turn out billfold parts. For the next four days, the prevailing silence of the shop was occasionally broken by either harsh criticism or fulsome praise of Sammy's outstanding workmanship. I did not risk replying to either impeachment or panegyric for fear of involvement in further situational deteriorations.

Twelve-hour days were creeping again at snail's pace. The strictly business communications were of no help, and the sporadic bursts of distaste or enthusiasm for Sammy's clicking ability helped very little. With the return of boredom, came a return of fatigue. My legs tired as the afternoons dragged on, and I became engaged in conscious efforts to rest one by shifting my weight to the other. I would pause in my work to stare through the barred windows at the grimy brick wall across the alley; and, turning my head, I would notice that Ike was staring at the wall too. George would do very little work after Ike left the shop at night. He would sit in a chair and complain of weariness and sore feet.

In desperation, I fell back on my game of work, my blues and greens and whites, my ovals and trapezoids, and my scraping the block. I came to surpass Boo, the energetic night worker, in volume of output. George referred to me as a "day Boo" (day-shift Boo) and suggested that I "keep" Sammy's machine. I managed to avoid this promotion, and consequent estrangement with Sammy, by pleading attachment to my own machine.

When Sammy returned to work, discovery of the cleavage between George and Ike left him stunned. "They were the best of friends!" he said to me in bewilderment.

George now offered Sammy direct, savage criticisms of his work. For several days the good-natured Sammy endured these verbal aggressions without losing his temper; but when George shouted at him "You work like a preacher!" Sammy became very angry, indeed. I had a few anxious moments when I thought that the two old friends were going to come to blows.

Then, thirteen days after Black Friday, came an abrupt change in the pattern of interaction. George and Ike spoke to each other again, in friendly conversation:

> I noticed Ike talking to George after lunch. The two had newspapers of fish at George's cabinet. Ike was excited; he said, "I'll pull up a chair!" The two ate for ten minutes.…It seems that they went up to the 22nd Street Exchange together during lunch period to cash pay checks.

The professor theme was dropped completely. George never again mentioned his Sunday walks on the Midway with the professor.

Theoretical Considerations

Possible contribution to ongoing sociological inquiry into the behavior of small groups, in general, and factory work groups, in particular, may lie in one or more of the following ideational products of my clicking-room experience:

1.   In their day-long confinement together in a small room spatially and socially isolated from other work areas of the factory, the Clicking Department employees found themselves ecologically situated for development of a "natural" group. Such a development did take place; from worker inter-communications did emerge the full-blown sociocultural system of consumatory interactions which I came to share, observe, and record in the process of my socialization.

2.   These interactions had a content which could be abstracted from the total existential flow of observable doings and sayings for labelling and objective consideration. That is, they represented a distinctive sub-culture, with its recurring patterns of reciprocal influencings which I have described as times and themes.

3.   From these interactions may also be abstracted a social structure of statuses and roles. This structure may be discerned in the carrying out of the various informal activities which provide the content of the sub-culture of the group. The times and themes were performed with a system of roles which formed a sort of peeking hierarchy. Horseplay had its initiators and its victims, its amplifiers and its chorus; kidding had its attackers and attacked, its least attacked and its most attacked, its ready acceptors of attack and its strong resistors to attack. The fun went on with the participation of all, but within the controlling frame of status, a matter of who can say or do what to whom and get away with it.

4.   In both the cultural content and the social structure of clicker group interaction could be seen the permeation of influences which flowed from the various multiple group memberships of the participants. Past and present "other-group" experiences or anticipated "outside" social connections provided significant materials for the building of themes and for the establishment and maintenance of status and role relationships. The impact of reference group affiliations on clicking-room interaction was notably revealed in the sacred, status-conferring expression of the professor theme. This impact was brought into very sharp focus in developments which followed my attempt to degrade the topic, and correlatively, to demote George.

5.   Stability of the clicking-room social system was never threatened by immediate outside pressures. Ours was not an instrumental group, subject to disintegration in a losing struggle against environmental obstacles or oppositions. It was not striving for corporate goals; nor was it faced with the enmity of other groups. It was strictly a consumatory group, devoted to the maintenance of patterns of self-entertainment. Under existing conditions, disruption of unity could come only from within.

Potentials for breakdown were endemic in the interpersonal interactions involved in conducting the group's activities. Patterns of fun and fooling had developed within a matrix of frustration. Tensions born of long hours of relatively meaningless work were released in the mock aggressions of horseplay. In the recurrent attack, defense, and counter-attack there continually lurked the possibility that words or gestures harmless in conscious intent might cross the subtle boundary of accepted, playful aggression to be perceived as real assault. While such an occurrence might incur displeasure no more lasting than necessary for the quick clarification or creation of kidding norms, it might also spark a charge of hostility sufficient to disorganize the group.

A contributory potential for breakdown from within lay in the dissimilar "other-group" experiences of the operators. These other-group affiliations and identifications could provide differences in tastes and sensitivities, including appreciation of humor, differences which could make maintenance of consensus in regard to kidding norms a hazardous process of trial and error adjustments.

6.   The risk involved in this trial and error determination of consensus on fun and fooling in a touchy situation of frustration—mock aggression—was made evident when I attempted to introduce alterations in the professor theme. The group disintegrated, *instanter.* That is, there was an abrupt cessation of the interactions which constituted our groupness. Although both George and I were solidly linked in other-group affiliations with the higher learning, there was not enough agreement in our attitudes toward university professors to prevent the interactional development which shattered our factory play group. George perceived my offered alterations as a real attack, and he responded with strong hostility directed against Ike, the perceived assailant, and Sammy, a fellow traveler.

My innovations, if accepted, would have lowered the tone of the sacred professor theme. Such a downgrading of George's reference group would, in turn, have downgraded George. His status in the shop group hinged largely upon his claimed relations with the professor.

7.   Integration of our group was fully restored after a series of changes in the patterning and quality of clicking-room interaction. It might be said that reintegration took place in these changes, that the series was a progressive one of step-by-step improvement in relations, that re-equilibration was in process during the three weeks that passed between initial communication collapse and complete return to "normal" interaction.

Notes

1. Donald F. Roy, "Work Satisfaction and Social Reward in Quota Achievement: An Analysis of Piecework Incentive," *American Sociological Review,* XVIII (October, 1953), 507–514.
2. All names used are fictitious.
3. Lucille Milner, *Education of An American Liberal,* Horizon Press, New York, 1954, p. 97.

LABS

Internet Exercise

Social Groups

Introduction

Sociologically, a *group* refers to a collection of individuals who interact repeatedly, in a structured way, because of shared values, interests, and goals. The central element to a group is that the members identify with one another and feel a sense of belonging. This element distinguishes a social group from aggregates, crowds, and categories. Example of a social group may be an athletic team, seminar class, or local union. An *aggregate* is a collection of individuals in one place who have little interaction or sense of belonging with one another. Mall shoppers or people on a plane are examples of aggregates. A *crowd* is a collection of individuals who come together temporarily for a common cause and are united by the situation. Fans at a football game or music concert are examples of crowds. The people do not identify with one another and only interact temporarily. A *category* is a set of people who share a common trait, but do not interact in a meaningful way. For instance, the local electrical union is a group, but the designation "electrician" is a category.

Sociologists also make a distinction between primary and secondary groups. A *primary group* is a small, intimate group whose members spend a lot of time together, have meaningful relationships, and show genuine concern for one another over an extended period of time. Primary groups are integral to socialization, learning roles associated with statuses, and helping to shape character. A clique of close friends is an example of a primary group. *Secondary groups* are larger and less intimate than primary groups. They are characterized by members that are less involved with each other. The interaction that takes place usually has a utilitarian purpose, rather than being simply for the enjoyment of the group relationships. An example of a secondary group is a college lecture class.

Another way to classify groups is by membership. An *in-group* is a social group in which individuals feel integrated and to which a sense of loyalty is felt. On the other hand, an *out-group* rivals and competes with the in-group. Public school students feel united with one another and may view private school students with disdain as the out-group. In-groups and out-groups can be trivial or very critical. For instance, if a Crip gang member comes face to face with an out-group Blood gang member, there could be fatal consequences. A *reference group* is yet another type of group, one which an outsider observes and uses as a point of reference. A reference group can help individuals know what is appropriate and thus guides future actions. In addition, reference groups can provide confirmation or disapproval of past or present actions. At any point in time, an individual may have multiple reference groups, in-groups, and out-groups.

Idea in Use

The July 2002 edition of the *Journal for Studies on Alcohol* included Cameron Wild's article entitled "Personal Drinking and Sociocultural Drinking Norms: A Representative Population Study." In his research, Wild examined the relationship between an individual's drinking behavior and the expectations and perceptions about alcohol use by members of his or her reference groups. Wild hypothesized that heavy drinkers were more likely to estimate that members of their reference groups would drink the same amount of alcohol as themselves. Using a nationally representative sample of Ontario residents who consumed alcohol in the previous 12 months, Wild confirmed his hypothesis. Heavy drinkers were more likely than light drinkers to overestimate how much alcohol members of three different reference groups consumed. Wild concludes that his research supports normative perceptions. That is, if heavy drinkers overestimate the amount of alcohol that their reference group members consumed, they may feel that their own drinking practices are appropriate and normal.

Activity Instructions

This internet exercise will explore the multitudes of on-line communities.

1. Go to www. egroups. com (you may choose another group portal if you are familiar with it, but be sure to identify which portal you use). Identify how many groups are available for your:

   a. University/College
   b. Place of Residence (start with your town and then build up to county/ nearest city if you don't find anything)
   c. Favorite Musician/Band
   d. Religion with which you most identify

2. For each of the categories above, indicate what types of on-line groups have been formed. For instance, in the University/College category, you may find on-line groups related to athletics, for international students, alumni classes, etc.

3. Now choose one group from each category. Identify how many members have joined the group, what information that the group description discloses, and how much activity the group has had in the past seven days.

   • Hint 1—you do not have to join the group to procur this information
   • Hint 2—you can find out this information even if the group is private

4. Finally, choose your primary hobby/interest and see if there are groups available that you would consider joining. What are these groups and why would you or would you not join?

5. Turn in your assignment to your instructor as directed.

Individual Writing Exercise

McDonaldization of Society

Introduction

An organization that represents bureaucracy and is representative of a shift in organizational principles within society is McDonald's. George Ritzer, a contemporary sociologist from the University of Maryland, introduced the concept of *McDonaldization* as a way to explain society. Ritzer theorized that people break down tasks into the smallest possible parts to be the most efficient. However, he realized this very process of becoming efficient created more inefficiency. Ritzer called this process "the irrationality of rationality." For instance, the drive-thru window (or windows at some places) was created to serve more people in a faster amount of time. More often than not the actual process of paying for and getting food take much longer than expected by the company headquarters and customers. It is important to understand that *McDonaldization* does not just occur in the fast food industry. Ritzer developed the concept in such a manner that it can be universally applied. The practice of *McDonaldization* can be seen within almost every large organization and is increasingly more problematic in the fields of education and medicine.

Ritzer identified four key aspects of the McDonaldization process: efficiency, calculability, predictability, and the use of non-human technology. *Efficiency* refers to using the optimum methods to achieve a given end. McDonald's employs efficiency when they use the customer to complete services. For example, the consumer must bus their own table and typically must get their own beverage and condiments. Sometimes, putting the consumer to work can slow down the entire process (have you ever been behind someone who doesn't know how to swipe their credit card at the checkout line?). It also limits the interaction between people, leading to a more solitary and isolated world. *Calculability* is the emphasis on quantitative aspects rather than on quality. This is easily evidenced at McDonald's where advertisements promote Big Macs, double and triple burgers, and super-sized meals (now no longer used—more about this below in *Idea in Use*) rather than eating healthily and in moderation. Notice how McDonald's never claims that their product is a quality product. *Predictability* emphasizes things such as discipline, routine, and consistency. The meals that McDonald's offers across the country and most of the world are identical and the customer knows what to expect. No matter where you go, a happy meal has the same arrangement of kiddie-sized food plus toy; a number two value meal is a quarter pounder with cheese, french fries, and a drink. Routine scripts are performed by the employees and direct the interaction between worker and customer. While predictability can put people at ease, it also limits experience, individuality, and innovations. Finally, Ritzer identified *control through the substitution of non-human technology for human workers* as a characteristic of organizations throughout society. Conveyor belts as well as the pushing of buttons to dispense the right amount of soda and condiments are evidence of such substitutions. While replacing humans with robots and other machines can limit the unpredictability, individuality, and inefficiency of humans, it also has serious implications for unemployment, segregation from society, limited social interactions, and an increased dependence on machines.

Idea in Use

Supersize Me, a movie by Morgan Spurlock, became a blockbuster hit in 2004. This creative documentary followed Spurlock's adventure in consuming only food from McDonald's for a full month. Following his three self-defined rules, Spurlock gained thirty pounds and a host of health problems. He interviewed dozens of people, from doctors and lawyers, to first graders who can identify Ronald McDonald but not Jesus or George Washington. Spurlock not only chronicles his experience but also looks at the costs for society. The poor health that fast food corporations, unhealthy school lunchrooms, and sugary soda confections contribute to have not only physical costs, but have legal, financial, emotional, and cultural implications. Since the movie was produced, McDonald's has disbanded the "supersize" advertising campaign and created a variety of salads.

Activity Instructions

In this individual exercise, you will be analyzing how McDonaldization fits in with Weber's bureaucracy and identifying areas in daily life which the McDonaldization process affects.

1. Compare Ritzer's four characteristics that are central to McDonaldization to the six elements that Weber identifies as key to ideal bureaucracy (you can find Weber's list of elements in any introductory sociology textbook, online, or in the introduction to the exercise entitled *Bureaucracy* in this section). How much do they overlap? What are the main differences between Ritzer and Weber?

2. Identify the franchises in your community and make a list according to type. For instance, one category can be fast food restaurants, another could be sit-down restaurants, clothing retail stores, and/or gyms.

3. Using the categories that you created in Question 2, identify and list independent stores that are in your community (Mom and Pop shops, etc.).

4. Write a brief summary of the stores you frequent more often. What is the appeal for the stores that you visit most often? How do efficiency, calculability, and predictability factor into the appeal or lack of appeal of stores for you?

5. Analyze how McDonaldization's elements are present in your university experience. Some possibilities are analyzing the application process, grading system, or classroom structures and interactions.

6. Turn in your assignment as directed by your instructor. You will be graded on the exhaustiveness of your lists and your thorough examination of McDonaldization.

Group Exercise

Bureaucracy

Introduction

Bureaucracy is a formal organization that is structured to achieve the maximum degree of efficiency. Businesses, colleges, hospitals, and other entities are bureaucracies when their organizational structure is specifically arranged to maximize production with minimal overlap and effort.

Max Weber, a German sociologist, identified six key characteristics of an "ideal type" bureaucracy. An ideal type bureaucratic organization is one that only exists in the abstract. An ideal type embodies all of the proscribed elements perfectly and serves as a model and reference point. *Specialization* is one element that Weber named as essential to bureaucratic organizations. Clear and extensive division of labor often characterizes specialization. *Hierarchy of authority* is another characteristic and specifies that organizations have vertical rankings of positions. It usually takes the shape of a pyramid, with many people at the base, and few holding office at the top. *Explicit, written rules and regulations* are another key element to bureaucratic organization and enhance predictability and efficiency. Often in the form of handbooks and manuals, the written manuscript provides descriptions, expectations, and regulations of specific jobs as well as references to contact in departments to answer questions, etc. *Impartial employment practices* refer to the hiring of individuals that embody the skills, qualifications, and ability needed to perform the job competently, rather than using nepotistic practices. This idea of impartiality is also applied in promotion situations. A fifth characteristic specified by Weber is the *impersonality* of the organization. Rather than taking feelings and emotions into account, the rules and regulations direct interactions. Uniform treatment of members of the organization as well as spectators or clients is mandated. Finally, there is an emphasis on *recordkeeping* and paperwork. The saving and filing of all transactions and correspondences among and between bureaucratic organizations is a fundamental element. The paper trail can set precedent in new cases and situations, as well as insure that the proper procedures and practices were followed.

Weber saw the bureaucratic process as an attempt to be the most efficient or *rational.* He theorized that modernity and rationalization occur simultaneously and occur in all aspects of social life. Therefore, he believed that the long-term consequences of rationalization were problematic. Believing that extremely rationalized institutions were impersonal, repressive, less spontaneous, and dehumanizing, Weber was pessimistic and envisioned an "iron cage" imprisoning our actions, emotions, traditions, and personality.

Idea in Use

The bureaucratization of educational institutions, particularly in higher education, has received attention in academics and in the public. In an effort to be more efficient, college and university administrators are looking for professional staff with little or no academic experience. The use of external constituencies such as governing boards of directors, trustees/regents, foundations, and other groupings of political and business leaders has shifted accountability, increased specialization, and shifted the hierarchy of authority. This is precisely what William Waugh suggests in a 2003 article in *The Annals of the American Academy of Political and Social Science.* In the article "Issues in University Governance: More 'Professional' and Less Academic," Waugh suggests that the transfer to a reliance on more external rather than internal constituencies has drained the power from faculty as well as students and de-emphasized academics. Waugh suggests various alternatives and resolutions to the increased bureaucratization of higher education. One suggestion is to return to traditional university governance processes rather than large, bureaucratic processes. Additionally, he suggests maintaining a clear and separate division between academic and non-academic components.

Activity Instructions

In this group exercise, you will relate how bureaucracies have affected your life and the lives of your peers.

1. Think back to the job you have held longest, or, if you have never formally worked, the club/group/association with which you have been most involved. Identify how your workplace or organization epitomizes Weber's ideal bureaucracy. For instance, how was specialization and division of labor organized in the organization? Make sure you identify aspects of your experience for each of the six elements.

2. In your small group, compare your answers to question one. Make a master document that illustrates all of the group members' answers and place an asterisk on any answers that multiple group members identified. Your master document should resemble this:

Specialization	Hierarchy of Authority	Written Rules/Regulations
Impartial Employment Practices	Impersonality	Recordkeeping

3. Rank, from one to six, the elements that your group believes have had the most influence at your work/organization (1 = most important, 6 = least important). Explain why you chose to rank the element as the most important/influential. Do you think that this may change as the type of job/organizational experience changes?

4. Finally, as a group, identify how this sociology class is like a bureaucratic organization (using the six ideal type elements that Weber identified).

5. Turn in your group's master document, rankings, and write-up from question four to your instructor as directed.

Social Stratification

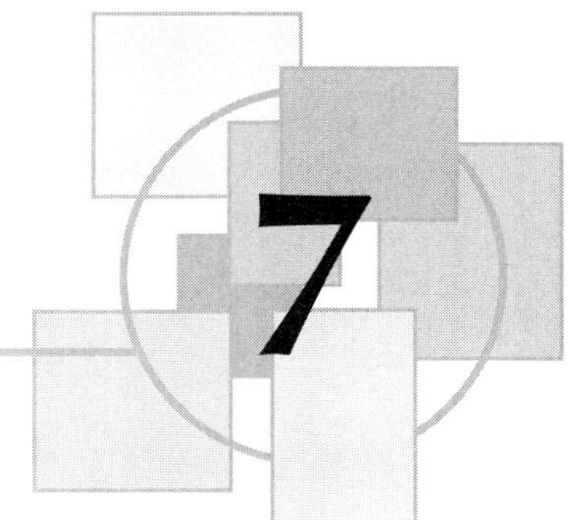

No Degree, and No Way Back to the Middle
Timothy Egan

Labs
Internet Exercise: Global Stratification
Individual Writing Exercise: Poverty in the United States
Group Exercise: Social Class in the United States

No Degree, and No Way Back to the Middle

Spokane, Wash.—Over the course of his adult life, Jeff Martinelli has married three women and buried one of them, a cancer victim. He had a son and has watched him raise a child of his own. Through it all, one thing was constant: a factory job that was his ticket to the middle class.

It was not until that job disappeared, and he tried to find something—anything—to keep him close to the security of his former life that Mr. Martinelli came to an abrupt realization about the fate of a working man with no college degree in 21st-century America.

He has skills developed operating heavy machinery, laboring over a stew of molten bauxite at Kaiser Aluminum, once one of the best jobs in this city of 200,000. His health is fine. He has no shortage of ambition. But the world has changed for people like Mr. Martinelli.

"For a guy like me, with no college, it's become pretty bleak out there," said Mr. Martinelli, who is 50 and deals with life's curves with a resigned shrug.

His son, Caleb, already knows what it is like out there. Since high school, Caleb has had six jobs, none very promising. Now 28, he may never reach the middle class, he said. But for his father and others of a generation that could count on a comfortable life without a degree, the fall out of the middle class has come as a shock. They had been frozen in another age, a time when Kaiser factory workers could buy new cars, take decent vacations and enjoy full health care benefits.

They have seen factory gates close and not reopen. They have taken retraining classes for jobs that pay half their old wages. And as they hustle around for work, they have been constantly reminded of the one thing that stands out on their résumés: the education that ended with a high school diploma.

It is not just that the American economy has shed six million manufacturing jobs over the last three decades; it is that the market value of those put out of work, people like Jeff Martinelli, has declined considerably over their lifetimes, opening a gap that has left millions of blue-collar workers at the margins of the middle class.

And the changes go beyond the factory floor. Mark McClellan worked his way up from the Kaiser furnaces to management. He did it by taking extra shifts and learning everything he could about the aluminum business.

Still, in 2001, when Kaiser closed, Mr. McClellan discovered that the job market did not value his factory skills nearly as much as it did four years of college. He had the experience, built over a lifetime, but no degree. And for that, he said, he was marked.

He still lives in a grand house in one of the nicest parts of town, and he drives a big white Jeep. But they are a facade.

"I may look middle class," said Mr. McClellan, who is 45, with a square, honest face and a barrel chest. "But I'm not. My boat is sinking fast."

By the time these two Kaiser men were forced out of work, a man in his 50's with a college degree could expect to earn 81 percent more than a man of the same age with just a high school diploma. When they had started work, the gap was only 52 percent. Other studies show different numbers, but the same trend—a big disparity that opened over their lifetimes.

Mr. Martinelli refuses to feel sorry for himself. He has a job in pest control now, killing ants and spiders at people's homes, making barely half the money he made at the Kaiser smelter, where a worker with his experience would make about $60,000 a year in wages and benefits.

"At least I have a job," he said. "Some of the guys I worked with have still not found anything. A couple of guys lost their houses."

Mr. Martinelli and other former factory workers say that, over time, they have come to fear that the fall out of the middle class could be permanent. Their new lives—the frustrating job interviews, the bills that arrive with red warning letters on the outside—are consequences of a decision made at age 18.

The management veteran, Mr. McClellan, was a doctor's son, just out of high school, when he decided he did not need to go much farther than the big factory at the edge of town. He thought about going to college. But when he got on at Kaiser, he felt he had arrived.

His father, a general practitioner now dead, gave him his blessing, even encouraged him in the choice, Mr. McClellan said.

At the time, the decision to skip college was not that unusual, even for a child of the middle class. Despite Mr. McClellan's lack of skills or education beyond the 12th grade, there was good reason to believe that the aluminum factory could get him into middle-class security quicker than a bachelor's degree could, he said.

By 22, he was a group foreman. By 28, a supervisor. By 32, he was in management. Before his 40th birthday, Mr. McClellan hit his earnings peak, making $100,000 with bonuses.

Friends of his, people with college degrees, were not earning close to that, Mr. McClellan said.

"I had a house with a swimming pool, new cars," he said. "My wife never had to work. I was right in the middle of middle-class America and I knew it and I loved it."

If anything, the union man, Mr. Martinelli, appreciated the middle-class life even more, because of the distance he had traveled to get there. He remembers his stomach growling at night as a child, the humiliation of welfare, hauling groceries home through the snow on a little cart because the family had no car.

"I was ashamed," he said.

He was a C student without much of a future, just out of high school, when he got his break: the job on the Kaiser factory floor. Inside, it was long shifts around hot furnaces. Outside, he was a prince of Spokane.

College students worked inside the factory in the summer, and some never went back to school.

"You knew people leaving here for college would sometimes get better jobs, but you had a good job, so it was fine," said Mike Lacy, a close friend of Mr. Martinelli and a co-worker at Kaiser.

The job lasted just short of 30 years. Kaiser, debt-ridden after a series of failed management initiatives and a long strike, closed the plant in 2001 and sold the factory carcass for salvage.

Mr. McClellan has yet to find work, living off his dwindling savings and investments from his years at Kaiser, though he continues with plans to open his own car wash. He pays $900 a month for a basic health insurance policy—vital to keep his wife, Vicky, who has a rare brain disease, alive. He pays an additional $500 a month for her medications. He is both husband and nurse.

"Am I scared just a little bit?" he said. "Yeah, I am."

He has vowed that his son David will never do the kind of second-guessing that he is. Even at 16, David knows what he wants to do: go to college and study medicine. He said his father, whom he has seen struggle to balance the tasks of home nurse with trying to pay the bills, had grown heroic in his eyes.

He said he would not make the same choice his father did 27 years earlier. "There's nothing like the Kaiser plant around here anymore," he said.

Mr. McClellan agrees. He is firm in one conclusion, having risen from the factory floor only to be knocked down: "There is no working up anymore."

LABS

Internet Exercise

Global Stratification

Introduction

Inequality is not just a trait of American social life. In fact, inequality *between* countries is much more pronounced. The classification terminology that relates to global stratification has changed over the years. Traditionally, sociologists used categories of "third world," "second world," and "first world" as a way to classify countries. This classification was based on the country's level of industrialization with "first world" referring to the most industrialized and "third world" meaning non-industrialized countries. There were several problems with this typology. First, the third-world grouping included over 100 countries with varying levels of wealth, development, and industrialization outlook. Second, the second world, which generally referred to communist countries, had vague requirements for inclusion and after the fall of the Soviet Union, became even more ambiguous. Therefore, alternative terminology has been created to focus on the economic development of the country rather than on industrialization and political status.

One new classification system, developed by the World Bank, groups countries according to income level. The three strata that make up this typology are high-income countries, middle-income countries (further sub-divided to lower-middle and upper-middle), and low-income countries. The level of income disparity between countries can be vast. For instance, the poorest people in high-income countries would likely be considered much better off than the richest of low-income countries. The extent and severity of poverty is far more marked in low-income countries. Another classification system that has been used extensively by sociologists relates to development level. This schema categorizes countries into developed, developing, and underdeveloped levels. One of the criticisms of this methodology is that it proposes that every country should develop/industrialize in a linear fashion.

There are three main theoretical perspectives that attempt to explain global stratification: *modernization theory, dependency theory,* and *world systems theory.* Modernization theory suggests that technology and culture account for differences in economy. Proponents believe that low-income countries will inevitably and irreversibly modernize once they rid themselves of barriers to advancement. The main criticisms of the theory is that it assumes that all nations should modernize in a similar fashion to the United States and thus it takes an ethnocentric slant that material and technological advancements are better than living simply. Another main criticism is that the theory essentially blames culture for the poverty experienced in the country.

Dependency theory takes a conflict perspective and blames rich nations for restraining the development of poor nations. This theory suggests that rich nations make other nations dependent on them. Rich nations provide manufactured goods (often hazardous) to developing countries, and obtain raw materials and cheap labor from the poor countries. There are several criticisms of this theory as well. The main critique is that it is too simplistic, blaming global poverty on rich countries. In fact, global stratification is a very complex problem.

The world systems theory recognizes that all countries take part in an international economic system. The level of participation in this world system, which is dominated by capitalism, differs by country. *Core* countries are rich, industrialized countries that benefit the most from the international market. *Semiperiphery* countries benefit off the periphery, but lose profits to the core. The *peripheral* countries are poor and their participation is often dictated by the conditions imposed on them by the core and semiperiphery countries. In this world systems theory, there are global partnerships, and politics and economics intermingle. Critics maintain that the world systems theory still has a very linear one-way network, benefiting the rich to the detriment of the poor.

Idea in Use

Albert Bergesen and Omar Lizardo use the world systems theory to explain international terrorism. In the 2004 publication of their article "International Terrorism and the World System" in *Sociological Theory,* the authors first identify how various theoretical perspectives can be used to understand international terrorism. Using a historical analysis, they disentangle the relationship between globalization and terrorism. They suggest that there are several factors that make international terrorism more likely. Specifically, they propose that a dominant nation-state is in a state of decline and there is growing instability and volatility within semiperiphery states. They emphasize that international terrorism is much more likely to be initiated by semiperiphery states than core or periphery zones. Bergesen and Lizardo detail several examples, including the United States' decline and the crisis for Arab-Islamic states that have precipitated the Iraq War and associated war on terror.

Activity Instructions

In this internet exercise, you will be identifying areas of stratification between global communities.

1. The World Bank is an organization that seeks to eliminate the suffering of people and countries in poverty. They provide extensive funding for education, healthcare, and debt relief. They also provide global statistics on the economic and social conditions of all countries. Go to their website at www.worldbank.org. You will first be selecting countries based on income level. Go to the "Countries" page and select the "Data" option on the left side menu, and then choose the "Country Classification" option. Under the "Definition of Groups" heading, click on the "View All Groups" hyperlink. Select two countries from each income heading. You do not need to select countries from the OECD option and only have to choose two countries from the low-middle or high-middle categories.

2. You will now be finding information about the social and economic climate in your selected countries. Go to the "Online Databases" section and access the Data Query. If you get lost in cyberspace, the address is: http://devdata.worldbank.org/dataquery/. You will input your selected countries and select the following series of indicators for all five years.

   - Gross Domestic Product (GDP—current US$)
   - Exports of Goods and Services (% of GDP)
   - Literacy Rates of Adult Males and Females
   - Immunization for Measles
   - Malnutrition Prevalence
   - School Enrollment (primary and secondary)
   - Paved Roads
   - Fixed Lines and Mobile Phone Subscribers

   Provide information for the latest year that reports the information. Some countries do not have data available. It is okay to include a selected country if most of the data is provided. However, if more than three of the indicators are missing for all years, you will have to select a new country from the same income level.

3. Return to the "Select Countries" option in the data query. Select high income, low income, and the middle income that corresponds to the countries you selected previously. Select the same indicators as you did in part two and run the query. Record the information for the most current year.

4. Create two tables. The first table should include the indicators as rows and your selected countries as the columns. Record the data you found and indicate to which year the data refers. The second table should be generated in a similar fashion, but instead of using countries as the columns, use the income level groupings.

5. Write a report (approximately two pages typed double spaced) that compares the countries, taking into consideration the income level.

   - How disparate are the living conditions?
   - What can you tell about the living conditions from the information you obtained?
   - Out of the six selected countries, which one would you most like to live in and why?
   - Compare how your selected countries relate to the overall conditions on the income level (i.e., compare your two high income countries to the information you found when you ran a query on the high income category).
   - Are your selected countries better or worse than the average experienced by the income grouping?

6. Finally, go to the statistics division of the United Nations found at: http://unstats.un.org/unsd/. Click on the "Demographic and Social Statistics Databases," the "Social Indicators" option, and then the "Statistics" link. Choose one of your selected countries from each income group to investigate. Create a table that shows:

   - Life expectancy at birth for males and females
   - Infant mortality rate
   - Estimated percentage of people that have access to improved drinking water sources for total, rural, and urban
   - Population distribution percentages for rural and urban

   Be sure to include the year to which the data refer. In some cases, there will be missing data.

7. Turn in all your tables and report to your instructor as directed.

Individual Writing Exercise

Poverty in the United States

Introduction

Public policy programs often target the issue of poverty, a complicated topic, which affects millions of people within the United States. Social scientists and governmental agencies often have a hard time agreeing on a definition of poverty, as well as its causes, prevention, and relief. The collection of reliable poverty data did not begin until the 1960s when the federal government created poverty threshold figures. The poverty threshold figures are what the government says is needed to support a minimally adequate standard of living and is based on the size and age composition of family. The poverty threshold is what the Census Department uses as a "statistical yardstick." Total family income is then compared to the threshold and poverty status is assigned if appropriate.

Absolute poverty refers to the absolute minimum that one needs to subsist. A person living in absolute poverty would have difficulty obtaining food, shelter, and other necessities, so survival is a struggle. People living in absolute poverty qualify for governmental aid, and are essentially powerless. *Relative poverty* is a comparative concept whereby one individual or category does not fare as well as another. Generally, relative poverty is not "keeping up with the Jones'." For instance, a family that meets all essential needs but cannot afford to go on vacation may consider themselves relatively poor if all the families in their neighborhood are capable.

While there are people living in poverty within every race, ethnicity, age, geographic area, and gender, there are certain demographic categories more susceptible to poverty. The *feminization of poverty* is a term that describes the increasing proportion of women in poverty. Women in poverty are often single mothers; therefore, children are also put at a risk of growing up in poverty. The feminization of poverty is not just a problem in the United States; it is a global trend that often has devastating effects.

The stereotypical image of a person living on welfare throughout life is not an accurate reflection of the majority of the poor. While there are some individuals who refuse to work, many living in poverty are too young or too old to work, ill, disabled, or poorly educated. The less educated are at a great disadvantage because the opportunities to find a full-time job that will sufficiently provide for a family are unlikely.

Idea in Use

William Julius Wilson is a prominent sociologist who has written extensively on urban poverty. His books, *The Truly Disadvantaged* and *When Work Disappears*, describe the plight of the underclass and attach blame to society. The underclass refers to people who lack basic skills and training and have experienced severe poverty for an extensive period of time. Wilson concentrates his analysis on the black underclass living in American cities. The main thesis is that the loss of work opportunities has created a situation that perpetuates poverty. Specifically, the loss of manufacturing jobs and the "suburbanization" of America has led to racial segregation in neighborhoods, poor education systems, and a pessimistic attitude. Wilson's work has contributed much to the "war on poverty" and he is one of the most significant contemporary sociologists. In 1996, he was named by *Time* magazine as one of America's 25 most influential people and received the National Medal of Science in 1998, the highest scientific award in the United States.

Activity Instructions

There are a lot of myths and stereotypes about poverty. In this exercise, you will be debunking common beliefs and learning more about poverty in the United States.

1. For the following set of questions, there are no right or wrong answers. Answer honestly about what amounts and percentages you think apply.

   - What do you think that the poverty threshold is for a single adult?
   - What do you think the poverty threshold is for a family of four (two adults and two children)?
   - What percentage of the population do you think is in poverty?
   - What percentage of whites live in poverty?
   - What percentage of African Americans live in poverty?
   - What percentage of Hispanics live in poverty?
   - What percentage of Asians live in poverty?
   - What is the poverty rate for children?
   - What is the poverty rate for the elderly?

2. Now you will be finding out the correct estimates for the previous questions. You can use any reference material that is appropriate (be sure to cite). Good places to start include the Joint Center for Poverty Research (www. jcpr. org), the Census Bureau poverty page, and other poverty research organizations.

3. There are many federal and state programs that assist the poor. Choose one program to learn more about from the list below. Find out what the requirements are to be eligible, the benefits of the program, the time limits to receive benefits, and whether you think that they are beneficial or of little consequence for people living in poverty. Your report should be at least two pages (typed, double spaced). Be sure to cite your references.

   - Food Stamps
   - Head Start
   - Housing Choice Vouchers (formerly Section 8)
   - Medicaid
   - Supplemental Security Income (SSI)
   - Temporary Assistance to Needy Families (TANF)
   - Women, Infants, and Children (WIC)

4. Turn in the assignment to your instructor as directed.

Group Exercise

Social Class in the United States

Introduction

Stratification in the United States takes many forms. One of the primary ways we experience stratification is by social class. The boundaries between social classes are often unclear, as is what is required to move in and out of a social class. However, unlike the caste system, people in the United States are able to move up and down the class system. The number of social classes can typically range from four to seven, depending on the classification system. For convenience, we will refer to a five-class system with *upper, upper-middle, middle, working,* and *lower* as our categories. The main determinant of which class you belong to has traditionally been income. Other factors that may shape social class are occupational prestige, schooling, power, and wealth (accrued assets unrelated to work income). Within each class, there can be debate about further classification. For instance, the upper class can be categorized as people with old money or new money, and levels of respect can vary depending on how the money was obtained (earned legally, illegally, inheritance, lottery, etc.).

The upper class is comprised of between one and five percent of Americans and generally holds much power and influence in local and national communities. With annual salaries of several hundred thousand dollars and more, members of the upper class tend to be white and male. However, this has been changing slowly as there have been record numbers of people becoming self-made millionaires. A 2005 survey conducted by the market research and polling company TNS Financial Services showed that there are over 8.9 million households in the United States that have achieved the distinction of "millionaire," and that most people did not generate the money solely from job income, but rather relied on investment opportunities.

About 10 to 15 percent of Americans are estimated to be in the upper-middle class. They hold local influence and normally earn at least one hundred thousand dollars a year. The middle class is the largest class comprised of 30 to 35 percent of American families. This class encompasses individuals with less-prestigious, white-collar occupations and some specialized blue-collar jobs. The middle class members typically have some college education, although they may not have graduated, and live modestly.

Dominated by blue-collar, pink collar, and manual labor jobs, another large social class is the working class. This social class is particularly vulnerable to financial problems if work is interrupted (laid off, disability, etc.) or they experience a personal crisis (fire, accident, etc.). Their income typically is less than the national average.

Finally, about 20 percent of American families are categorized as lower class and are disproportionately more likely to be black, Latino, and/or single mothers. While the majority of the lower class work, their wages (typically minimum wage) provide little respite to economic disadvantage. The lower class has little power to enact change in political or social institutions and often experiences impoverished schooling and healthcare.

Idea in Use

The Trivers-Willard hypothesis states that there are class differences in the expectations for and investment in offspring. Specifically, high-status individuals invest more in sons than daughters while low-status families invest and expect more from daughters. Rosemary Hopcroft tested this hypothesis using the General Social Survey cumulative files. Her research published in *Social Forces* in 2005 did find support for the Trivers-Willard hypothesis. In particular, Hopcroft found that sons of high-status fathers received more education than daughters and that daughters of low-status fathers received more education than sons. While the research in "Parental Status and Differential Investment in Sons and Daughters: Trivers-Willard Revisited" does support the hypothesis, it is important to note that Hopcroft looked at only educational attainment as a means of investing in offspring.

Activity Instructions

This group exercise focuses on how we perceive social class in our daily lives.

1. One of the main ways we ascertain social class is occupational prestige. For the following list of occupations, as a group, rank the occupations in terms of prestige (1 = most prestigious, 20 = least prestigious). Star any occupations that were a source of discussion or problematic to rank as a group.

_______ Accountant	_______ House Painter
_______ Actor	_______ Lawyer
_______ Bartender	_______ Logger
_______ Bookkeeper	_______ Musician
_______ Bus Driver	_______ Police Officer
_______ Chemical Engineer	_______ Social Worker
_______ Electrical Engineer	_______ Sociologist
_______ Farmer	_______ Surgeon
_______ Firefighter	_______ Welder
_______ Hair Dresser	_______ Window Washer

2. As a group, come up with five other points that you can use as indicators of social class.

3. Finally, as a group, think about some prime time television shows. Make a list of shows that feature lower class, middle class, and upper class individuals and/or families. Write a statement of what you used to classify the shows. Are there demographic themes that you find? Specifically, how do race, gender, age, urban/rural location come into play (if at all)?

4. Turn in your assignment to your instructor as directed.

Deviance

A Career Perspective on Heroin Use and Criminal Behavior
Charles E. Faupel

Labs
Internet Exercise: Crime Statistics
Individual Writing Exercise: Criminal Court System
Group Exercise: Deviance

A Career Perspective on Heroin Use and Criminal Behavior

The idea of "career" is popularly associated with professions and other middle-class occupations. But sociologists have been using this concept for many years to refer to criminal and deviant activities. The concept was first introduced into the deviance literature by Goffman (1959) in his treatment of the moral career of mental patients, and was later extended by Becker (1963) to deviant careers in general. Since then, career has been used as an interpretive framework for understanding numerous types of deviance, including prostitution and other sexual behaviors, professional crime, fencing, skid-row alcoholism, gambling, and narcotics addiction. Despite the stereotypes associated with them, all these activities can be understood in terms of career. For purposes of this article, we may define career as a series of meaningfully related statuses, roles, and activities around which an individual organizes some aspect of his or her life over a period of time.

I will here analyze heroin use and heroin-related criminal behaviors from the perspective of a career. The research that informs this perspective was conducted in the Wilmington, Delaware, area in 1979 to 1981. A total of thirty hard-core urban street addicts were interviewed for 10 to 25 hours each about all aspects of their drug-using and criminal behavior.

Heroin Use As a Career

Occupational careers typically begin when individuals choose and enter a career field. They first make some decision about whether or not to go on to college and, if so, what to major in. After graduating from college, they seek their first job that ideally is related to their field of study. Career heroin users experience a similar phase of initiation. Typically, someone *turns them on* (introduces them) to heroin, though they have experimented with a variety of other drugs. Similarly, all the heroin users that I interviewed engaged in criminal or quasi-criminal activities as a means of supporting their habits. These *hustles* are cultivated and fine tuned over a period of time, often under the tutelage of older, more experienced addicts.

During the course of a career, one encounters obstacles and opportunities, successes and failures, or "ups and downs," that define one's career path. Heroin addicts also encounter these vicissitudes in their career. A typical experience involves *getting hooked* and *jones-ing*—becoming addicted and then suffering periodic withdrawal from heroin when supplies are unavailable. Over time, most addicts develop a *main hustle*, a criminal specialization that provides them with increased income and stature in the subculture of heroin use. But they also suffer setbacks in their careers, as when they get *busted* by the police, either for crime or drug possession.

Finally, people with conventional careers eventually *retire*, or leave one career to begin another. Heroin users refer to this last career phase of theirs as *burning out* or *shaking the monkey*. Like conventional careerists who come back out of retirement, addicts often return to *the life*, becoming involved again in heroin use and criminal activities. Also, like conventional careerists, criminal addicts often make "career shifts" by abandoning old *hustles* to pursue new ones.

Contingencies of Heroin-Using Careers

Social and biographical factors profoundly affect the careers of heroin addicts. A major *score* (proceeds from a criminal act) may establish the reputation of an addict as a big-time hustler, thereby launching a new criminal career or enhancing an existing one. Getting *busted*, on the other hand, may force the addict to abandon a particular criminal career, at least temporarily. But such major events in the addict's life do not completely shape the addict's career. Even far less significant occurrences also affect the addict's career. For example, learning how to prepare and self-inject heroin enables the addict to stop depending on others in the subculture to *get off* (shoot heroin). Whether the events are major or minor, they have much to do with at least two important contingencies in the addict's career: whether drug is available and whether the addict's life structure is disrupted.

Drug Availability

Drugs are not always easy to get. Eddie, a white addict in his late twenties reflected, "You might have money in your pocket and you go up there and you wait until five o'clock that afternoon [for a dealer]; or you might go up there and he's sitting there at ten o'clock and you don't have any money. By the time you get money, he's gone." Such difficulties in connecting with a dealer are part of the challenge of the addict life style. But there is more to drug availability than simply finding a dealer. Because heroin is so expensive, even a modest habit for an addict using street dope is extremely costly. Hence, a critical factor in drug availability is affordability. There are two ways of making heroin more affordable.

One way involves *increasing income* through criminal means. Regular heroin users commonly report a heavy reliance on criminal activity to obtain the necessary funds to support their drug habit. This is because using heroin on a regular basis requires substantially more money than most addicts can earn through a conventional job. Sometimes, in order to make more money, addicts would take up a new *hustle* that is more more profitable than the current one. Consequently, they consume more drugs. This career shift is not unique to heroin addicts, though. It occurs in conventional occupations as well. Employees may get promoted within their own companies or with new companies, which offers significantly more income. When this occurs, the individuals usually spend more money by, say, purchasing a new car, in the same way as heroin addicts buy more drugs.

Another way of making heroin more affordable is *lowering its cost*. This often involves purchasing heroin in large quantities, usually by the *bundle* (the equivalent of about 25 bags), which costs much less than if 25 bags are bought individually. Experienced addicts usually buy one or more bundles, sell four or five bags from each, for a large profit, to less experienced users at street prices, and then use that money to *re-up* (buy another bundle). By getting heroin this way, which addicts call *juggling*, they can use more of the drug. There are other methods of reducing the cost of heroin. Women addicts sometimes move in and live with dealer-boyfriends, from whom they can get all the dope they want. Other addicts become *testers* for dealers by injecting into themselves a quantity of a drug to test for its purity. For their service, testers do not have to pay for the test drug and often are remunerated with additional quantities.

Making drugs affordable, either through increased income or lowered cost, is not the only condition that enhances availability. Addicts may acquire a sizable *stash* (supply) of heroin, but if they cannot get it into their bloodstream they have not enhanced availability at all. They must learn to *cook* (prepare) the drug, *tie up* (expose a vein), and *spike* (inject). Until these skills are learned, the novice user is dependent on others in the subculture to *get off*, a favor which is usually done on a fee-for-service basis. Older, experienced, but temporarily down-and-out junkies will offer this service for a share of the dope. This obviously will reduce drug availability for the inexperienced addict. Learning to self-inject, then, makes one's stash available for consumption at all times.

Life Structure

Heroin addicts participate in a myriad of activities in their daily lives. These activities constitute the addict's *life structure*. It involves settling into a daily routine of conventional and criminal activities. The conventional routine may include going to school, going to work, doing household chores, running errands, drinking beer with friends, and so on. The criminal routine involves regularly performing certain acts required by the type of crime to be committed. There are various examples of criminal routine. In burglary, addicts spend time staking out business establishments or residential areas to determine the best locations and times to strike. In shoplifting, they typically establish *runs*, regular sequences of stores from which they *boost* (shoplift), during certain times of the day, while reserving other times to sort and *fence* (sell) what they have stolen. In prostitution, they keep a busy evening and night-time work schedule, which normally runs from about 7 P.M. to 3 A.M., while sleeping in the morning and discharging domestic responsibilities in the afternoon. It is within this structure of conventional and criminal activities that *copping, juggling*, and *shooting* dope take place.

In conventional society, cigarette smokers and coffee drinkers often consume much more nicotine and caffeine during "off" times, such as when they are at home during the holidays or on vacation. These are the times when they are out of their usual routine—their life structure is in effect disrupted, though temporarily. Similarly, disruption to the heroin addict's life structure can have a profound impact on drug consumption. In fact, during such times, the addict's drug habit often gets out of control. As Old Ray, a veteran addict, explained, "Usually the person that gets involved in drugs is not totally involved in anything else. I was on the street at the time [I started using more]. I just got laid off.... I had encountered a situation of economic castration. This made me susceptible to the street."

A Typology of Heroin-Using Careers

Both drug availability and life structure profoundly influence the addict's career phases. As shown in Figure 8.1, there are four possible career phases dependent on whether drug availability is relatively limited or unlimited and whether life structure is relatively stable or unstable.

The Occasional User

The "occasional use" phase, defined by relatively stable life structure and limited drug availability, is typical of addicts very early in their careers. Most heroin users begin their careers quite young, and many are still in school when they first start experimenting with the drug. Those who are beyond school age are often employed or maintain a stable structure of domestic and child-care responsibilities. To cite a few examples: Mario was working as an apprentice for a local optician when he first began using heroin; Eddie was a full-time student at the local university; Bertha worked as a barmaid and cared for an infant son; and Mona was living at home with a stable family and working full-time doing clerical work. Such routines provide insulation from becoming heavily addicted. Further, these conventional routines fail to provide relatively unlimited drug availability that often comes with lucrative criminal routines. While most young users have had some criminal experience prior to using heroin, this early criminality is typically sporadic, not sufficient to provide a dependable income.

Occasional users have not yet spent enough time in the drug subculture to be fully cognizant of, much less to have internalized, its normative proscription against turning others on. They have not yet attended the "school of hard knocks." They have not yet *done time* (been jailed or imprisoned) and may have never even been arrested. They are unlikely to have experienced their first *jones* (withdrawal from heroin). Therefore, they tend to do things that more experienced addicts would not do, especially turning neighborhood friends on to heroin. But this is tantamount to sharing with friends the excitement of their first sexual experience. The rather graphic image of the drug peddler as a "merchant of death" seeking to victimize innocent youth, then, is a highly distorted stereotype and, in most cases, simply wrong. The more realistic image of how drug use is spread is a much more innocent one: It consists of young friends sharing drugs in the same way as adolescents sneaking behind the barn to share a cigarette purloined from a father's coat pocket.

Life Structure

	Stable	Unstable
Availability		
Limited	The Occasional User	The Street Junkie
Unlimited	The Stable Addict	The Free-Wheeling Addict

Figure 8.1   A Typology of Heroin-Using Career Phases

This early, occasional phase of heroin-using careers is also a time of experimentation with crime for most users. By the time they have had their first encounter with heroin, most addicts have had some criminal experience. This early criminality is usually less serious and profitable than later criminal activities. Harry's first crime, for example, was stealing a bicycle at age 13. He stole the bike to demonstrate his worthiness for being accepted into a neighborhood street gang. It was not until several years later that he became involved in burglary and drug dealing on a regular basis.

Finally, in this early phase of heroin-using careers, drug use does not lead to criminal activity. The major reason is that occasional users are still far from being heavily involved in heroin, hence they have no need to turn to sustained criminal activity for quick, lucrative income required for heavy drug use.

The Stable Addict

This is a seasoned, mature addict, enjoying relatively unlimited drug availability and stable life structure. The addict can get a constant supply of heroin at reasonable cost. This has much to do with the addict's relatively stable life structure, which is largely supported by criminal routines that regularly or reliably produce the needed income for drug use.

According to popular belief, it is heavy use of drugs that compels the user to commit crime as a way of getting money for the next fix. In other words, drug use is widely assumed to precede criminal activity. But my research shows just the reverse: Criminal activity precedes drug use. This explains why the more profit an addict gets from crime the more drugs he or she consumes. As Stephanie said, "The better I got at crime, the more money I made; the more money I made, the more drugs I used." She went on to explain, "I think that most people that get high, the reason it goes to the extent that it goes . . . is because they make the money like that. I'm saying if the money wasn't available to them like that, they wouldn't be into drugs as deep as they were."

While stable addicts are heavy users of heroin, they do not use too much of it. Instead, they impose a certain limit on their drug use, so that they are unlikely to die from drug overdose. The reason is the relative stability of their life structure, whose criminal and conventional routines regulate drug use. If their life structure is disrupted, the already heavy use of heroin will likely become uncontrollably excessive, as is often found in the next career phase of heroin addiction.

The Free-Wheeling Addict

In this career phase, the addict uses heroin to uncontrolled excess. An important factor is the relatively unlimited availability of the drug. But, as suggested, far more important is the disruption of the addict's life structure, because it often sharply escalates drug use. Loss of a conventional job, forced abandonment of a criminal routine, or some other negative event may disrupt a life structure. But more often it is a highly positive experience, such as an unprecedented success at a criminal enterprise, that disrupts the addict's routine life. When this occurs, the addict is likely to become a free-wheeling one, using heroin with a vengeance.

A typical example is Harry's experience. His main hustle had been burglary, which provided a reliable, though not greatly lucrative, income. One momentous day, his long-time friend Bart offered him an opportunity that he could not turn down. As Harry said, "I got hooked up with these people that Bart was hanging around with, and they were into [armed robbery of grocery stores] . . . . So there was a string of those that went down, and we went hogwild." After Harry abandoned his burglary routine for this far more profitable venture, his income soared. This sharply increased his drug availability. But, more important, he no longer had to maintain a rigorous routine as a burglar. Now his work in armed robbery was far from routine. It required only two or three hours per day in a three-day work week, and there was too little time for planning and executing the heists. This, then, disrupted Harry's life structure that had been established by his many burglaries. As a result, his heroin use increased dramatically. This free-wheeling, uncontrolled drug use lasted for nearly eight months, after which he ended his armed-robbery binge and returned to his old hustle as a burglar.

The Street Junkie

Like the free-wheeling addict, the street junkie has an unstable life structure. But the junkie's unstable life is a result of problems, difficulties, failures, or some other negative experiences. Such distressing experiences tend to greatly increase the addict's desire for drug consumption. But, unfortunately, by causing addicts' income to plummet, the same negative events in their life severely limit the availability of drugs. Therefore, they become down-and-out junkies desperate for a fix. This desperation often compels the junkies to commit crimes that would have been unthinkable before, such as mugging poor elderly women for their meager money.

Summary

The life styles of heroin addicts parallel professional and other conventional careers in many ways. Like professionals exploring various career options before choosing one they like, heroin addicts experiment with different types of drugs and criminal activities to sustain their drug use before settling into a preferred drug and crime. Heroin addicts also encounter the vicissitudes of upward and downward mobility in their drug-criminal world. Most important, heroin use among addicts is comparable to consumer behavior among conventional careerists, and criminal activities among addicts are analogous to income-producing jobs among conventional careerists.

The connection between drug use and crime in the world of addiction is also similar to the connection between consumer behavior and income-producing activity in the world of professions. More specifically, crime produces income that makes drug use possible in the same way as a profession generates income that makes consumer activity possible. Thus, the more income crime produces, the greater the quantity of heroin is used, just as the more income a profession produces, the greater the quantity of merchandise is purchased. Moreover, when the addict's life routine is disrupted, heroin use increases. This is basically the same as the situation when the professional's life routine is disrupted and consumer activity increases.

References

Becker, Howard S. 1963. *Outsiders: Studies in the Sociology of Deviance*. Glencoe, IL: Free Press.
Goffman, Erving. 1959. "The Moral Career of the Mental Patient." *Psychiatry* 22: 123–142.

LABS

Internet Exercise

Crime Statistics

Introduction

Crime statistics are a useful way for social scientists to study criminal deviance in society. There are two primary collections of general crime statistics at the national level: the Uniform Crime Reports and the National Crime Victimization Study. Although both sets of statistics collect data on similar crimes, they utilize different methodologies and at times use different definitions of particular crimes. Therefore, the two programs are meant to complement one another and are not strictly comparable.

The Uniform Crime Reports (UCR) began in 1930 under the auspices of the FBI. Local law enforcement agencies from around the country report their crime data to the FBI. Although submitting data to the UCR is voluntary, an overwhelming majority of agencies participate (though this was not always the case). The FBI compiles and standardizes the data submitted by each jurisdiction and annually publishes the collection of statistics in a report called *Crime in the United States*. The data are solely from law enforcement agencies and no information is provided from court proceedings, medical examiner or coroner reports, or any other criminal justice agency. The crimes that are recorded as "Part I" or "Index Crimes" in the UCR are: murder, forcible rape, robbery, aggravated assault, burglary, larceny-theft, motor vehicle theft, and arson. In addition, there are 21 categories of less serious offenses recorded in "Part II" of the UCR. The UCR employs a hierarchy rule, which states that when there are multiple offenses in a single crime event, only the most serious crime is reported to the UCR. For instance, if a case involves the rape and murder of a victim, the law enforcement agency will only report the murder. Therefore, it is important to note that the UCR is not a complete representation of crimes in the United States, although it does provide a very good estimate of incidents, especially violent offenses.

The National Crime Victimization Study (NCVS) was created in 1973 to complement the UCR. The data are collected through phone interviews with adult members of approximately 50,000 different households each year. The crimes that are integrated in the NCVS statistics are rape, sexual assault, personal robbery, aggravated and simple assault, household burglary, theft, and motor vehicle theft. The information in the NCVS focuses on specific characteristics of the victim and offender, as well as details about the actual crime. Many of the crimes reported in the NCVS are not reported to the police, and therefore not recorded in the UCR. These crimes captured by the NCVS, but not reported to the police are called, collectively, the *dark figure of crime*.

Both the UCR and the NCVS report crimes as *raw numbers* and as *rates*. Rates are calculated by dividing the number of crimes by the total population for a given jurisdiction, and multiplying that number by the unit of population designated for the rate. For example, if one wanted to determine the rate per 100 people (which is essentially a percentage), he or she would divide the number of crimes by the total population and multiply by 100. The UCR uses a rate based upon a unit of *100,000* population, while the NCVS bases its rate on a unit of *1,000* population.

Idea in Use

Police reports and victim surveys, while reporting different overall *levels* of crime, usually report parallel trends. Karin Wittebrood and Marianne Junger found sharply divergent trends, however, when they analyzed the police statistics and victimization statistics of the Netherlands. In their 2002 article in *Social Indicators Research*, they revealed that police statistics reported a sizeable increase in crime over two decades while the victimization statistics showed no such increase and have remained relatively stable over the decades. They hypothesize about the cause of this discrepancy and suggest that the main contributor of the increase in crime reported by police statistics is the introduction of more formalistic and regulatory collection practices by police in recent years. They indicate that there may have been a slight increase in violence in the Netherlands but nothing as substantial as police statistics would indicate.

Activity Instructions

You will be comparing UCR and NCVS statistics, determining *rates* and *dark figures.* You may want to print out the specific information from the UCR and NCVS pages to help you complete this exercise. To determine the dark figure for each crime, you will need to take the difference between the UCR rates and the NCVS rates. **REMEMBER:** the rate for the UCR is the number of crimes per ***100,000*** persons while the rate for NCVS is per ***1,000*** persons. The formula for a crime rate as calculated by the UCR (per 100,000) inhabitants is:

$$\frac{incidents}{population} \times 100,000$$

To determine the crime rate as reported by the NCVS (per 1,000) inhabitants you would simply replace the 100,000 with the 1,000. Therefore, since you have the number of incidents, determined the population, and can standardize the rate per inhabitant with the other crime set, you can calculate the rate and compare.

1. You will visit the websites for each collection of criminal statistics and then answer a set of questions.

   a. Go to the FBI home page to find the UCR data for the most current year. The FBI home page is http://www.fbi.gov. You can get to the Uniform Crime Reports in several ways. One way is to click the "Use Our Resources" heading and search the area under "Get Information I Need" for crime stats. Once you are at the main page for the Uniform Crime Reports, select the latest year that has complete data available. You may want to read through the appendix, which provides a full description of data collection methods, a comparison of UCR and NCVS, and other valuable information. Click on *Section II: Offenses Reported* and then on burglary (you may have to expand the table of contents). The headings are *"Narrative Comments – Property Crime – Burglary."* Keep this page open.

   b. Open a new web browser window and go to the Bureau of Justice Statistics home page to find the comparative NCVS data. The homepage is located at: http://www.ojp.usdoj.gov/bjs/. You will then need to select criminal victimization and scroll down to publications. Find the criminal victimization data for the same year as you did for the UCR. Click on the acrobat file at the bottom of the page.

   c. You will be using the two open web pages to answer the following questions about burglary.

2. For the UCR data:

   - Does the page provide a definition of burglary? If yes, how is it defined?
   - How many burglaries occurred in the most recent year?
   - What is the population figure provided in the UCR for burglary for that year?
   - What is the rate of burglary for the United States?

- How has the rate of burglary changed from the previous year? In the last ten years? Provide specific numbers.
- Are you surprised by any of your findings?

3. For the NCVS data:

   - Does the page provide a definition of burglary? If yes, how is it defined?
   - How many burglaries occurred in the most recent year?
   - What is the population figure provided in the NCVS for burglary for that year?
   - What is the rate of burglary for the United States?
   - How has the rate of burglary changed from the previous year? In the last ten years?
   - Are you surprised by any of your findings?

4. What is the dark figure for burglary (show calculations)?

   What are the differences that you found for the rates of burglary with the two sets of data? What are some causes of the disparity between the two datasets? (NOTE: Remember to take into account the differences in the population units upon which the rates are determined for the UCR and NCVS before you analyze the differences. Since the UCR is based upon 100,000 population rather than 1,000 population, a rate of 5,000 in the UCR, for example, would be the same as a rate of 50 in the NCVS.)

5. Finally, determine about how much crime is prevalent in your community. Return to the UCR webpage that had the latest year's worth of data (right before you clicked Section II in part 1). Depending on your community, you will be using Table 8 or 8A. Identify the city/town that you are reporting on and provide the counts of:

   - Murder
   - Forcible Rape
   - Robbery
   - Aggravated Assault
   - Property Crime
   - Are you surprised by any of your findings?

6. Turn in your assignment as directed by your instructor.

Individual Writing Exercise

Criminal Court System

Introduction

The police, the courts, and corrections are the three components that make up the criminal justice system in the United States. They serve to enforce a code of standards and impose formal social control so that future criminal behaviors are deterred and society is protected from potential harm. The judicial system is a critical component in the enforcement of laws and social order. It is a fascinating structure that is often surrounded by controversy. Social issues such as abortion, affirmative action, and marital rape are often debated within Superior, Circuit, and/or Appellate courts. While preserving social order, they also facilitate social change. Because the court is a prominent and influential component, there has been growth in the study of the court system which is part of a field called the *sociology of law.*

The court system in the United States is based on the *adversarial process.* This entails the presumption of innocence until proven guilty and requires the aggressive work of prosecutor and defense in a neutral and fair court. The complicated criminal justice system rarely allows all cases to be heard in court, however. Lawrence Friedman and Robert Percival depicted how the criminal court system works with an illustration of a wedding cake. The small, top layer represents celebrated cases. These are the cases that receive major media attention, often involve expensive defense teams and extensive numbers of witnesses and experts, and tend to be jury trials. For instance, the Scott Peterson case, Kobe Bryant trial, and of course the OJ Simpson trial are prominent examples. The next layer of the "wedding cake" is composed of serious felony cases such as murders, rapes, and burglaries. The third layer includes less serious felonies, typically the victim and offender know each other, and the punishment is typically light if convicted. The bottom layer consists of the majority of cases: misdemeanors.

The lower the "layer" in the hierarchy of cases, the less adversarial the court experience is likely to be. In fact, only about 10 percent of all criminal cases will ever appear before a court. Plea-bargaining negotiations typically resolve most cases and save time and money for both the prosecutor and accused. Plea-bargaining in itself is controversial for at least two reasons. First, it results in some offenders pleading to a lesser charge. This allows some offenders to be released earlier from incarceration or completely spared the jail-time. On the other hand, some defendants may feel pressured into pleading guilty to a crime that they haven't committed because of the physical and emotional expense of a trial.

Idea in Use

It is often maintained that each level of the criminal justice system is racially discriminatory. Stephen Demuth and Darrell Steffensmeier tested this assertion by evaluating race and ethnicity effects on sentence outcomes. Using data from the 1990s for sixteen counties across the United States, they found that white defendants were more likely to receive lighter sentences (less likely to be incarcerated and when incarcerated, for less time) than black or Hispanic defendants. This is especially true in drug cases where the odds of incarceration for black and Hispanic defendants are 59 percent and 53 percent higher than the odds of incarceration for white defendants. For the full research findings, see their article "Ethnicity Effects on Sentence Outcomes in Large Urban Courts: Comparisons Among White, Black and Hispanic Defendants" in the December 2004 edition of *Social Science Quarterly.*

Activity Instructions

You will be observing the media and/or realistic representations of criminal court cases. Also, you will be reviewing governmental publications that relate to the area of criminal courts.

1. If possible, attend a criminal case at your local courthouse. Each state has a different name for the court that hears felony cases: usually the state calls it the "County Court," "Circuit Court," or the "Superior Court." It is suggested that as a courtesy you call your local courthouse and ask when a criminal court is in session or search the internet to see if your local court has a calendar on the web. Explain that you are taking a sociology course and would like to attend a session. Adult court trials are open to the public, although juvenile and family cases are generally closed.

2. If it is not possible to attend an actual trial, utilize a media representation of a courtroom session. Watch a session of a real criminal trial on Court TV (at least an hour and a half of a single trial).

3. You will have to allow plenty of time to observe the case. Make notes of the environment of the courtroom—an actual physical description or sketch—and an account of the key players in the courtroom. Describe the case that is at the center of the plot or session. Pay special attention to the behaviors of the judge, suspect, witnesses, and jury.

4. Identify any problems that you see with the defense or prosecutor tactics.

5. Before the actual verdict is revealed, indicate what verdict you would have found.

6. Please summarize your findings and indicate any surprises or expectations that were realized.

7. Turn in your observations and summary of the criminal court case that you observed to your instructor as directed.

Group Exercise

Deviance

Introduction

Deviance is a subjective, relative concept that refers to acts, behaviors, beliefs, or conditions that violate the norms and values that society expects to be upheld. Many associate deviance with crime, but sociologists make distinctions between the two terms. Crimes are violations of formal, culturally defined laws. Therefore, some acts can be deviant but not criminal (actions of paranoid schizophrenia), criminal but not deviant (speeding), or both criminal and deviant (murder). Because everyone has varying values and norms that they hold to be correct, everyone has labeled others as deviant. People can also be defined as deviant by others if they don't fit in or conform to the group's prescribed notions of what is appropriate or "the norm." For example, some may view those afflicted with mental and physical disabilities as deviant, even though those afflicted did not choose their disability.

There are two types of norms that can be violated: *mores* and *folkways*. Mores and folkways refer to how central to a society's value system a particular norm is, and are usually determined by how strongly people react when violated. Norms may also be classified according to whether they are formal or informal. Formal norms are those that have been codified into law or official policy. Informal norms, by contrast, are those that are commonly recognized and are those to which most people adhere because of custom and common understanding. Figure 8.2 is a typology depicting the intersection of the two dimensions of "centrality" and "formality" and provides examples of each of the four types of norms that emerge from this intersection.

Conformity and deviance are behaviors that are constructed by society to some extent. We learn expected behaviors through socialization. Since every culture has varying expectations about behavior, each culture defines deviant acts differently. Even within the United States, there are conflicting determinants of deviance. Place and time are two variables that alter the way behavior/beliefs/condition is perceived. Purchasing alcohol in grocery or convenience stores is accepted in many states, but outlawed and deviant in others. Homosexuality and interracial relationships were once considered deviant but have become socially accepted in recent decades.

Idea in Use

Gambling is a deviant act that is completely legal in some states, but criminalized in others. Sports betting is only legal in one state (Nevada), yet this 'deviant and criminal act' receives considerable attention, with "lines" published in national and regional newspapers. Phyllis Coontz qualitatively evaluated professional sport bookmakers in an effort to understand this criminal but not deviant notion. In the 2001 *Deviant Behavior: An Interdisciplinary Journal* article "Managing the Action: Sports Bookmakers as Entrepreneurs" Coontz finds that while bookies acknowledge the illegality of their job, they do not self-identify as criminal nor deviant. Coontz suggests that this

		Formality	
		Formal	**Informal**
Centrality to Value System	**Mores**	Murder	Urinating on crucifix
	Folkways	Parking ordinances	Rules of personal space

Figure 8.2   Typology of Norms

is because the job is well organized, so well organized that there is a good career trajectory, more akin to entrepreneurship than criminality.

Activity Instructions

This group exercise will help you differentiate between deviant and criminal acts, how the labeling of acts, belief, or circumstances as deviant is conditional on time and place, and some of the ways that sociologists account for deviance in society.

1. There are several groups of people that have been labeled as deviant. Although these people have not violated any criminal laws, they are often targets of informal sanctions. Identify as many groups of people that are considered deviant (but not criminal) because of behaviors, beliefs, and conditions. You should have at least five examples for each category. An example is provided below.

Behavior	Belief	Condition
Nudity in Public Places	Vegan	Morbidly obese

2. Choose three of your answers from the previous part (they can but don't have to be all from one category of deviance). Identify places or times in history where the behavior, belief, or condition was not deviant.

3. There are two contrasting ways to think about deviance. One way is to think that deviant behaviors are abnormal and something pushes an individual to be deviant. The other way is to believe that all people are inherently deviant but we constrain, or pull in our behaviors to fit a more appropriate niche. Discuss the two approaches within your group and write a position paper about what your group majority believes. Be sure to cite examples from your daily life. For instance, you may want to talk about how every group member feels a need/desire to steal items that they need, but that the majority deny those urges after considering possible punishment or embarrassment if caught. Feel free to use specific theories of deviance to support your answer.

4. Turn in your group assignment to your instructor as directed.

Sex and Gender

A Woman Can Learn Anything a Man Can
Carolyn Turk

Labs
Internet Exercise: Gendered Institutions
Individual Writing Exercise: Gender Socialization
Group Exercise: Women's and Men's Movements

A Woman Can Learn Anything a Man Can

When I was a kid, everything in my bedroom was pink. I have two sisters and we had a complete miniature kitchen, a herd of My Little Ponies and several Barbie and Ken dolls. We didn't have any toy trucks, G.I. Joes or basketballs. We did have a Wiffleball set, but you would have been hard-pressed to find it in our playroom. Tomboys we weren't.

So some people may find it ironic that I grew up to be a mechanical engineer. In fact, I am the only female engineer at my company. In order to get my college degree, I had to take a lot of math and science classes. I also had to work with a team of students as part of a national competition to convert a gas-guzzling SUV into a hybrid electric vehicle—that's where I learned how to fix cars. I'm proud to say that I got A's in all my classes, including multivariable calculus and differential equations. I've always been pretty good at math and design, but I didn't understand where that could take me. I was expected to go to college, but no one ever told me I'd make a good engineer someday.

When I was in high school, I didn't know the first thing about engineering. I couldn't have distinguished a transmission from an alternator. The car I drove needed some work but I was afraid to take it to the mechanic. Because honestly, the mechanic could have shown me an electric can opener and said, "This is part of your car and it's broken—pay me to fix it," and I wouldn't have known any better.

At the end of my junior year of high school, I heard about a summer program designed to interest girls in engineering. The six-week program was free, and students were given college credit and a dorm room at the University of Maryland. I applied to the program, not because I wanted to be an engineer, but because I was craving independence and wanted to get out of my parents' house for six weeks.

I was accepted to the program and I earned six engineering credits. The next year I entered the university as an engineering major. Five years later I had a degree and three decent job offers.

I can't help shuddering when I hear about studies that show that women are at a disadvantage when it comes to math. They imply that I am somehow abnormal. I'm not, but I do know that if I hadn't stumbled into that summer program, I wouldn't be an engineer.

When I was growing up I was told, as many students are, to do what I am best at. But I didn't know what that was. Most people think that when you are good at something, it comes easily to you. But this is what I discovered: just because a subject is difficult to learn, it does not mean you are not good at it. You just have to grit your teeth and work harder to get good at it. Once you do, there's a strong chance you will enjoy it more than anything else.

In eighth grade I took algebra. On one test I got only 36 percent of the answers correct. I failed the next one, too. I started to think, Maybe I'm just no good at this. I was lucky enough to have a teacher who didn't take my bad grades as a judgment of my abilities, but simply as an indication that I should study more. He pulled me aside and told me he knew I could do better. He let me retake the tests, and I pulled my grade up to an A.

I studied a lot in college, too. I had moments of panic while sitting underneath the buzzing fluorescent lights in the engineering library on Saturday afternoons, when I worried that the estrogen in my body was preventing me from understanding thermodynamics. But the guys in my classes had to work just as hard, and I knew that I couldn't afford to lose confidence in myself. I didn't want to choose between my femininity and a good career. So I reminded myself that those studies, the ones that say that math comes more naturally to men, are based on a faulty premise: that you can judge a person's abilities separate from the cultural cues that she has received since she was an infant. No man is an island. No woman is, either.

Why are we so quick to limit ourselves? I'm not denying that most little girls love dolls and most little boys love videogames, and it may be true that some people favor the right side of their brain, and others the left. But how relevant is that to me, or to anyone, as an individual? Instead of translating our differences into hard and fast conclusions about the human brain, why can't we focus instead on how incredibly flexible we are? Instead of using what we know as a reason why women can't learn physics, maybe we should consider the possibility that our brains are more powerful than we imagine.

Here's a secret: math and science don't come easily to most people. No one was ever born knowing calculus. A woman can learn anything a man can, but first she needs to know that she can do it, and that takes a leap of faith. It also helps to have selective hearing.

LABS

Internet Exercise

Gendered Institutions

Introduction

Social institutions figure prominently in the socialization of gender. While expectations about gender roles are generally shaped by the family, primary peers, and media messages, social institutions such as the workplace and educational systems can reinforce norms or provide new models of gender. Spheres of politics, military, higher education and the business world offer new avenues of advancement for women.

Women have always worked, both at and away from the home. The number of women who participate in the paid labor force has greatly increased since the 1960s. However, as women enter the workplace they have been subjected to occupational segregation, wage gaps, a "second shift" at home, and a glass ceiling.

Women are concentrated in service oriented (waitress, child care, etc.) and administrative support (secretary, etc.) jobs, often called, pink-collar jobs. This so-called "women's work" pays less, has limited promotion opportunities, is less prestigious, and usually employs men as a boss or supervisor. While there has been slow progress to lower occupational segregation, there is often sex segregation within the industry or company. In the medical field for instance, women have been entering the profession at greater numbers. However, they are often concentrated in lower-paying fields such as family practice and gynecology-obstetrics while men dominate the more affluent specializations, such as surgery.

The wage gap refers to the difference between men and women's pay even when controlling for education and experience. On average, full-time working women make 77 cents per every dollar that a full-time working man earns. This can really add up over time. For instance, a woman who has her Bachelor's degree will earn about 1.2 million dollars less in her lifetime than a male who graduates with the same degree, from the same college, in the same graduating class (www.wageproject.org).

Finally, a woman has historically been expected to do the majority of housework and child-rearing at the home. While more women have entered the paid labor market, they are still expected to complete the less prestigious and unpaid work at home. Oftentimes called the "second shift," women complete significantly more housework than men, regardless of how many hours of paid labor she works.

While there is no doubt that the social conditions for women have improved over time, gender inequality still persists within and among social institutions. The inequality of pay, opportunity, and prestige can greatly compound over time, to insure that women remain disadvantaged and subordinate to men. Moreover, the combination of race, class, and gender can have interactive effects that compound the disadvantage.

Idea in Use

Through the institution of Title IX in 1972, the amount of monies and attention that university athletic programs devote to women has been brought up to the level of men. However, research has shown that gender representation in *NCAA News* and other media outlets has been quite uneven, with the majority of stories and pictures relating to men, and when space is given to collegiate women's endeavors, the locating of the stories and pictures is in less desirable locations. Cunningham, Sagas, Sartore, Amsden, and Schellhase update the literature on gender representation in the

NCAA News in their 2003 *Sex Roles* article "Gender Representation in the NCAA News: Is the Glass Half Full or Half Empty?" They found that coverage of women's sports has improved over time and that the coverage of women is equitable when compared to the standard of the proportion of female student-athletes. However, when using a standard of the proportion of teams allocated to women and men, the coverage of women is inequitable. They conclude that the glass can be considered "one-quarter empty."

Activity Instructions

In this exercise, you will be expected to use the internet to witness the level of gender stratification in the workplace and other social institutions.

1. The number of women in politics has increased over time. However, women holding elected offices are still an under-represented minority. Go to the Center for American Women and Politics website at http://www.cawp.rutgers.edu to answer the following questions. You should be able to find most answers in the "Facts and Findings" page, but feel free to explore.

   - How many women are in the U.S. Senate? What is the percentage?
   - How many women are in the House of Representatives? Percent?
   - What is the party affiliation for most of the women that hold office at the national level?
   - Now you will be investigating the number of women that hold office in the state where you currently are (or should be) a registered voter.

     - Historically, how many women in that state have held the post of governor, lieutenant governor, and attorney general?

       - Place a star next to any name of a woman that holds office currently.

     - What is the number and percentage of women in your state legislature for the most current year available? Where does your state rank in terms of the percentage of women in the state legislature?

2. Women have also increasingly joined the military and have been taking leadership positions within the military. You will be visiting multiple websites to answer the questions.

   - Go to the Women's Research & Education Institute (WREI) website at www.wrei.org and find the "Women in the military" page under projects.

     - Using Table 1, determine which branch of the military (army, navy, marines, air force, and coast guard) has:

       - The highest number of women (total of enlisted and officers)
       - The largest percentage of women in the branch (total of enlisted and officers)
       - The highest number of women officers
       - The highest percentage of women officers
         (Be sure to cite the branch and the raw number or percentage)

     - In the "Did you Know" section, find out:

       - What percentage of the troops serving currently in Afghanistan and Iraq are women?
       - What percentage of the active duty women officers and what percentage of active duty enlisted women are African American?

- Go to the comprehensive website of "Captain Barb" at: http://userpages.aug.com/captbarb/ to answer the following questions.

  - In the "Stars on their Shoulders" section find:

    - Who are the first three star women generals/admirals?
    - What was the first year that any women received a "Star"?

  - In the "Medals" section identify:

    - The woman who won the "Medal of Honor"
    - The first woman since WWII to win the Silver Star
    - The woman who is the most decorated woman in military history—identify her and how many medals she earned

  - Finally go to the Women in Military Service for America Memorial website at http://www.womensmemorial.org. To answer the following questions you will need to go to the History and Collections site and then the History section.

    - How many women were Prisoners of War (POWs) during World War II?
    - How many women casualties were there in Desert Storm?
    - When did the Marines first name a woman General?

3. According to the 2005 *Women in the Labor Force: A Databook* published by the Bureau of Labor Statistics, the jobs with the highest concentration of women are dental hygienists (98.8%), preschool and kindergarten teachers (98.1%), and secretaries and administrative assistants (96.9%). You will need to visit the query builder at http://data.bls.gov/PDQ/outside.jsp?survey=nc to find out about wages for these jobs.

   - Select the 'View Areas Within an Occupation' button
   - Select the occupations listed above (you will have to enter each one individually, run the query, and start over with the next occupation)
   - Get the wage estimate for the entire United States (leave the work level as the default—no work level)
   - Record the wages for the most current year

4. Women in sports have also celebrated recent advancements. Title IX was a major factor in balancing the playing field for women. Briefly describe what Title IX is and its effect on college athletics. Write a paragraph about your stance on Title IX. You can find information about Title IX at the following websites, but feel free to use your own resources.

   - Feminist Majority Foundation—www.feminist.org
   - Gender Equity in Sports—http://bailiwick.lib.uiowa.edu/ge/
   - Women's Sports Foundation—http://www.womensportsfoundation.org/

5. Turn in your assignment to your instructor as directed.

Individual Writing Exercise

Gender Socialization

Introduction

Sex and gender are two related concepts that are often used interchangeably. However, distinctions should be made with both terms. *Sex* refers to the biological assignment of male or female at birth. *Gender* refers to a cultural assignment that often places specific attitudes, activities, and behaviors on a particular sex. Basically, gender consists of designated masculine and feminine roles that one is expected to take on as a male or female. For instance, the ability to carry a child is a matter of sex assignment. The cultural notions of motherhood and different work roles are related to gender. The socialization of gender roles begins even before birth with questions to parents about boy's and girl's potential names, color theme for baby's room, and masculine or feminine appropriate toys. While today, there may be less emphasis on the traditional socialization of gender roles, they do in fact exist and still play an integral part in shaping an individual.

The primary agents of socialization (parents, peers, education, and mass media) teach us about gender. In the United States, and to a much larger degree in other countries, there is a boy preference prior to birth. Reasons are varied, but many propose that there is a desire for boys to carry on the surname, and that raising boys is less costly and simpler than bringing up girls. Once children enter the world, they are placed with gender expectations about appearance and behavior. This is reinforced by clothing choices (e.g., boys in bold colors, girls in subdued pastels), toys, and the steering of behaviors and attitudes. In the educational sphere, there has been much research about teachers' different interactions with and responses to males and females, specifically related to frequency and content. For example, boys are typically directed into math and science programs, while girls are steered toward the humanities and fine arts. This is achieved not only through personal interactions, but also through the depictions and examples of gender in textbooks. Fortunately, research about gender socialization in schools has received considerable public attention and changes in lesson planning, classroom teaching styles, and educational materials is becoming evident.

Idea in Use

Children learn about gender norms at a very young age and as Judith Owen Blakemore evidenced, make judgments about norm violators. In her article "Children's Beliefs About Violating Gender Norms: Boys Shouldn't Look Like Girls, and Girls Shouldn't Act Like Boys" published in a 2003 edition of *Sex Roles*, Blakemore investigates the knowledge and beliefs that children aged three to eleven hold. Children were asked about their knowledge of norms (e.g., who usually plays with Barbies), if it is possible for norms to be violated (e.g., is it possible for boys to play with Barbies), and how much they would like being friends with a person who violated the norm (i.e., how would you feel about a boy who plays with Barbies). Generally, Blakemore found that boys were more devalued when they violated gender norms of *appearance* than when girls violated such norms. On the other hand, girls who *acted* in a more masculine way were viewed more negatively than boys who played in feminine styles. Encouragingly, gender norms related to occupations were not devalued when gender norms were violated.

Activity Instructions

In this independent exercise, you will be reflecting on the gender roles that you have personally experienced or observed. You will also be analyzing how agents of socialization can shape gender norms.

1. Thinking back to when you were a child, what were some of the things that your caregivers did or said that shaped the gender roles you experienced? Examples could include what kinds of toys you played with, clubs/groups/sports you joined, what style of hair and dress your caregiver accepted, or terms that were used to describe you (tomboy, girlie boy, macho, etc.). Were/are there any areas that you rejected in attempts to socialize your identity as more masculine or feminine? If you had a sibling of the opposite sex, were there differences in how your caregivers treated each of you?

2. Now identify areas where masculine or feminine stereotypes of adult behavior have affected your life. Do you generally accept traditional gendered roles and expect others to do the same? For instance, do you expect that women do most of the household chores, while the man is the breadwinner? If male, would you consider a typically female job such as nurse? If female, would you ever consider being in a typically "male" field such as construction?

3. While watching television, observe how gender is used in commercials. For at least ten different commercials, detail what the product is for and whether the advertisement is geared toward males or females. For instance, are the women featured in advertisements for home domestics while men are in bank commercials? Who does the majority of voiceovers within commercials—males or females?

4. Turn in your assignment as directed by your instructor.

Group Exercise

Women's and Men's Movements

Introduction

Women's movements that promote gender equality are often referred to as *feminist* or related to *feminism*. These two words conjure up a multitude of images for both men and women. *Feminism* refers to the belief that men and women should be treated equally in the social, political, and economic spheres. A *feminist* is someone who espouses feminism and therefore, both males and females can be feminists. Feminism can take several forms of expression and it has changed over time.

The history of the feminist movement has entailed various positions. The evolution of feminism has taken place in what sociologists refer to as "three waves." The first wave of feminism refers to the abolitionist and suffragist movements. For example, first wave feminists successfully earned the right for women to vote, own and inherit land, divorce, and the right of joint custody. The second wave of feminism began in the mid-1960s. The push for the legalization of birth control pills and abortion, the attention to domestic violence and sexual harassment, and the Equal Rights Movement were at the forefront of the second wave. Some scholars suggest that the second wave is currently in progress. Others however, believe we entered the third wave of feminism in the early 1990s. This third wave is a continuation of the second wave, but with special emphasis of including younger generations and the persistent push for equality between sexes.

There are many types of feminism. Four main types of feminism that address social change are: liberal feminism, socialist (often called Marxist) feminism, radical feminism, and black feminism (or more broadly—multicultural or womanist). *Liberal feminists* work within the existing social structure to gain equal opportunities for both men and women. *Socialist/Marxist feminists* argue that inequality is due directly to class structure and men's oppression of women. They espouse an eradication of the existing patriarchal capitalist system with a state-centered economic base. *Radical feminists* are perhaps the most extreme, suggesting that only an elimination of gender and all notions of gender would create equality. Radical feminists envision a society that separates the body from reproduction and using technology for reproduction. *Black feminists* see the link of race, class, and gender and want to see feminism cross all boundaries of class and race. Black feminists hope to achieve empowerment for all women by acknowledging the legacy of struggles and the importance of voice and action in everyday life.

Men's movements are also varied in type and convictions. Many organized men's movements began in support of the feminist movement. Such groups were created to achieve equality between sexes, but tended to focus on personal change rather than sweeping institutional change. Such pro-feminist organizations include Meninists as well as the National Organization for Men Against Sexism (NOMAS). Other men's groups suggest promasculinist ideas and ban women from participating in organizations. For instance, the Million Man March did not invite women to participate and the Promise Keepers accept women volunteers and prayers from women but suggest that they "have found that men tend to feel much freer and more open . . . in the company of other men" and perhaps women at meetings would infringe on the expression of "celebration and other emotions" (see www.promisekeepers.org). While men's movements have had fleeting success, their longevity and impact has not been as substantial as some women's movements.

Idea in Use

The overwhelming majority of rapes involve a female victim, thus making the crime of interest to feminists. It is often suggested that there is a negative relationship between gender equality and rape. That is, rape is hypothesized to be more common in places with less gender equality. However, different types of feminists have proposed different relationships between rape and gender equality. Whereas, liberal feminists are more likely to believe in the negative relationship, others such as radical and socialist feminists would believe in a positive association between the two variables. These feminists suggest that without completely eliminating the existing social structures to achieve equality, men will continue to perpetrate rapes to maintain their dominance. These feminists would expect a backlash effect; that is, men would have to exert their dominance with rape if they no longer could exert dominance with jobs, wealth, education, etc. After providing a review of the differing feminist perspectives of the relationship, Roy Austin and Young Kim used a cross-national sample to examine gender equality and rape. In a 2000 publication of *International Journal of Offender Therapy and Comparative Criminology*, they discuss their findings that support a positive relationship between gender equality and rape, as well as the implications for feminist theories.

Activity Instructions

In this group exercise, it is best to be in a gender-mixed group. You will be evaluating attitudes and ideas of women and men's movements.

1. Before you join your group, take some time to think about and answer the following questions for yourself:

    - What does a feminist look like?
    - Would you classify yourself as a feminist?
    - Do you believe that women and men should be paid the same amount if they are working the same job?
    - Should men have the right to bar women from places (i.e., clubs, golf courses, etc.)? Should women be allowed to do the same?
    - Who should have the primary responsibility of raising children? If both parents work, who should take off when the child is sick?
    - Why do you think rape occurs?

2. In your group, nominate someone to record and organize your answers. For each of the questions above, write each answer provided and indicate whether the answer came from a male or female. For instance, for question two, how many men and how many women identify as a feminist? Write a paragraph about the gender differences or similarities among answers.

3. When your group hears the word feminist, do the majority of members believe that this has negative or positive connotations? What other terms (if any) would be more positive? What are some of the reasons for group members believing that the term is or is not positive?

4. Turn in your group's write-up to your instructor as directed.

Race and Ethnicity

Anatomy of Environmental Racism
Robert D. Bullard

Labs
Internet Exercise: Race in the United States
Individual Writing Exercise: Racial Group Relations
Group Exercise: Prejudice, Stereotypes, and Discrimination

Anatomy of Environmental Racism

Despite the many federal laws, mandates, and directives by the federal government to eliminate discrimination in housing, education, and employment, government rarely addresses discriminatory environmental practices. People of color (African Americans, Latino Americans, Asian Americans, and Native Americans) are disproportionately affected by industrial toxins, dirty air and drinking water, and the location of noxious facilities such as municipal landfills, incinerators, and hazardous-waste treatment, storage, and disposal facilities.[1]

Impact of Environmental Racism

All communities are not created equal. Some are subjected to all kinds of environmental assaults. Many differences in environmental quality between communities of color and white communities result from institutional racism. Institutional racism influences local land use, enforcement of environmental regulations, industrial facility siting, economic vulnerability, and where people of color live, work, and play. Environmental racism is just as real as the racism that exists in housing, employment, and education.

The roots of institutional racism are deep and difficult to eliminate.[2] Discrimination is a manifestation of institutional racism. Even today, racism permeates nearly every social institution. Environmental institutions of both governmental and nongovernmental bodies are no exceptions. Racism influences the likelihood of exposure to environmental and health risks as well as accessibility to health care.

People-of-color communities have borne a disproportionate burden of this nation's air, water, and waste problems as well as the siting of sewer treatment plants; municipal landfills; incinerators; hazardous-waste treatment, storage, and disposal facilities; and other noxious plants. Residents of many of these same communities live in housing contaminated with lead, whose problems are further complicated by hospital closures and inaccessible health clinics.

People of color have been systematically excluded from (or allowed minimal participation in) decision-making boards, commissions, and staffs of governmental bodies. Business elites promote jobs, an expanded tax base, and economic development as selling points for local residents to accept risky industries. Jobs are often promoted over the environment, especially when the community discovers how many jobs are created, the skills required, the pay scale, and *who* will actually end up getting the jobs.

Environmental racism disadvantages people of color while providing advantages (i.e., privileges) for whites. A form of illegal exaction forces people of color to pay costs of environmental benefits for the public at large. Determining who pays and who benefits from our current urban and industrial policies is central to an analysis of environmental racism. Exclusionary zoning and unequal protection have created environmental sacrifice zones where residents pay with their health. Racial barriers in housing limit mobility options available to people of color.

Racism influences every social and economic strata of people of color. Moreover, environmental inequities do not result solely from differences in social class. In the United States, race interpenetrates class and creates special health and environmental vulnerabilities. People of color are exposed to greater environmental hazards in their neighborhoods and on the job than are their white counterparts. Studies find elevated exposure levels by race, even when social class is held constant.[3] For example, research indicates race to be independent of class in the distribution of air pollution,[4] contaminated fish consumption,[5] location of municipal landfill and incinerators,[6] abandoned toxic-waste dumps,[7] and lead poisoning in children.[8]

Lead poisoning is a classic example of an environmental health problem that disproportionately affects children of color at every class level. Lead affects between three and four million children in the United States—most of whom are African Americans and Latino Americans who live in urban areas. Among children five years old and younger, the percentage of African American children who have excessive levels of lead in their blood far exceeds the percentage of whites who do at all income levels.[9]

The federal Agency for Toxic Substances Disease Registry (ATSDR) found that, for families earning less than $6,000, 68 percent of African American children had lead poisoning, compared with 36 percent for white children. In families with income exceeding $15,000, more than 38 percent of African American children suffer from lead poisoning, compared with 12 percent of whites.[10] Even when income is held constant, African American children are two to three times more likely than their white counterparts to suffer from lead poisoning.

People of color do not have the same opportunities as whites to escape unhealthy physical environments.[11] Most environmental-justice activists challenge an environmental ethic that allows individuals, workers, and communities to accept health risks others can avoid by virtue of their skin color. For example, African Americans, no matter what their educational or occupational achievement or income level, experience greater environmental threats because of their race.[12]

Institutional barriers such as housing discrimination, redlining by banks, and residential segregation prevent African Americans from buying their way out of health-threatening physical environments. The ability of an individual to escape a health-threatening physical environment usually correlates with income. However, racial barriers complicate this process for millions of African Americans.[13] An African American who has an income of $50,000 is as residentially segregated as an African American on welfare.

Some communities, located on the "wrong side of the tracks," receive different treatment in the delivery of public services, including environmental protection. In the heavily populated South Coast air basin of Los Angeles, for example, over 71 percent of African Americans and 50 percent of Latino Americans reside in areas with the most polluted air, while only 34 percent of whites live in highly polluted areas.[14]

The Dumping Grounds

Apartheid-type housing and development policies limit mobility, reduce neighborhood options, diminish job opportunities, and decrease environmental choices for millions of Americans.[15] Why do some communities get dumped on and others do not? Waste generation directly correlates with per-capita income. Therefore, public officials neither propose nor locate many waste facilities in the suburbs.

The Commission for Racial Justice's landmark study, *Toxic Wastes and Race*, found race to be the most important factor (i.e., more important than income, home ownership rate, and property values) in the location of abandoned toxic-waste sites.[16] The study also found that three out of five African Americans live in communities with abandoned toxic-waste sites; 60 percent (fifteen million) African Americans live in communities with one or more abandoned toxic-waste sites; three of the five largest commercial hazardous waste landfills are located in predominantly African American or Latino American communities, accounting for 40 percent of the nation's total estimated landfill capacity; and African Americans are heavily overrepresented in the population of cities with the largest number of abandoned toxic-waste sites, a list that includes Memphis, St. Louis, Houston, Cleveland, Chicago, and Atlanta.[17]

In addition to racial composition, economic factors combine to increase the likelihood of a community hosting a hazardous-waste incinerator. A 1990 Greenpeace report, *Playing with Fire*, found that the minority portion of the population in communities with existing incinerators is 89 percent higher than the national average; communities where incinerators are proposed have minority populations 60 percent higher than the national average; average income in communities with existing incinerators is 15 percent less than the national average; property values in communities close to incinerators are 38 percent lower than the national average; and in communities where incinerators are proposed, average property values are 35 percent lower.[18]

Garbage dumps are not randomly scattered across the landscape. These facilities are often located in communities that have high percentages of poor, elderly, young, and minority residents.[19] In 1979, one of the first studies to link race with the location of municipal solid waste sites focused on Houston.[20] From the early 1920s to the late 1970s, all of the city-owned municipal landfills, and six out of eight of the garbage incinerators, were located in African-American neighborhoods.

From 1970 to 1978, three out of four of the privately owned landfills that were used to dispose of Houston's garbage were located in African American neighborhoods. Although African Americans made up only 28 percent of Houston's population, 82 percent of the municipal landfill sites, public and private, were located in African American neighborhoods.

Siting inequity is not confined to Houston. African American communities from South Central Los Angeles to the southeast side of Chicago to West Harlem are vulnerable to waste facility siting. As recently as 1991, Residents Involved in Saving the Environment (RISE), a biracial community group challenged the King and Queen County, Virginia, Board of Supervisors for selecting a 420-acre site for a regional landfill, located in a primarily African American community. King and Queen County population is nearly evenly split between African Americans and whites. The group charged the board with racial discrimination in landfill siting and zoning since all three of the county-run landfills are located in predominantly African American communities.

In June, 1991, a U.S. district judge for the Eastern District of Virginia in *RISE v. Kay* ruled that the selection of the mostly African American area in King and Queen County did not violate the equal-protection clause, despite the county's historical placement of landfills in African American areas.[21] Although the court acknowledged that the placement of landfills in the county from 1969 to 1991 had a disproportionate impact on African American residents in the county, it failed to find discrimination.

Siting inequities are not unique only to facilities for dumping household garbage. The southern United States, our own Third World, is rapidly becoming the dumping ground for household garbage and hazardous waste. Historically, the South scored at or near the bottom on almost all indicators of well-being (e.g., education, income, economic development, environmental quality, and health care). The region has a long history of exploitation of land and people, especially African Americans, dating from slavery. There is a clear link between the region's lax enforcement of regulations designed to protect public health and the environment, lax enforcement of laws designed to protect the civil rights of its African American citizens and race relations.

Findings in *Dumping in Dixie* show that African Americans in the South bear a disparate burden in the siting of hazardous-waste landfills and incinerators, lead smelters, petrochemical plants, and a host of other noxious facilities.[22] South Louisiana's "Cancer Alley" and Alabama's "blackbelt" epitomize disparate waste facility siting.

Emelle, Alabama, hosts the nation's largest commercial hazardous-waste landfill, dubbed the "Cadillac of dumps." In Emelle, a rural community in the heart of Alabama's "blackbelt," African Americans make up over 90 percent of the population and 75 percent of the residents in Sumter County. The Emelle landfill receives wastes from Superfund sites and wastes from all forty-eight contiguous states.

Dallas, on the other hand, has a long history of allowing lead smelters to be sited in African American and Latino American neighborhoods. The dangers of lead have been known since the Roman era. The lead contamination problem in the mostly African American West Dallas neighborhood was documented by the Dallas Health Department as far back as 1969. A 1983 federal study established that the local smelter was the source of elevated blood lead levels in children who lived in West Dallas.[23] Cleanup delays by the EPA has amounted to "waiting for a body count."[24] One wonders if the residents of the mostly white North Dallas neighborhoods would receive the same treatment as the residents of West Dallas.

Comprehensive cleanup activity began in the West Dallas site in January, 1992—nearly twenty years after the first published report of the problem. An estimated 30,000 to 40,000 cubic yards of lead-contaminated soil will be removed from several West Dallas sites, including school property and the yards of some private homes. The soil is scheduled to be dumped at the Magnolia landfill in Monroe, Louisiana, a community that is over 60 percent African American.[25]

Siting inequities were identified by the U.S. General Accounting Office (GAO) nearly a decade ago. After protests sparked by the siting of a PCB landfill in the mostly African American Warren County, North Carolina, the GAO initiated its own investigation of a hazardous waste facility siting in the EPA's Region IV. The government agency found a strong relationship between the location of off-site hazardous-waste landfills and race and socioeconomic status of the surrounding communities in the EPA's Region IV.[26]

The GAO identified four off-site hazardous-waste landfills in the eight states (Alabama, Florida, Georgia, Kentucky, Mississippi, North Carolina, South Carolina, and Tennessee) that comprise the EPA's Region IV. The four sites included Chemical Waste Management (Sumter County, Alabama), SCA Services (Sumter County, South Carolina), Industrial Chemical Company (Chester County, South Carolina), and the Warren County PCB landfill (Warren County, North Carolina). African Americans made up the majority of the population in three of the four communities with off-site hazardous-waste landfills.

In 1983, African Americans were clearly overrepresented in communities with waste sites since they made up only about one-fifth of the region's population, and three-fourths of the landfills were located in African American communities. Siting imbalances that were present in 1983 have not disappeared. In 1992, African Americans still make up about one-fifth of the population in Region IV. However, the two currently operating off-site hazardous-waste landfills in the region are located in codes where African Americans are a majority of the population. . . .

Conclusion

A new form of grass-roots environmental activism has emerged in the United States that emphasizes securing environmental justice for communities of color. Knowing that environmental racism is a major barrier to achieving environmental and economic justice for people of color, grass-roots activists have not limited their attacks to noxious facility siting and toxic contamination issues. Instead they have begun to seek change in destructive industrial production processes, wasteful consumptive behavior, urban land use and transportation, spatial housing patterns and residential segregation, redlining, and other environmental problems that threaten public safety.

People-of-color groups have begun to build a national movement for environmental justice. However, a national policy is needed to address environmental problems that disproportionately affect people-of-color, working class, and low-income communities. All communities deserve to be protected from the ravages of pollution. No one segment of society should have to bear a disparate burden of the rest of society's environmental problems.

Finally, pushing "risky" technologies and "dirty" industries off on people as a form of economic development is not a solution to the underdevelopment in impoverished Third World-like communities in this country and in similar communities around the world. Social-justice and equity goals must be incorporated into all levels of environmental decision making and policy formulation.

Notes

1. See Robert D. Bullard, *Dumping in Dixie: Race, Class, and Environmental Quality* (Boulder, Colo.: Westview Press, 1990).
2. See J. A. Kushner, *Apartheid in America: An Historical and Legal Analysis of Contemporary Racial Segregation in the United States* (Frederick, Md.: Associated Faculty Press, 1980); Robert D. Bullard and Joe R. Feagin, "Racism and the City," in M. Gottiender and C. V. Pickvance, eds., *Urban Life in Transition* (Newbury Park, Calif.: Sage, 1991), 55–76.
3. Bunyan Bryant and Paul Mohai, eds., *Race and the Incidence of Environmental Hazards: A Time for Discourse* (Boulder, Colo.: Westview Press, 1993).
4. See Myrick A. Freeman, "The Distribution of Environmental Quality," in Allen V. Kneese and Blair T. Bower, eds., *Environmental Quality Analysis* (Baltimore: Johns Hopkins University Press, 1971); and Michel Gelobter, "The Distribution of Air Pollution by Income and Race" (paper presented at the Second Symposium on Social Science in Resource Management, Urbana, Ill., June 1988).

5. Patrick C. West, J. Mark Fly, and Robert Marans, "Minority Anglers and Toxic Fish Consumption: Evidence from a State-Wide Survey in Michigan," in Bryant and Mohai, *Race and the Incidence of Environmental Hazards.*

6. Robert D. Bullard, "Solid Waste Sites and the Black Houston Community," *Sociological Inquiry* 53 (Spring 1983): 273–288; and Robert D. Bullard, *Invisible Houston: The Black Experience in Boom and Bust* (College Station, Tex.: Texas A&M University Press, 1987).

7. United Church of Christ Commission for Racial Justice, *Toxic Wastes and Race in the United States: A National Study of the Racial and Socioeconomic Characteristics of Communities with Hazardous Waste Sites* (New York: United Church of Christ, 1987); Paul Mohai and Bunyan Bryant, "Environmental Racism: Reviewing the Evidence," in Bryant and Mohai, *Race and the Incidence of Environmental Hazards.*

8. Agency for Toxic Substances Disease Registry, *The Nature and Extent of Lead Poisoning in Children in the United States: A Report to Congress.* Atlanta: U.S. Department of Health and Human Resources, 1988, pp. 1–12.

9. Ibid.

10. Ibid.

11. Bullard, *Dumping in Dixie,* 7; Gerald Jaynes and Robin M. Williams, *A Common Destiny: Blacks and the American Society* (Washington, D.C.: National Academy Press, 1989), 144–145.

12. See Nancy Denton and Douglas Massey, "Residential Segregation of Blacks, Hispanics, and Asians by Socioeconomic Status and Generation," *Social Science Quarterly* 69 (1988): 797–817; and Robert D. Bullard, "Endangered Environs: The Price of Unplanned Growth in Boomtown Houston," *The California Sociologist* 7 (Summer 1984): 84–102; Bullard, *Dumping in Dixie.*

13. Denton and Massey, "Residential Segregation of Blacks," 814.

14. See Paul Ong and Evelyn Blumenberg, "Race and Environmentalism," Graduate School of Architecture and Urban Planning, UCLA (unpublished paper, March 14, 1990): 9; and Eric Mann, *LA.'s Lethal Air: New Strategies for Policy, Organizing, and Action* (Los Angeles: Labor/Community Strategy Center, 1991), 31.

15. Joe T. Darden, "The Status of Urban Blacks: 25 Years after the Civil Rights Act of 1964," *Sociology and Social Research* 73 (1989): 160–73; Robert D. Bullard, "Solid Waste Sites and the Black Houston Community," *Sociological Inquiry* 53 (Spring 1983): 273–288; Joe R. Feagin, *Free Enterprise City: Houston in Political and Economic Perspective* (New Brunswick, N.J.: Rutgers University Press, 1987); and Robert D. Bullard, ed., *In Search of the New South: The Black Urban Experience in the 1970s and 1980s* (Tuscaloosa, Ala.: University of Alabama Press, 1989).

16. Commission for Racial Justice, *Toxic Wastes and Race,* pp. xiii–xiv.

17. Ibid., 18–19.

18. Pat Costner and Joe Thornton, *Playing with Fire* (Washington, D.C.: Greenpeace, 1990), 48–49.

19. Michael R. Greenberg and Richard F. Anderson, *Hazardous Waste Sites: The Credibility Gap* (New Brunswick, N.J.: Rutgers University Center for Urban Policy Research, 1984), 158–159; and Bullard, *Dumping in Dixie,* 4–5.

20. Bullard, "Solid Waste Sites," 273–288.

21. "Landfill Didn't Violate Equal Protection," *National Law Journal* (22 July, 1991): 28.

22. See Bullard, *Dumping in Dixie,* chapter 1.

23. U.S. Environmental Protection Agency, "Report of the Dallas Area Lead Assessment Study," (Dallas, Tex.: U.S. Environmental Protection Agency Region VI, 1983), 8.

24. Jonathan Lash, Katherine Gillman, and David Sheridan, *A Season of Spoils: The Reagan Administration's Attack on the Environment* (New York: Pantheon Books, 1984), 135–136.

25. Randy Lee Loftis, "Louisiana OKs Dumping of Tainted Soil," *Dallas Morning News,* February 12, 1992, A1 and A30.

26. U.S. General Accounting Office, *Siting of Hazardous Waste Landfills and Their Correlation with Racial and Economic Status of Surrounding Communities* (Washington, D.C.: U.S. Government Printing Office, 1983), 1.

LABS
Internet Exercise

Race in the United States

Introduction

The United States is certainly diverse in population, with countless racial and ethnic groups living throughout the country. This introduction will provide a very brief review of the largest minority groups living in the United States.

Native Americans have had a troubled and long history of struggle, mostly at the hands of whites and the government. Today, there are 562 federally recognized tribes and approximately 300 reservations across the United States. Approximately 20 percent of the Native American population lives on reservations. Reservations are often impoverished communities, with per capita income just under $8,000 in 2000. Native Americans have low rates of adequate telephone and utility service. Unfortunately, civil rights advances have done little to change the condition of Native Americans and their struggle is essentially invisible to the mainstream.

African Americans started to enter the United States in significant numbers in the early 1600s. Arriving first as indentured servants and then as slaves, they were continuously and cruelly mistreated, and often referred to as property rather than human beings. In the mid to late 1800s, several Constitutional amendments were passed that gave African Americans more rights. However, these actions were chiefly superficial as they had to endure the Jim Crow era (when discrimination and segregation were essentially legalized by states) and associated violence. The civil rights movement of the 1950s and 1960s brought about much deeper reformation and outlawed overt discriminatory behaviors as well as institutional segregation. Progress has been made, especially illustrated by the growth of the black middle class. However, African Americans categorically still lag behind non-Hispanic whites in areas such as median income and educational attainment and have higher rates of health problems, poverty, and single headed households.

Hispanic Americans have diverse origins and settling patterns. According to the 2000 U.S. Census, Hispanics comprise the largest single racial or ethnic minority within the United States. The three countries that contribute the largest numbers to the American Hispanic population are Puerto Rico, Cuba, and Mexico. However, other counties within Central and South America are quickly contributing large numbers to the Hispanic population in America. Latinos (collective term referring to Hispanics with origins in Latin America) first settled in gateway cities within the United States and have slowly spread throughout the country. Hispanic American groups often have very differing social well-being outcomes. Typically Cuban Americans fare better (i.e., have higher job earnings, etc.) than Mexican Americans or Puerto Ricans. Ethnic enclaves within cities (e.g., Little Havana in Miami) help new Hispanic Americans in their adjustment to American society and provide a familiar and safe environment.

Asian Americans comprise several nationalities and language origins. Despite having diverse languages and cultures and thus differing experiences within the United States, Asian Americans are collectively referred to as the "model minority." This is due to the achievements (high educational attainment, low unemployment, etc.) that they have accomplished in a relatively short span. Chinese ancestry is the most common with over two million Chinese Americans living in the United States. Other large contributors to the population of Asian Americans are those of Filipino, Asian Indian, and Vietnamese descent.

Idea in Use

The number of biracial and multiethnic individuals in the United States has increased and there has been a conscious effort to recognize the multiplicity of races and ethnicity within the country. However, there has been little investigation into whether biracial individuals differ from monoracial people in terms of identity, development, and self esteem. In "Examining Ethnic Identity and Self-Esteem Among Biracial and Monoracial Adolescents," Jeana Bracey, Mayra Bámaca, and Adriana Umaña-Taylor found that biracial adolescents did differ significantly from monoracial adolescents on both self-esteem and ethnic identity. Specifically, they found that biracial adolescents reported higher self esteem than the Asian monoracial group but significantly less self esteem than black individuals. Additionally, biracial high school students reported more ethnic identity than whites, but were significantly less attached to ethnic identity than blacks, Latinos, and Asian adolescents. Finally, the authors found that adolescents who scored high on self-esteem also reported higher ethnic identity. The authors anticipate that the article, published in a 2004 edition of the *Journal of Youth and Adolescence*, could serve as a springboard for more analyses of the unique class of biracial.

Activity Instructions

In this exercise you will be using the internet to judge how accurately you perceive race in the United States.

1. Before you consult any resources, record what percentage you believe the different racial groups make up in the United States population, using the groups below (your answer should total 100%):

Race/ethnic group	My preliminary estimate (percent)	Actual census percent
White		
Black		
American Indian/Alaskan Native		
Asian		
Pacific Islander		
Hispanic/Latino		
Other		

Now, go to the U.S. Census table that details the actual racial and ethnic composition that was reported in 2000. You can find it by going to the American FactFinder page at the census website (www.census.gov) and selecting the "Fact Sheet." Make a table showing what your guesses were and the actual percentages you found at the website.

As you could probably tell by your results for question one, people often have a difficult time accurately estimating the share of racial groups in the United States.

2. Often it is difficult to be acutely aware of our hidden prejudices concerning racial groups. Go to https://implicit.harvard.edu/implicit/demo/measureyourattitudes .html to test yourself. After reading some of the information provided about the test and research results, proceed to the next page. Here, you will find a listing of tests. Select one test to take from the following list: Race IAT, Native IAT, Asian

IAT, or Skin-tone IAT. What were your results (you will not be marked down for biased results)? Were you surprised with the results? Do you think that the test was accurate?

3. Choose to investigate one of the following racial group's history in the United States: African Americans, American Indians, or Asians. Create a timeline of the significant historical events that has helped to shape the race of today. For instance, if you choose blacks you will definitely want to investigate the civil rights movement, for American Indians you should cover the Trail of Tears, and for Asians there should be inclusion of internment camps, etc. You need not detail all the events you find, just the ones you find to be the most significant. Be sure to reference the websites you used. Good places to start your investigation include:

   - AlternaTime—http://www2.canisius.edu/~emeryg/time.html
   - Ancestors in the Americas—http://www.cetel.org/timeline.html
   - American History Timeline—http://www.animatedatlas.com/timeline.html

4. Finally, within a race or ethnicity there can be several distinct populations. The fastest growing minority group within the United States is Hispanic/Latino and the category comprises of diverse cultures. Go to the Lewis Mumford Center for Comparative Urban and Regional Research at http://mumford.albany.edu/census/HispanicPop/HspPopData.htm. The five states with the largest percentage of Hispanics/Latinos are: California, New York, Texas, Florida and New Jersey. For these states, use the "select a state" option and determine for all five states the 2000 Mumford estimate of:

   - Percent Hispanic/Latino in the state
   - The percent change in the Mumford estimates from 1990 to 2000 for the percent Hispanic/Latino
   - The country of origin that contributes most to the percent Hispanic/Latino (i.e., Cuba, Mexico, Puerto Rico, or Dominican Republic)

   Write a brief summary (1 page, typed, double-spaced) of the major findings.

5. Turn in your assignment to your instructor as directed.

Individual Writing Exercise

Racial Group Relations

Introduction

There are many ways to describe the intergroup relationships and interaction patterns between the majority and minority racial groups. Sociologists have concentrated on four distinct models of group interaction: *assimilation, pluralism, segregation,* and *genocide.*

The process in which minorities lose their distinctive cultural identity and take on the dominant group's cultural practices and traditions is called *assimilation.* There are levels of assimilation. First, there is cultural assimilation, often referred to as acculturation and involves only the actions of the minority group. This requires the shifting of visible cues of identity. For instance, minority group members will adopt the clothing styles, language, religion, norms, etc. of the dominant group. Another level of assimilation is structural assimilation, which involves the integration of minority groups into the majority group's neighborhoods, workplaces, schools, and other important social spheres. Finally, the ultimate step is biological assimilation. This requires intermarriage of racial groups and reproduction. A very popular critique of the assimilation model is that it requires the adaptation of minority group members, while the dominant group has to change very little. This is evidenced by calls to make English the official legal language within the United States, Anglo dress codes at work and school, and immigrants who Anglo-size their names when entering the country. There are many dynamics that make assimilation an easier process for certain groups, while dominant groups may still be resistant to acceptance of all minority groups.

Another model of interaction that has received considerable attention is *pluralism.* Pluralism, often known as multiculturalism, allows minority group members to retain their individualized, distinct cultures while also remaining free of discriminatory or prejudicial practices. Pluralism celebrates diversity and implies that there is no need to impose on behaviors and beliefs on the majority group. A salad bowl in which each component adds flavor without losing its distinctiveness is often used as a visual to illustrate the ideal of pluralism. One central issue within pluralism is evident when a majority group's practices, rituals, or behaviors offends a minority group or vice versa. For instance, Columbus Day celebrations can be insulting or hurtful to Native Americans.

Segregation is the physical and social separation of minority groups from the dominant group. Segregation is most often involuntarily imposed, although at times certain groups may choose to isolate themselves. Neighborhoods, schools, and social institutions are often racially segregated despite governmental policies. While the situation has slowly improved over time, Douglas Massey and Nancy Denton found that blacks are hypersegregated in many cities. Hypersegregation is an accumulation of segregation measures and implies that blacks in inner cities have very little contact and social interaction with the dominant group, thus remaining removed from the opportunities afforded to the dominant group.

A fourth form of race group social interaction is genocide. *Genocide* is the systematic murder of one or more minority groups. The most devastating example of genocide was Adolf Hitler's extermination of Jews. About six million people were killed during the Holocaust. In the United States, Native Americans were systematically killed. Even though there is a global moral condemnation of genocide it still occurs in contemporary times. For instance, Rwandan Hutus killed about 600,000 Tutsis in 1994 and there was considerable carnage in Bosnia and Herzegovina in the 1990s.

Idea in Use

Segregation can have lasting effects even when one moves out of a residentially segregated area. Using the National Longitudinal Survey of Freshmen, Camille Charles, Gniesha Dinwiddie, and Douglas Massey found that blacks who came from segregated neighborhoods experienced 70 percent more family stress (death, crime, social problems, etc.) than whites encountered and about double what Asians had experienced. The authors also found that African Americans experienced more health problems and spent more time with their family than whites, Asians, and Latinos and that the extent of involvement with family and greater health problems increased as the level of segregation increased. Finally, they determined in multivariate analyses that those who previously resided in segregated areas have lower grade point averages. The authors theorize that individuals who come from segregated neighborhoods experience more family stress, which in turn increases the number of health (mental and physical) issues that they have to personally deal with and also increases the amount of involvement and attention devoted to the family. This can create obstacles to the amount of time college students spend on their studies and thus negatively effect their overall academic achievement. For the full article entitled "The Continuing Consequences of Segregation: Family Stress and College Academic Performance" see the December 2004 edition of *Social Science Quarterly.*

Activity Instructions

In this individual activity, you will be investigating the forms of minority-dominant group patterns of social interaction.

1. Segregation is common in both cities and suburbs, as well as within social arenas. Investigate whether racial segregation is evident where you previously and currently live and attend school.

   - Refer first to where you grew up and discuss the racial composition of your neighborhood and school.
   - If you live off-campus, walk around a five-block radius of your dwelling and observe the racial composition of your neighborhood.
   - If you live on-campus, talk about segregation within your dorm and in the cafeteria.
   - Finally, observe groups of people on campus that are voluntarily socializing. What are the racial compositions of these groups?

2. It is common for college campuses to enroll international students and neighborhoods around schools can have a number of immigrants living and working within them. Briefly interview an international student or immigrant about their experience since arriving in the United States. Do they feel a need to assimilate or do they see a multicultural dynamic within America? Other topics you may want to address are if they have experienced problems or obstacles, if they came with a family or to rejoin a family, and why they chose the city/town in which to reside. If you are an international student, please write about your experiences. Write a short synopsis of your findings (2–3 pages, typed, double-spaced).

3. Turn in your write-ups to your instructor as directed.

Group Exercise

Prejudice, Stereotypes, and Discrimination

Introduction

Minority groups are categories of people that are set apart by a physical or cultural distinction and subordinated by the majority because of the difference. While minority groups are typically smaller in number than the majority group, this is not necessarily the case. Women, for example, comprise a minority group in America even though there are slightly more women than men in this society. What defines a minority group, rather, is the relative lack of power and autonomy they experience in relation to the majority group. Race and ethnicity are often used as the bases for minority identification because the physical attributes are often clearly observable. Because race is socially constructed, majority members with power can create and change racial categories to remain distinct and dominant. Prejudices, stereotypes, and discrimination are important terms that are generally applied to attitudes, beliefs, or acts related to keeping certain racial groups as minority groups in number and in power.

Prejudice refers to preconceived ideas about an entire category of people without a systematic examination of facts. Prejudices about a minority group can be both negative and favorable, though typically prejudices are negative in their content. Prejudices refer to attitudes and beliefs, and not actual behaviors. These generalizations about a group, often made on the basis of a limited personal experience or a handful of observations, are entrenched within cultures and transmitted through generations.

Stereotypes are very closely related to prejudices. Stereotypes are specific characterizations that people have for the members of a group viewed with prejudice. For instance, a person who is prejudiced against the elderly may believe that all senior citizens are bad drivers. A person who stereotypes does not see any individual differences among the members of the minority groups.

Discrimination refers to the actual acts and behaviors that serve to control minority groups. Discrimination denies or restricts minority members' access to opportunities and capital. Degrees of discrimination vary on a continuum of subtle to obvious, as well as a continuum of negative to positive. It is important to note that while prejudice and discrimination are often joint occurrences, prejudice and discrimination can happen independently of one another. There are two main forms of discrimination: individual and institutional. *Individual discrimination* is quickly condemned by most and refers to an individual's hateful actions that are borne out of prejudice. *Institutional discrimination* occurs as a result of structures and institutions that favor majority members. This form of discrimination can be even more harmful than individual acts of discrimination. For instance, schools can claim to accept all students that pass certain criteria (i.e., test scores, recommendations, extracurricular activities) regardless of race. This practice however assumes that the educational opportunities for all students have always been equal. Rather, the massive racial segregation that exists in elementary and middle schools has produced systematic differences in the quality of education that inner-city black children receive in relation to suburban white children. By failing to consider legacies of injustices, the colorblind treatment can be seen as evidence of indirect institutional discrimination.

Idea in Use

Racism is a related concept and refers to the ideology that holds one race superior to all others. Eduardo Bonilla-Silva wrote a compelling book entitled *Racism Without Racists: Color-Blind Racism and the Persistence of Racial Inequality in the United States* that seeks to uncover the racial rhetoric often employed by whites. In chapter three, Bonilla-Silva discusses how the dominant racial group often talks to project their non-racist ideology. However, he puts forward that qualifiers such as "I am not racist, but . . ." and "some of my best friends are black" perpetuate color-blind racism. Another main component of the book is Bonilla-Silva's analysis of color-blind racism's racial stories, such as "If Jews, Italians, and Irish have made it, how come blacks have not?" and "The past is in the past." Bonilla-Silva's book and research provides a clear analysis of the dominant form of racism and the associated racial discourse.

Activity Instructions

In this group exercise you will be identifying stereotypes and patterns of discrimination that exist in society, as well as evaluating how racial discrimination could be alleviated.

1. In your group, identify and list stereotypes that you have heard about people of *your own* race, ethnicity, gender, region of residence (southerner, Midwestern, etc.) and your nationality/ancestry. Include positive and negative stereotypes. For instance, many people positively stereotype Asians as brilliant in math and science and negatively stereotype Asians as having a short stature.

2. Does your group, as a whole, believe that racial discrimination is still a relevant issue in American society?

   - If yes, give examples of the discrimination you see or have experienced.
   - If no, give the group's rationale and reasons for this belief and whether another form of discrimination (e.g., sexual orientation) has taken over in importance.
   - Does your group believe that protective programs, such as affirmative action, are still necessary and vital to ensuring an even playing field? Why or why not?

3. Turn in your group assignment to your instructor as directed.

Political and Economic Sociology

The Power Elite
C. Wright Mills

Labs
Internet Exercise: Economy Types
Individual Writing Exercise: Types of Governmental and Political Systems
Group Exercise: Politics in the United States

The Power Elite

The powers of ordinary men are circumscribed by the everyday worlds in which they live, yet even in these rounds of job, family, and neighborhood they often seem driven by forces they can neither understand nor govern. 'Great changes' are beyond their control, but affect their conduct and outlook none the less. The very framework of modern society confines them to projects not their own, but from every side, such changes now press upon the men and women of the mass society, who accordingly feel that they are without purpose in an epoch in which they are without power.

But not all men are in this sense ordinary. As the means of information and of power are centralized, some men come to occupy positions in American society from which they can look down upon, so to speak, and by their decisions mightily affect, the everyday worlds of ordinary men and women. They are not made by their jobs; they set up and break down jobs for thousands of others; they are not confined by simple family responsibilities; they can escape. They may live in many hotels and houses, but they are bound by no one community. They need not merely 'meet the demands of the day and hour'; in some part, they create these demands, and cause others to meet them. Whether or not they profess their power, their technical and political experience of it far transcends that of the underlying population. What Jacob Burckhardt said of 'great men,' most Americans might well say of their elite: 'They are all that we are not.'[1]

The power elite is composed of men whose positions enable them to transcend the ordinary environments of ordinary men and women; they are in positions to make decisions having major consequences. Whether they do or do not make such decisions is less important than the fact that they do occupy such pivotal positions: their failure to act, their failure to make decisions, is itself an act that is often of greater consequence than the decisions they do make. For they are in command of the major hierarchies and organizations of modern society. They rule the big corporations. They run the machinery of the state and claim its prerogatives. They direct the military establishment. They occupy the strategic command posts of the social structure, in which are now centered the effective means of the power and the wealth and the celebrity which they enjoy.

The power elite are not solitary rulers. Advisers and consultants, spokesmen and opinion-makers are often the captains of their higher thought and decision. Immediately below the elite are the professional politicians of the middle levels of power, in the Congress and in the pressure groups, as well as among the new and old upper classes of town and city and region. Mingling with them, in curious ways which we shall explore, are those professional celebrities who live by being continually displayed but are never, so long as they remain celebrities, displayed enough. If such celebrities are not at the head of any dominating hierarchy, they do often have the power to distract the attention of the public or afford sensations to the masses, or, more directly, to gain the ear of those who do occupy positions of direct power. More or less unattached, as critics of morality and technicians of power, as spokesmen of God and creators of mass sensibility, such celebrities and consultants are part of the immediate scene in which the drama of the elite is enacted. But that drama itself is centered in the command posts of the major institutional hierarchies.

1

The truth about the nature and the power of the elite is not some secret which men of affairs know but will not tell. Such men hold quite various theories about their own roles in the sequence of event and decision. Often they are uncertain about their roles, and even more often they allow their fears and their hopes to affect their assessment of their own power. No matter how great their actual power, they tend to be less acutely aware of it than of the resistances of others to its use. Moreover, most American men of affairs have learned well the rhetoric of public relations, in some cases even to the point of using it when they are alone, and thus coming to believe it. The personal awareness of the actors is only one of the several sources one must examine in order to understand the higher circles. Yet many who believe that there is no elite, or at any rate none of any consequence, rest their argument upon what men of affairs believe about themselves, or at least assert in public.

There is, however, another view: those who feel, even if vaguely, that a compact and powerful elite of great importance does now prevail in America often base that feeling upon the historical trend of our time. They have felt, for example, the domination of the military event, and from this they infer that generals and admirals, as well as other men of decision influenced by them, must be enormously powerful. They hear that the Congress has again abdicated to a handful of men decisions clearly related to the issue of war or peace. They know that the bomb was dropped over Japan in the name of the United States of America, although they were at no time consulted about the matter. They feel that they live in a time of big decisions; they know that they are not making any. Accordingly, as they consider the present as history, they infer that at its center, making decisions or failing to make them, there must be an elite of power.

On the one hand, those who share this feeling about big historical events assume that there is an elite and that its power is great. On the other hand, those who listen carefully to the reports of men apparently involved in the great decisions often do not believe that there is an elite whose powers are of decisive consequence.

Both views must be taken into account, but neither is adequate. The way to understand the power of the American elite lies neither solely in recognizing the historic scale of events nor in accepting the personal awareness reported by men of apparent decision. Behind such men and behind the events of history, linking the two, are the major institutions of modern society. These hierarchies of state and corporation and army constitute the means of power; as such they are now of a consequence not before equaled in human history—and at their summits, there are now those command posts of modern society which offer us the sociological key to an understanding of the role of the higher circles in America.

Within American society, major national power now resides in the economic, the political, and the military domains. Other institutions seem off to the side of modern history, and, on occasion, duly subordinated to these. No family is as directly powerful in national affairs as any major corporation; no church is as directly powerful in the external biographies of young men in America today as the military establishment; no college is as powerful in the shaping of momentous events as the National Security Council. Religious, educational, and family institutions are not autonomous centers of national power; on the contrary, these decentralized areas are increasingly shaped by the big three, in which developments of decisive and immediate consequence now occur.

Families and churches and schools adapt to modern life; governments and armies and corporations shape it; and, as they do so, they turn these lesser institutions into means for their ends. Religious institutions provide chaplains to the armed forces where they are used as a means of increasing the effectiveness of its morale to kill. Schools select and train men for their jobs in corporations and their specialized tasks in the armed forces. The extended family has, of course, long been broken up by the industrial revolution, and now the son and the father are removed from the family, by compulsion if need be, whenever the army of the state sends out the call. And the symbols of all these lesser institutions are used to legitimate the power and the decisions of the big three.

The life-fate of the modern individual depends not only upon the family into which he was born or which he enters by marriage, but increasingly upon the corporation in which he spends the most alert hours of his best years; not only upon the school where he is educated as a child and adolescent, but also upon the state which touches him throughout his life; not only upon the church in which on occasion he hears the word of God, but also upon the army in which he is disciplined.

If the centralized state could not rely upon the inculcation of nationalist loyalties in public and private schools, its leaders would promptly seek to modify the decentralized educational system. If the bankruptcy rate among the top five hundred corporations were as high as the general divorce rate among the thirty-seven million married couples, there would be economic catastrophe on an international scale. If members of armies gave to them no more of their lives than do believers to the churches to which they belong, there would be a military crisis.

Within each of the big three, the typical institutional unit has become enlarged, has become administrative, and, in the power of its decisions, has become centralized. Behind these developments there is a fabulous technology, for as institutions, they have incorporated this technology and guide it, even as it shapes and paces their developments.

The economy—once a great scatter of small productive units in autonomous balance—has become dominated by two or three hundred giant corporations, administratively and politically interrelated, which together hold the keys to economic decisions.

The political order, once a decentralized set of several dozen states with a weak spinal cord, has become a centralized, executive establishment which has taken up into itself many powers previously scattered, and now enters into each and every cranny of the social structure.

The military order, once a slim establishment in a context of distrust fed by state militia, has become the largest and most expensive feature of government, and, although well versed in smiling public relations, now has all the grim and clumsy efficiency of a sprawling bureaucratic domain.

In each of these institutional areas, the means of power at the disposal of decision makers have increased enormously; their central executive powers have been enhanced; within each of them modern administrative routines have been elaborated and tightened up.

As each of these domains becomes enlarged and centralized, the consequences of its activities become greater, and its traffic with the others increases. The decisions of a handful of corporations bear upon military and political as well as upon economic developments around the world. The decisions of the military establishment rest upon and grievously affect political life as well as the very level of economic activity. The decisions made within the political domain determine economic activities and military programs. There is no longer, on the one hand, an economy, and, on the other hand, a political order containing a military establishment unimportant to politics and to money-making. There is a political economy linked, in a thousand ways, with military institutions and decisions. On each side of the world-split running through central Europe and around the Asiatic rimlands, there is an ever-increasing interlocking of economic, military, and political structures.[2] If there is government intervention in the corporate economy, so is there corporate intervention in the governmental process. In the structural sense, this triangle of power is the source of the interlocking directorate that is most important for the historical structure of the present.

The fact of the interlocking is clearly revealed at each of the points of crisis of modern capitalist society—slump, war, and boom. In each, men of decision are led to an awareness of the interdependence of the major institutional orders. In the nineteenth century, when the scale of all institutions was smaller, their liberal integration was achieved in the automatic economy, by an autonomous play of market forces, and in the automatic political domain, by the bargain and the vote. It was then assumed that out of the imbalance and friction that followed the limited decisions then possible a new equilibrium would in due course emerge. That can no longer be assumed, and it is not assumed by the men at the top of each of the three dominant hierarchies.

For, given the scope of their consequences, decisions—and indecisions—in any one of these ramify into the others, and hence top decisions tend either to become co-ordinated or to lead to a commanding indecision. It has not always been like this. When numerous small entrepreneurs made up the economy, for example, many of them could fail and the consequences still remain local; political and military authorities did not intervene. But now, given political expectations and military commitments, can they afford to allow key units of the private corporate economy to break down in slump? Increasingly, they do intervene in economic affairs, and as they do so, the controlling decisions in each order are inspected by agents of the other two, and economic, military, and political structures are interlocked.

At the pinnacle of each of the three enlarged and centralized domains, there have arisen those higher circles which make up the economic, the political, and the military elites. At the top of the economy, among the corporate rich, there are the chief executives; at the top of the political order, the members of the political directorate; at the top of the military establishment, the elite of soldier-statesmen clustered in and around the Joint Chiefs of Staff and the upper echelon. As each of these domains has coincided with the others, as decisions tend to become total in their consequence, the leading men in each of the three domains of power—the warlords, the corporation chieftains, the political directorate—tend to come together, to form the power elite of America.

Notes

1. Jacob Burckhardt., *Force and Freedom* (New York: Pantheon Books, 1943), pp. 303 ff.
2. Cf. Hans Gerth and C. Wright Mills, *Character and Social Structure* (New York: Harcourt, Brace, 1953), pp. 457 ff.

LABS

Internet Exercise

Economy Types

Introduction

The economy is a social institution that deals with the means of production, distribution, and consumption of goods and services. There are two broad types of economic systems that are found globally: capitalism and socialism. Capitalism and socialism represent the poles of a continuum that reflect the ownership of natural and manmade resources, as well as the means of production. *Capitalism* is based on private ownership of resources and production systems of goods and services. *Socialism,* on the other hand, refers to a system where all the resources and means of production are collectively owned. Since capitalism and socialism are ideal types of economies, there is always some blurring. Generally, culture and government of the society can dictate the form of economy and the direction the economy tilts. Therefore, there are many different specific sub-types of economies found across the globe.

There are several key characteristics of capitalism that clearly distinguish the system from all others. First, there must be an emphasis on private ownership. In ideal capitalism, individuals can own land, buildings, factories, companies, natural resources, raw materials, and any other kind of property with no interference from government. Secondly, the pursuit of wealth is emphasized and the belief that profits should be maximized is highlighted. Lastly, there is an emphasis on competition and a supply and demand principle regulates this competition. Competition is not only seen in the quest to make the most profit, but also in getting the desired product at the best cost. Pure capitalism, or *laissez-faire* capitalism, refers to a hands-off policy in which the government does not interfere with the free market system. The United States' economic system is capitalistic, but modified from *laissez-faire* capitalism in that the government does regulate market competition to prevent monopolies from forming and safeguarding consumers and employees.

Pure socialism is characterized by a) collective ownership of resources and the means of production, b) renunciation of the pursuit for individual wealth in favor of collective goals and insurance that all members of society has access to the basic necessities of life, and c) governmental control and influence. Ideally, the socialist government collects the wealth and uniformly distributes it back to the people in the form of medical care, transportation, education, housing, and other services. In practice, this is highly variable depending on the government intentions. The former Soviet Union was based on a socialist economy and China currently uses socialist principles.

Sociologists also often refer to mixed economies, also known as social democracies or welfare capitalism. These terms refer to a state economy that has features of both capitalism and socialism. Specifically, there is a free market system typical of capitalism in place, but a very organized system of state based social welfare programs (i.e., nationalized healthcare, educational systems, etc.). To accumulate the capital needed to start and maintain the social welfare systems, taxes are rather high in these countries. Sweden has adopted this form of economic system.

Idea in Use

There is some debate that the rise in social democracies and mixed economies in Europe has dampened the social capital within the area. The argument is made that since the government increases its presence in all spheres of society, the need for family and social networks is decreased. For instance, decisions and discussion about childcare that once was relegated to families is now solved by national childcare programs. Those who believe in this argument also extend the argument and suggest that informal solidarity is slowly eradicated. There is an opposing position that argues that welfare states, especially those in Scandinavia, create greater social capital. They contend that since the government manages most of the spheres of society, citizens have more time to contribute to voluntary organizations and civil society. A 2005 article in *Policy and Politics* by Wim van Oorschot, Wil Arts, and Loek Halman sought to empirically test the hypotheses offered by opposing sides. Using the 1999/2000 European Values Study, the authors found that at the national level, higher welfare spending was associated with decreased feelings of solidarity towards needy groups (elderly, unemployed, and immigrants) but increased participation and social capital (more active in volunteering, spending time with friends, and more trusting of others and institutions).

Activity Instructions

You will be learning more about the types of economies found globally through this web-based exercise.

1. For the following countries, characterize their economies as socialist, capitalist, or mixed. Also take note of the unemployment rates within the country, how the labor force is divided (state or non-state sectors), the distribution of the labor force, and household income or consumption by percentage share (not all countries will have data for each category).

China	Norway
Cuba	Taiwan
El Salvador	Turkey
Italy	Uzbekistan

   Websites that may be valuable to visit include:
   CIA-The World Factbook—www.cia.gov/cia/publications/factbook
   The Library of Congress—http://lcweb2.loc.gov/frd/cs/

   Are the results what you would expect based on the type of economy (particularly how the wealth is distributed within the country)?

2. Visit the Celebrate Capitalism website at www.celebratecapitalism.org. How does this organization define capitalism and what is their primary purpose as a group? List the "big seven" official thinkers of capitalistic thought and identify one to learn more about. Write a brief summary (1–2 pages, typed, double-spaced) about what the individual contributed to creating and promoting capitalism.

3. Go to the World Socialist Movement homepage at www.worldsocialism.org and explore the site to answer the following questions:

   - Does the group believe that a capitalist country can become socialist without a revolution?
   - How does the group respond to the sentiment that 'people are too greedy' to be socialist?
   - Who owns the world? (hint: discuss global inequality)

4. Turn in your assignment to your instructor as directed.

Individual Writing Exercise

Types of Governmental and Political Systems

Introduction

Political and governmental structures have changed and developed since the beginning of time. However, the one constant characteristic in differing government systems is the bestowing of power and authority upon leaders. The distribution and amount of power varies according to the four styles of political systems: *authoritarian, totalitarian, monarchical,* and *democratic.*

Authoritarian governments reject any involvement and input of the citizens in decision making, selection of leaders, and policy making. The rulers are often characterized as tyrants, dictators, or despots that have unquestioned authority and power. New ideas and dissent among the public is quickly and severely repressed. Countries with single political parties or run by military junta such as Kuwait and Sudan are often authoritarian in style.

Totalitarian governments are perhaps even more restrictive than authoritarian governments since totalitarian systems closely control nearly all aspects of life. Power is concentrated solely within the government and the government controls all social institutions. Information produced in mass media outlets and provided in schools is determined by the government. Surveillance is a typical feature of totalitarian states. North Korea and China are two countries that have totalitarian governments.

Monarchies are government types in which the power is held by one ruling family and is inherited from one generation to another. Monarchies vary in the degree of control that the government exercises over the people. *Absolute monarchies* deny any power distribution and retain complete domination. They can also be totalitarian or authoritarian in nature, but the power stems from the family. Saudi Arabia has an absolute monarchy today. Other monarchies are simply figureheads or symbolic leaders that allow the governing body to be elected by the people. This is called a *constitutional monarchy.* Constitutional monarchies are very visible throughout European countries, such as Denmark and England.

Finally, *democracies* are governments that allow participation in the electoral process of leaders, the organization and distribution of power, and allow the ability to voice opposition to the direction of policy. Theoretically, all people have an equal voice and can voice their opinions through voting for and electing their representatives. In practice, class inequalities have limited the voice of many. The United States and Kenya are two examples of countries that are democratic in style.

Idea in Use

Dictatorships are common in totalitarian and authoritarian governments and absolute monarchies. Juvenal Habyarimana assumed leadership in Rwanda in 1973 through a military *coup d'etat* and eliminated all other political parties and opposition within the country. Philip Verwimp in the *European Journal of Political Economy* article entitled, "The Political Economic of Coffee, Dictatorship, and Genocide" analyzes how Habyarimana manipulated loyalties and obtained power as the country's main export and state revenue producer, coffee, started to fall in value. It is important to realize that coffee exports accounted for over 70 percent of the country's revenue and that Habyarimana's regime depended on the product. As Verwimp indicates, "coffee price and the production of coffee determine the dictator's budget and supply of loyalty of the population." The late 1980s and early 1990s began a period of decline for coffee production and consumption. Thus to maintain his dictator role, Habyarimana had to increase power and repression of the people. The increased repression was needed to maintain loyalty from peasants and other Rwandans. At first, Habyarimana began confiscating property, but then he and his regime began using arbitrary arrests, rape, and massacres as the way to maintain power. Verwimp claims that by attempting to maintain loyalty from one ethnic group, the Hutus, Habyarimana began targeting the extermination of another group, the Tutsis. He did this by planting a genocidal ideology into the mindset of the Hutus. While the Rwandan genocide did not officially begin until after Habyarimana was killed in 1994, the ideological framework of genocide was in place because of Habyarimana's quest for loyalty and totalitarian political power. Verwimp makes it clear that the genocide was not created because of the fall of coffee prices, but rather the coffee was incidental to Habyarimana remaining in power. See volume 19 of *European Journal of Political Economy*, published in 2003, for more details and to see how conditions in Rwanda have contributed to increased consciousness of fair trade coffee.

Activity Instructions

This is an individual exercise which explores different types of governments at the global and local levels.

1. Choose one country (other than the United States) to learn about their governmental style. Do some research and write a brief (1–2 pages, typed, double-spaced) paper summarizing the history of the government (have there been changes from dictatorship to democracy, etc.), the leaders (symbolic and actual, etc.) that have been most prominent throughout time, how often are elections (if they have elections), the main political parties and any other key characteristics that you learn. Be sure to cite your references and characterize the country as totalitarian, authoritarian, democracy, or monarchy.

2. Choose one non-American leader from any place or time that has influenced world politics. Write a brief paper (1–2 pages, typed, double-spaced) about how they led their country and how they wielded their power. Be sure to cite your references.

3. Finally, colleges across the country have student electoral bodies that work to make the campus a better community. In addition, there are various clubs and organizations that seek to diversify and entertain students. Select a student leader from your campus to interview. This person could be from student government or a student group. Ask your subject how they were elected (could all students vote, only full-time seniors, etc.), how the electoral process was organized (time span, major rules, etc.) and any obstacles or problems they encountered. Also be sure to ask them about how candidates are nominated or selected to the leadership positions. Write up a concise review of your interview.

4. Turn in your reports to your instructor as directed.

Group Exercise

Politics in the United States

Introduction

Democracy has reigned in the United States since the Revolutionary War ended. Therefore, the political system is based on plurality rule where the winner needs only one more vote than his or her opponent to win the election. Political parties are created to insure that their candidate is supported and generates at least the one additional vote to win the contested seat. Political parties identify their position on social and economic issues and create a party platform. While there are several different political parties within the United States, it is predominately a two-party country. The Democratic Party is associated with liberal positions such as greater governmental intervention and more welfare based programs that help disadvantaged groups. The Republican Party is considered conservative and is associated with desiring less government involvement and more economic freedom.

Special interest groups, political action committees, and lobbyists are influential in the creation and management of party positions on particular issues. Special interest groups work on a variety of issues such as education, medical research funding, farming, and gun ownership. Special interest groups often hire lobbyists, who are individuals paid to pressure elected officials for their support on the issue. Lobbyists can represent a variety of interests, from non-profit organizations and volunteer groups to international governments and multinational corporations. Political action committees are special interest groups that invest money in political officials and parties to try to swing support in their favor. Political action committees are restricted in their giving to individual candidates (upper limit of $5,000) so often they transfer monies to the party. Elections and campaigns can be shaped greatly by these financial contributions and therefore campaign finance reform has received unenthusiastic support from members already on Capitol Hill.

Idea in Use

There has been much attention to how religious group membership can drive political elections. News media outlets often speculate about how the religious right can provide an advantage to the Republican Party. Clem Brooks and Jeff Manzo meticulously analyzed religious group membership and political outcomes from 1972 through 2000 to determine whether such membership could drive elections and produce a Conservative outcome. In their article "A Great Divide? Religion and Political Change in U.S. National Elections, 1972–2000" published in *The Sociological Quarterly,* they found that the partisanship of evangelical Protestants and Catholics had transferred toward the Republican Party. Specifically, they found that Catholics had moved from a Democratic Party ideology to a more Republican ideology and that evangelical Protestants had intensified their Republican identification. However, they caution that since there is little evidence of a widening gap of religion and voting practices throughout the study period the term of a 'great divide" is exaggerated and misleading. Rather, they suggest that the relationship between religious group membership and political outcomes is multi-dimensional and depends on a variety of circumstances such as group size, turnout, partisanship, and voting behaviors.

Activity Instructions

Your small group will investigate how much you know about the political system in the United States and discuss current issues in American politics.

1. One of the main problems with the political process is that many citizens have voter apathy and fail to vote in local, state, and national elections. Since turning 18 and being of legal age to vote, determine who in your group has registered to vote and who has actually voted. Keep a list that indicates how many years each person has voted and at what level (local, state, national, all, etc.). If the group as a whole feels uncomfortable with linking their voting activity with their names, use identification numbers (1, 2, 3, etc.) instead of names. After the list has been created, answer the following questions:

   - Is there a specific election (presidential, senate, etc.) that people in your group tend to vote on more often?
   - What are the main reasons that your group members don't vote (i.e., don't know where polling place is, not aware of who is running, unsure of candidate's position on issues, absentee voting problems, registering problems, etc.)?
   - For the people who did vote in your group, how did they become aware of the information that those who did not vote were uninformed about? For instance, if a major issue identified in the above answer is that people did not know where the polling places are, how did the voters know where to go?
   - Is anyone in your group involved in organizations that are politically related (e.g., rock the vote, moveon.org, smackdown your vote, etc.)?

2. Another problem related to politics in the United States, is ignorance about the political process and knowledge of elected officials. As a group, answer the following questions.

   - When is Election Day?
   - Who are your U.S. Senators?
   - Name one U.S. Representative from your state.
   - Who is the Governor of your state and what is his or her party affiliation?
   - Who is the mayor in your city, town, or township?
   - As a whole, what color is your state (red = Republican, blue = Democrat)?
   - How many electoral votes does your state have?

3. Finally, political contests are determined by the candidates' positions on the issues. What does your group believe are the three most important issues facing the United States currently? What are the general positions of the major political parties (Democrat and Republican) concerning the three issues you identified?

4. Turn in the write-ups—either individually or a collective summary, as directed by your instructor.

The Family

Love, American Style
Lisa E. Phillips

Labs
Internet Exercise: Trends in Families and Households
Individual Writing Exercise: Family: Concepts and Functions
Group Exercise: Union Formation and Dissolution

Love, American Style

Blame it on the boomers: Generation X is making marriage work for them.

Love is in the air, but marriage must be in the water. How else to explain Americans' attraction to matrimony? According to "Marital Status and Living Arrangements: March 1998," a recently updated U.S. Census Bureau report released last month, about 56 percent of all American adults were married and living with their spouses last year (111 million people). Not surprisingly, California, Texas, New York, Florida, and Nevada were the top five states, respectively, for marriages in 1996. That's a pretty rosy picture of family values, even taking into consideration the downside of the report: that about 10 percent of adults (19.4 million) were "currently divorced" last year. It's the word currently that defines us: Hope springs eternal. Divorce isn't forever.

"People aspire to what they don't have," says Steve Kraus, a director at Yankelovich Partners, explaining the behavior patterns of boomers who are marrying, divorcing, and remarrying, versus Generation Xers, many of whom are holding off on making that big commitment for the first time.

"Not every Gen Xer is a child of divorce," he adds, "But the eighties were their formative years, when divorce rates skyrocketed."

That's why, according to a recently released Yankelovich poll, Gen Xers—the half that aren't already hitched—are delaying marriage, as shown by the current median age at the time of first marriage: 25 years for women and 26.8 years for men in 1997. Boomers, by contrast, were marrying young: In 1970, the median age for marriage for women was 20.8 years, and for men, 23.2 years.

Yankelovich's survey of some 2,500 Gen Xers shows that those who are still single are planning to enjoy themselves, while those who are married are nesting with a vengeance. Fifty-eight percent of single Xers say their social life is a high priority, compared to only 38 percent of married Xers. Some 61 percent of singles feel it's vital to keep up on media trends, compared to 49 percent of their married friends. And when it comes to fun, 68 percent of single Xers expect to have "more fun" this year, while a mere 52 percent of married people are counting on it.

Kirsty Doig, vice president of New York City-based Youth Intelligence, hasn't found that attitude among the Gen Xers she's spoken to. "They don't feel they lose their identity by getting married, and they're not looking at marriage as an end to their fun," she says.

Gen Xers, she adds, felt abandoned as they grew up. "They were latch-key kids, many were the children of divorce, and the media told them they were stupid," Doig says. "So they turned to their peers for support."

Nationally, there is nearly one divorce for every two marriages, according to census data from 1996, the most current year available. Preliminary figures from the Monthly Vital Statistics Report for the first seven months of 1998 don't indicate a major shift in that trend.

But on average, Americans are staying married longer. The median duration of marriages ending in divorce has lengthened—from 6.7 years in 1970 to 7.2 years in 1990, according to the U.S. National Center for Health Statistics.

And we're older when we finally call it quits. The median age at divorce for men was 35.9 years in 1990, or 2.7 years older than in 1970. Women's median age at the time of their divorce in 1990 was 33.2, up 3.4 years from 1970.

The rate of remarriage has slowed, as well. In 1970, 12.3 percent of divorced women and 20.5 percent of divorced men remarried. By 1990, just 7.6 percent of divorced women and 10.6 percent of divorced men were heading back to the altar.

Still, the Census Bureau is predicting an upswing in Gen X marriages by 2010. About half of them are married now, and census projections indicate about two-thirds will be hitched by 2001, when the true millennium rolls around. By 2010, 85 percent will be settling down.

Tradition with a Twist

But settling down to what? Traditional family values, on their own terms. Something edgier, with more irony than their parents. "They want to do traditional family things, like spend time on the family photo album," Kraus notes. "But instead of putting the pictures in a book, they'll scan them into their computers and put them on a Web site."

Youth Intelligence's Doig agrees. "Marriage isn't a locked jail to Gen Xers," she says. "They may not be more committed to it than their parents, but they're redefining it for themselves." If, for example, Gen Xers wish to stay at home with their children, they'll find ways to telecommute or jobs that will allow them to share the responsibility.

Both Doig and Kraus use the word nostalgic to describe Xers' view of hearth and home. The Xers, though, are nostalgic for the childhood that boomers supposedly had. It's informed their model for the perfect, traditional marriage.

"The stereotypical boomer grew up watching Leave It To Beaver," says Kraus. "The stereotypical Gen Xer grew up watching The Brady Bunch. Their impression of family life was, 'Hey, let's go find a bunch of strangers to live with us.'" It's a wonder they want to get married at all.

GEN X MARRIAGES IN Y2K+

Marital Status, Projections by Age for Years 2000 and 2010

Characteristics	# (000s)		Percent Distribution	
	2000	**2010**	**2000**	**2010**
Total population 18+	203,852	225,206	100 %	100 %
Never married/single	44,459	50,747	21.8%	22.5%
Married at least once	159,393	174,459	78.2%	77.5%
Population 25–34 years	37,233	38,521	100 %	100 %
Never married/single	12,288	5,660	33.0%	14.7%
Married at least once	24,946	32,860	67.0%	85.3%
Population, 35–54 years	81,689	78,847	100 %	100 %
Never married/single	8,232	4,741	10.1%	6.0%
Married at least once	73,458	74,108	89.9%	94.0%

Source: Census Bureau, Current Population Reports, P25-1129, and American Demographics.

In general, Generation X is putting off marriage—at least for another decade, according to current Census Bureau projections. Boomers, on the other hand, are taking the plunge—some over and over again.

Virginia Is: Counties Where Single Population is Greater than the Married Population

Name	State	Single	Married	Ratio (S/M)
1) Williamsburg City	VA	6,721	2,645	2.54
2) Radford City	VA	8,568	4,222	2.03
3) Lexington City	VA	3,425	1,963	1.74
4) District of Columbia	DC	242,035	146,213	1.66
5) Harrisonburg City	VA	13,712	9,196	1.49
6) Claiborne	MS	4,242	2,877	1.47
7) Suffolk	MA	270,440	185,906	1.45
8) Shannon	SD	2,830	2,048	1.38
9) New York	NY	571,206	435,595	1.31
10) Clarke	GA	35,051	27,183	1.29

Source: 1990 Census, CACI.

Virginia and neighboring Washington, D.C., take the country's top five places for number of singles-to-married couples. However, college kids at William and Mary, not to mention Georgetown, George Washington University, and the Catholic University of America, make up a great deal of the single population in Williamsburg and Washington, while Clarke County, Georgia, is home to the University of Georgia.

LABS

Internet Exercise

Trends in Families and Households

Introduction

The typical image of a progression from courtship to marriage to having and raising children came with clear roles and obligations. Now, more options have become increasingly popular and accepted within American society. Choices such as cohabitation, living as homosexual partners, remaining single throughout life, and non-traditional family formations have provided diversity that many celebrate while others raise concerns.

While marriage is still the predominant household form, cohabitation and remaining single have grown in popularity. In the decade from 1990 to 2000, the United States Census indicates that the number of married family households decreased (from 55.2 percent to 51.7 percent), while the number of individuals living alone experienced an increase of 1.2 percent (from 24.6 percent to 25.8 percent) and the number of cohabiting couples increased slightly to account for 5.2 percent of American households. Additionally, the percentage of female-headed family households increased in the same decade. Looking at a longer time period, we see that there has been a steady increase of never married people. In 1950, 26 percent of men and 19 percent of women were never married. In 2000, 31 percent of men and 25 percent of women have never married. The percentages of never married are greatly influenced by those opting to marry later in life. Whereas in 1950 it was typical to marry when one was in his or her early 20s, in 2000 the mean age of marriage has increased to the mid and late 20s. Several factors play a role in the increasing number of unmarried adults. Certainly, the acceptance of cohabitation is one influence, as are the growing population of women in the labor force, increases in life expectancy, population growth, and divorce rates.

The count of homosexual relationships has been problematic to obtain. Often, surveys and studies will differ on the definition of homosexuality (i.e., preference vs. behavior) and this will lead to different estimates of the homosexual population. Additionally, while homosexuality has become more accepted in society, there is still a stigma associated with this lifestyle and thus undercounts are a threat. The General Social Survey shows that since 1973 there has been increased tolerance of same sex relationships. However, even in the latest data (2004) a majority of respondents (62.4 percent) reported that they felt that sexual relations between two adults of the same sex are always or almost always wrong. Nevertheless, from 1990 to 2000, there was a significant increase in the number of people who reported they live in same sex, unmarried households, from about 145,000 to 595,000.

Trends in reproduction, childbearing, and childcare have also provided diverse options for families and households. Artificial insemination, surrogate parenting, and in-vitro fertilization have increased the opportunities for previously infertile couples to conceive. On the flipside, more effective birth control options and increased availability and safety of abortions have limited unwanted pregnancies. Another trend related to families and households is the increasing percentage of grandparents raising their grandchildren.

Idea in Use

The idea of states legalizing same sex marriages and recognizing homosexual civil unions spurs great controversy. Debate has ensued at various levels and has led to the implementation of new political acts (e.g., the 1996 Federal Defense of Marriage

Act) and calls for Constitutional amendments banning same-sex marriages. Nevertheless, several states (notably Vermont, Hawaii, and Alaska) have created homosexual friendly climates by considering same-sex marriage and civil unions in the state legislature. Scott Barclay and Shauna Fisher in a 2003 edition of *The Policy Studies Journal* report on their multivariate analysis of what characteristics of states make them particularly likely to ban lesbian and gay marriages. In "The States and the Differing Impetus for Divergent Paths on Same-Sex Marriage, 1990-2001" they examine how states previously decided on homosexual unions, partisan politics, and elections (e.g., election year, percent Democrat, etc.), the constituency characteristics (e.g., racial diversity, education, etc.), religious factors (e.g., percent Catholic, etc.) and how the presence of gay, lesbian, and bisexual residents within the state effect the enactment of anti-same-sex laws. Not surprisingly, they found that states that have previously enacted pro-same-sex marriages and unions were less likely to then ban such relationships, as were states with highly educated citizenry. However, there were some unexpected relationships. For instance, religious variables were *not* significant and as the percent of same-sex couple households increased in the state there was an increased likelihood of states passing anti-same-sex marriage laws. They suggest that perhaps religious membership is not as important as previously thought and that a backlash effect was in place in some states. Overall, their findings suggest that previously accepted notions about influences in the legislation of homosexual unions should be evaluated more and that the state's impetus to legislate such relationships move (or don't move) at varying speeds.

Activity Instructions

This exercise will require you to visit internet sites to gain more information about the contemporary trends in families and households.

1. Go to the Human Rights Campaign website which is a page dedicated to equality regardless of sexual orientation. The site is at www.hrc.org. Click on "Laws In Your State" from the left side menu. Select the state from which you currently reside. First, determine what the percentage increase of same-sex partners in your state from 1990–2000 was according to the U.S. Census. Then, select the hyperlink that directs you to "View Current Laws." From this page, find the information that reports the status or details of the laws pertaining to the following:

   - Adoption Law
   - Donor Insemination
   - Non-Discrimination
   - Surrogacy Law
   - Marriage/Relationship Recognition

   Repeat this process for two more states of your choice. Report your findings and summarize which of the states that you examined were more favorable or restrictive of gay, lesbian, bisexual, and transgender families. You may also want to look at the current legislation page to find out more about the study states.

2. Go to the Census website (www.census.gov) and select the American FactFinder page and then select the "People" tab from the left side menu. You will be examining the rates of various types of families and households at three levels: the national, state, and local level. For each level, determine what the rates are for the following characteristics (you will have to scroll down to the "Relationships" box to find the appropriate tables):

   - The percentage of males and females over the age of 15 who have never married
   - The percentage of males and females over the age of 15 who are divorced
   - The number of heterosexual cohabiters

- The number of same-sex male cohabiters
- The number of same-sex female cohabiters
- The number of grandparents raising their grandchildren
- The number of households

Create a table that compares the percentage of never married and divorced people by sex, the percentages of households that have heterosexual, same-sex male, and same-sex female cohabiters (you will need to calculate using the household count that you found), and the number of grandparents raising their grandchildren. Is there much variation across the levels of geography? What might account for differences or similarities?

3. Finally, you will be investigating one of the numerous types of reproductive technologies that are used to assist couples desiring children. Select one treatment type (e.g., artificial treatment, surrogacy, in-vitro fertilization, etc.) to describe. Write a very brief summary (1–2 paragraphs) of what the treatment involves. Helpful websites include the National Infertility Association (www.resolve.org) and the American Fertility Association (www.theafa.org), but feel free to use (and cite) any other reliable website that you find.

4. Turn in your assignment to your instructor as directed.

Individual Writing Exercise

Family: Concepts and Functions

Introduction

The social institution that is primarily in charge of the socialization of children is the family. Family can take many forms and serves many functions for society. While government agencies and some organizations define family quite narrowly, consisting of only married individuals with or without offspring, most sociologists prefer to use a more inclusive definition of family.

Family structures differ across the globe and within the United States. The *nuclear family*, consisting of two parents and their children residing together, is the most common family structure in the United States. A modified-nuclear family refers to households that consist of two or more related individuals (through marriage, blood, or adoption). *Extended family* is a form common in rural areas and in less developed countries, and consists of multigenerational households of parents, their children, and other relatives.

Descent is another concept that is often attached to the study of families. This concept refers to how a society traces kinship and inheritance through generations. *Patrilineal descent* is most common in agrarian and pre-industrial societies and traces kinship through the father. *Matrilineal descent* refers to societies that trace kinship by the mother, and property flows from mother to daughter. This is common in horticultural societies. Finally, high income nations, including the United States, are characterized by *bilineal descent.*

Still another dimension across which families vary is in the nature of their *authority structure. Patriarchal authority* places primary authority and decision making in the hands of males—husbands and fathers. Most western families are rooted in traditions of patriarchal authority. Some nations and tribal groups are characterized by *matriarchal authority.* Here, authority and decision making is located with females—wives and mothers. Finally, many societies, including the United States, are moving toward *egalitarian authority* within the family. Here, husbands and wives, fathers and mothers, share in decision-making responsibilities and quite typically negotiate areas of authority and decision making according to their interests and talents. It is also worth noting that the pattern of lineage discussed above quite typically follows the pattern of authority. That is, societies characterized by patriarchal authority in families are also characterized by patrilineal descent patterns, and vice versa.

The institution of the family also performs many functions for society. First, the family is responsible for the reproduction of humans and also regulating sexual behavior. For instance, incestuous relationships are forbidden in the United States and families uphold this regulation. Secondly, the socialization of children primarily occurs within families. Language, cultural norms, and values are taught to children within families. Additionally, families provide all kinds of support: financial, emotional, physical, etc. Finally, families give individuals a social place or location, such as social class and identities of race, ethnicity, and religion.

Idea in Use

Surnames have often been a key symbol to others about the pattern of lineage in families. Traditionally in American families, newly married women take their husband's last name and any offspring that the couple produces would also be given the father's last name suggesting a patrilineal family system. The number of married women who hyphenate their surnames or keep their maiden names (as either a surname or middle name) has risen in the past few decades. The practice of naming children when parents have different last names has been investigated very little. David Johnson and Laurie Scheuble were one of the first to examine the issue in their *Social Science Journal* article "What Should We Call Our Kids? Choosing Children's Surnames when Parents' Last Names Differ" (2002). They found that while married women who had non-traditional surnames (kept their own surnames or hyphenated versions) were overwhelmingly still likely to give their child the father's surname, they were also more likely to include their own surname in their child's name than those women who took their husband's last name. Women who had liberal sociopolitical views and/or were highly educated were also factors that contributed to an increased likelihood of the mother's surname being included in the child's name.

Activity Instructions

In this individual exercise you will be analyzing how the mass media (specifically television) has portrayed families throughout the past few decades.

1. Family sitcoms from the 1950s to the 1970s differ greatly from the programs offered in the 1980s forward. Identify a family sitcom of the 50/60/70s era and watch an episode. Programs such as *Leave it to Beaver, Bewitched,* and *The Brady Bunch* are some examples of popular shows that fit the criteria set above. You can find these shows (and others that qualify) on Nick at Nite, on Nickelodeon or TVLand. If you have no access to cable, you can rent videos of old sitcoms at your local video rental store.

2. Now identify a family sitcom that you either currently watch or watched as a child. Possible options include *Roseanne, The Cosby Show,* and *Everyone Loves Raymond.*

3. Watch at least one episode of each show you selected to analyze. Create field notes and specify the plot and main characters. Be sure to pay special attention to the treatment of family. Describe the demographic makeup of the family (race, single parent, stepfamily, married, nuclear, extended, etc.) from each show. Also, note how the family interacts (e.g., does father provide discipline and/or emotion) in working to solve the problem at hand.

4. Organize your field notes and, using the above directions as prompts, create a brief paper (2–3 pages, typed, double-spaced) that summarizes your findings. Be sure to examine if and how the two sitcoms differed in their treatment of families. Also, discuss whether you think that the families in your selected sitcoms represent the typical family of their time.

5. Turn in your field notes and paper to your instructor as directed.

Group Exercise

Union Formation and Dissolution

Introduction

Union formations through marriage vary in several ways across the globe. First, the number of partners can vary based on cultural norms. *Monogamy*, involving the union of two partners, is typically practiced in developed countries. *Polygamy*, the practice of uniting three or more people in a marriage, is more typically accepted in less-developed countries. Second, there are cultural norms that proscribe who you can marry. *Endogamy* refers to the norms that require a potential spouse to marry within specific social categories. Therefore, marriage may be restricted to individuals of the same village, age, race, social class, or religion. *Exogamy* refers to rules that require marriage between people of differing social categories. The most common form of exogamy in the United States is the requirement to marry outside one's own family (i.e., biological siblings cannot marry.)

Another way that marriage formation differs by culture is the notion of how marriage partners are selected. Arranged marriages, typical of preindustrial societies, align families with endogenous characteristics and can be set by parents with little or no input for the betrothed. In industrial societies, marriages are entered into because of romantic love that potential marriage partners feel for one another. The process of finding a partner involves courtship, dating, and formalization of the union through cohabitation and/or marriage.

Unfortunately, many times marital unions become distressed and couples seek a divorce. The United States has the highest divorce rate in the world, with most researchers agreeing that a newly married couple has about a 40 percent likelihood of eventually divorcing. Divorces are now legally easier to obtain and have become socially acceptable which may influence more people to divorce rather than staying in unsatisfying relationships. Immunity against divorce is not possible. However, there are certain characteristics of relationships more prone to divorce. Couples who marry at a young age, and couples with lower socioeconomic standing are more likely to divorce than others. Ironically, highly educated couples are also more likely to divorce. Additionally, children of divorced parents and pairs that experienced a traumatic event or loss are more likely to divorce. Those people who do remarry after divorcing are more susceptible to divorce again.

Remarriages are also typical within American society, with about 80 percent of divorcees re-entering into marriage. Divorced men are more likely than divorced women to remarry. Remarriage often creates the blending of families where children from one or both of the newly married spouses have to adjust to a new family and household. But blended families also offer opportunities for more diverse family types.

Idea in Use

The number of racially exogenous relationships has slowly increased in number and acceptance. Many race scholars and demographers use the rates of interracial marriages to study social distance. This typically involves estimating the odds of an interracial marriage if all racial groups were indifferent to the race of their spouse and were equally likely to marry someone from another racial group as someone from their own. These studies typically rely on national-level data. David Harris and Hiromi Ono in a 2005 article from *Social Science Research* make the case that it is not appropriate to use national-level data to estimate potential marriage. Rather, they suggest that looking at the local marriage markets, where mates predominately meet, are more appropriate. In "How Many Interracial Marriages Would There Be If All Groups Were of Equal Size in All Places? A New Look at National Estimates of Interracial Marriage" they report that the estimates of a national marriage market tend to overexaggerate the social distance of the races. The estimates of observed interracial marriage rates at the local level more closely correspond with the expected rates. Harris and Ono plead for researchers to consider local marriage markets rather than a single national market so that future research does not produce misleading images of patterns in interracial marriage and social distance between races.

Activity Instructions

In this group activity you will be discussing the progressions involved in relationship formations as well as discussing what you think the norms for marital dissolution should be.

1. In the search for a lifetime partner, what kind of characteristics would you look for in a mate? Have a discussion with your small group about your preferences. Have a group make a list of everyone's requirements and next to each characteristic, indicate whether this would create endogenous or exogenous relationships. For instance, a group member may have a preference to commit to someone who shares the same religion, which would be endogenous.

2. Trends in marital rates and cohabitation have fluctuated in recent years. Within your small group, poll the members about whether they desire to marry. Discuss the reasons behind the desires to either marry or not marry. Also, for those who want to marry, what do you consider the ideal age to join in such a union? For those who would prefer to remain single or cohabit, identify the reason for this preference and whether this would affect decisions on having children in the household.

3. Divorce and remarriage are now common in the United States. Make a list of reasons why you think that relationships end in divorce (economic, emotional, etc.—but be specific). Are there certain dealbreakers that make divorce necessary or should the marital covenant always be honored? Also discuss in your group how many marriages are too many. For instance, while it may be common for a second marriage to occur, someone entering his or her fifth marriage may not be viewed as natural.

4. Prepare your lists and documents in a single report and turn in to your instructor as directed.

Religion

A Peculiar People
William Kephart and William W. Zellner

Labs
Internet Exercise: Religiosity in the United States
Individual Writing Exercise: Religion: Concepts and Functions
Group Exercise: Types of Religious Organizations

...A Peculiar People

In their olden attire and horse and buggy, the Old Order Amish appear to be driving out of yesterday. Actually, they are more than simply old-fashioned. Conservatism is part of their religion, and as such it permeates their entire life.

The followers of Jacob Amman believe in a literal interpretation of the Bible and rely heavily on the statement, "But ye are a chosen generation, a royal priesthood, an holy nation, a peculiar people" (1 Peter 2:9). And because they have been specifically chosen by God, the Amish take great pains to stay "apart" from the world at large. They do this not only by living apart, but by rejecting so many of the standard components of modern civilization: automobiles, radio and television, high school and college, movies, air conditioning, jewelry and cosmetics, life insurance, cameras, musical instruments. The list goes on and on.

This is not to say that the Old Order Amish reject all change. As will be shown later, some of the changes have been fairly far-reaching.[1] But in general, the followers of Jacob Amman resist converting to what they believe to be harmful worldly ways.

Appearance and Apparel

Sociologists often use the term *in-group* to depict those who think of themselves as a unit, in contrast to the *out-group*, or nonmembers. An in-group is generally characterized by the loyalty, like-mindedness, and compatibility of its constituents. Members refer to the in-group as "we," and to the out-group as "they." For the Amish, wearing apparel is one of the most distinguishing features of the in-group.

Men's hats—probably the most characteristic feature of their attire—are of low crown and wide brim; smaller models are worn by the youngsters. Coats are without collars or lapels, and almost always include a vest. (An Amishman and his vest are not easily parted.) Wire hook-and-eye fasteners are used on suit coats and vests.

Amish men's trousers deserve special mention, because (1) they never have creases or cuffs; (2) they are always worn with suspenders (belts are taboo); and (3) most are without zippered or buttoned flies. Instead, the flap or "broadfall" type is used.[2] Also, with the exception of their shirts, Amish men's attire is predominantly black.

Following the biblical injunction, Amish women keep their heads covered at all times: indoors, by a small white lawn-cap; outdoors, by the familiar black bonnet. Cosmetics and makeup, of course, are prohibited at all times.

Dresses are of a solid color—blues and purples are quite common—with (variable) long skirts and aprons. In public, women also wear shawls and capes. Scott explains the latter practice as follows:

> The kerchief or cape is worn by nearly all plain women. It is also found in many surviving folk costumes of Western Europe. Its wide appeal to pious country women is no doubt based on the modesty it provides. The extra covering is seen to conceal the neckline and the form of the bosom, and provides privacy when nursing a baby.
>
> A 19th-century English woman remarked on…the cape, "Certainly the most ingenious device ever contrived for concealing all personal advantage."[3]

For Amish women, stockings must be black, and shoes are the black, low-heeled variety. Interestingly enough, in recent years young boys and girls have taken to wearing jogging shoes. In fact, the two most popular forms of footwear for the youngsters are jogging shoes and bare feet! For both sexes, all jewelry (including the wedding ring) is taboo, because whatever is worn is presumed to be functional.[4] An ornamental exception might be the Amishman's beard, though this does have recognition value: prior to marriage young men are clean-shaven, whereas married men are required to let their beards grow. Mustaches—which in the European period were associated with the military—are completely taboo.

Amish males wear their hair long, unparted, in a Dutch bob, with the necessary trimming done at home. Amish females also have their own special hairdo, both cutting and curling being forbidden. (Shaving their legs and plucking their eyebrows are also taboo.) Their hair braiding is distinctively Amish, however, and a classroom of twenty Amish girls—all with identical hairstyles—is an unusual sight for an outsider to behold!

The Old Order Amish are quite cognizant of the fact that they look different, and they have no intention of changing. On the contrary, their "difference" makes them feel close to one another and accentuates the in-group feeling.

Some observers believe that, because the Amish are thrifty, they deliberately use clothing that never goes out of style. This is not the reason, however. True, the followers of Jacob Amman are indeed thrifty. With the exception of shoes, stockings, and hats, they make nearly all their own clothing. They also wear their clothes until they are literally worn out. But the basic reason they will not change styles is that they consider such change to be worldly—and worldliness has negative connotations.

Stephen Scott, an authority on the subject, writes that

> The plain people…feel the world is controlled by Satan and the forces of evil. And so, they reason, conformity to the fads and fashions of popular society indicates identity with the world's system.

The plain people insist that the church, guided by the Word of God and not the dictates of fashion, should decide what a Christian should wear. They point out that the fashion centers have not been known for their righteousness. Economically, they judge the fashion industry to be a deceitful, greedy force. Keeping up with the latest styles is seen as wasteful, planned obsolescence.[5]

Scott notes also that the basic guidelines for the plain people in matters of dress and appearance stem from the Bible:

From [biblical] verses the plain people learn that their dress should be modest, simple, and economical, and that jewelry and elaborate hairdo are inappropriate for the Christian. By a lack of emphasis on external beauty, the plain people believe the inner virtue of the heart can better shine through. They also think that if one's mind is not preoccupied with beautifying one's body, a person can be free to do the Lord's work.[6]

General Lifestyle

It was Thorstein Veblen, one of the early giants of sociology, who first used the term *conspicuous consumption*, by which he meant the tendency to gain attention through the overt display of one's wealth. But whereas such display might be expected on the part of many Americans, it has no place in the Amish community. Their homes, for example, some of which have surprisingly modern features, would never contain elaborate furniture, fancy wallpaper, or Oriental rugs. Clothes, as we have seen, are plain and functional, and neither sex will wear adornments of any kind.

With their emphasis on humility, the Old Order Amish dislike all types of public recognition. Pride, in fact, is considered a cardinal sin. As a consequence, actions that are more or less commonplace in society at large are seldom encountered in Amishland. Boasting is rare. Having one's portrait painted or picture taken is prohibited; indeed, cameras are completely taboo. Such behavior would be considered a sign of self-aggrandizement.[7]

Bicycles, motorcycles, and automobiles are strictly *verboten* in the Lancaster County settlement, and any adult who bought one would be subjected to severe group pressures. The automobile is the best-known case in point, and—as will be shown—the Amish lifestyle is strongly influenced by their being a horse-type rather than an automobile-type culture.

The Old Order Amish are a slow-tempo community. They value such traits as obedience, modesty, and submission, rather than mobility and competitiveness.[8] The hustle and bustle that characterize so much of society at large will not be found in Amishland. Seeing an adult Amish person in a hurry would be rather unusual!

In their business ventures, the Amish follow a fairly conservative route. They have no interest in stocks, bonds, or other forms of "speculation." They are staunch believers in private enterprise, however, and will take out mortgages, borrow money from banks, and use checking accounts. Banks consider them excellent customers and excellent credit risks.

The followers of Jacob Amman have no strong interest in politics. Although they do vote—in local more than in national elections—voter turnout is relatively low. Hostetler reports that when they register, most do so as Republicans.[9] The Amish themselves have never held a major office of any kind, for a good reason: the church would not permit it.

The Old Order Amish tend to reject various forms of commercial insurance, including life insurance. However, they do have a fairly comprehensive network of mutual-aid organizations and self-help programs, some of which involve monetary assessments. A sick farmer can count on his fields being tended, and even harvested, by his neighbors.

Self-Help, Medicine, and Health

Should an Amish family's barn burn down, up to a hundred neighbors will gather, and in a day or two raise a new barn. Barn raisings have attracted nationwide publicity, but Amish construction skills are sometimes put to good use in erecting other kinds of less publicized buildings.

For example, in the late 1980s a young pediatrician, Holmes Morton, discovered that a genetic disease, glutaric aciduria, disproportionately affects Amish and Mennonite children in Lancaster County. According to Frank Allen, the disease "strikes suddenly and with devastating results, attacking the liver and nervous system, including the brain. Many victims lapse into comas and die within 48 hours. Most of those who survive the initial episode suffer progressive paralysis. Until Dr. Morton came along, the disease had never been correctly diagnosed in the community."[10]

In his efforts to buy building materials to establish a clinic and diagnostic equipment, Dr. Morton attempted to take out a second mortgage on his home. But that wasn't necessary. On November 19, 1990, the *Wall Street Journal*, hearing of Morton's efforts, printed a front-page article telling of his dream.

Donations were not solicited; nevertheless, more than 250 readers from thirty-seven states chose to contribute to the project. Two of the donors gave $100,000. Hewlett-Packard Corporation donated diagnostic equipment valued at $85,000. And an Amish farmer donated three prime acres of Lancaster County farmland for a building site.

On a rainy Saturday in late November 1990, more than one hundred Amish met within a mile of the barn raised for the movie *Witness*, and had their first Amish clinic-raising.

The clinic has become home for the latest in gene therapy, a relatively new medical field. It appears that the Amish have a higher rate of inherited diseases than most communities. Today's 75,000 Amish are all descended from just 47 families. In the last decade, Morton's clinic has become one of the most advanced gene research clinics in the country.

Rare diseases with odd names are the bane of the Amish. During July 1999, Holmes Morton and his colleagues began treating "three children stricken with Crigler-Najjar, a rare liver disease.... About 300 people worldwide have Crigler-Najjar: 16 trace their ancestry to Lancaster's Plain sects and are being treated by Morton."[11]

Morton plans to use a treatment called chimeraplasty, "which involves tricking the body into correcting a gene mutation. If successful, the technique could be used to treat up to 80% of all genetic diseases."[12]

The Amish have even rejected social security benefits. In the mid-1950s, they sent a delegation to Washington bearing a petition signed by some 14,000 members. The petition stated that they were quite willing to make social security *payments*. What they were asking Congress for was special legislation exempting them from social security *benefits*.

Knowing that "most people come to Washington to get something," Congress was flabbergasted at the request. The law was eventually changed, and today Amish farmers neither make payments nor receive benefits of any kind, including retirement, disability, and Medicare.[13]

Actually, a good deal of logic was behind the Amish offer. The Amish community has no rest homes, convalescent homes, or homes for the aged. Each family takes care of its own aged and infirm members, and no Amish person has ever been on welfare. Leaders were afraid that once social security checks started to arrive, the entire self-help program would be undermined, with a corresponding weakening of both family and community.

It is this system of intrafamily support, group solidarity, mutual aid—and, of course, faith in God—that prompts the followers of Jacob Amman to reject insurance. When trouble strikes, they know that help is no farther away than their Amish neighbors. But how much can be expected of even the best of neighbors?

In the spring of 1991, the *Philadelphia Inquirer* reported that an Amish child had died from a genetic defect that crippled his immune system. The condition was treatable, but the drug "cost $2,200 a treatment, not counting laboratory tests and periodic hospitalizations. Altogether, the cost of therapy would have been $190,000 a year, probably for life."[14] Ultimately, the manufacturer that produces the drug offered it without charge, but the family refused. They did not feel that it was fair to ask the community to contribute $70,000 a year toward required therapy.

At one time the Amish were reluctant to patronize doctors and hospitals at all, and some members still refuse to do so. In early 1991, for example, four hundred cases of rubella (German measles) had been reported in six Pennsylvania counties, as well as in other Amish settlements. During the previous year, there were only 1,093 such cases reported for the entire United States.[15]

Nevertheless, despite some reluctance to use doctors and hospitals, most Amish now use medical facilities when the situation calls for it. The majority of Amish women, though, have their babies at home, delivered by a midwife.[16]

During March 1990, after criminal charges were brought against an uncertified midwife, legislation was introduced in Harrisburg to allow midwifery without credentials. The "plain people," not ordinarily disposed to political involvement, gathered at the state capitol in support of the legislation. Afraid that the state would intrude on their centuries-old childbearing practices, more than five hundred Amish and Mennonites attended the rally. They carried signs but said little. Nevertheless, one Amish farmer told a reporter that two of his children were delivered by midwives, and the other was born in a hospital. He further said that "I would never go to the hospital again. It is so much more relaxed to do it at home and it's a lot cheaper. We don't have any bright lights or fancy trim or any TVs. When we go into the hospital we feel strange."[17]

Sadly, even the Amish with their conservative, rural lifestyle are not exempt from AIDS. Lancaster County ranks seventh in Pennsylvania in the number of AIDS cases reported. One preacher told Larry Lewis of the *Philadelphia Inquirer*, "We are not perfect. There is some premarital sex in the sect, probably a small amount of drug use, and some sexual straying."[18] He went on to say that he even knew of an older member of the community who had visited prostitutes at the county seat.

It should be mentioned, in connection with medicine and health, that the Old Order Amish are conservative in death as well as in life. Their funerals are plain: no flowers, no metal caskets, no music, no decorations, no mourning bands, no crepe. Most districts permit embalming, but a few do not. There are no Amish undertakers, however, and even funeral parlors are taboo. The wooden coffin is made by an Amish carpenter, services are held at home, and an Amish bishop presides. The olden custom of holding a wake—sitting up all night around the body of the deceased—is still practiced in most areas.

One unusual custom—not found outside of Amishland—was reported by Scott: "In many Amish communities, it is a common practice to hold two funeral services simultaneously for the same person. Usually one service is held in the house, and another in the barn or another farm building. This is necessary because of the large number of people who attend—over a thousand in some cases."[19]

Amish cemeteries are startlingly plain. There are no flowers, no decorations, no elaborate tombstones, and no mausoleums. In fact, there is not even a caretaker, so that the graves sometimes have a run-down look. In general, the only handmade signs are small, uniform headstones, with the name and dates of the deceased—no scrolls, epitaphs, or other inscriptions. Most Amish cemeteries are off the beaten track. For the most part, they are—or were—part of an Amish farmer's land, and there is no charge for the use of burial lots.

As might be imagined, the entire cost of an Amish funeral and burial is only a fraction of that normally spent by the "English" (non-Amish).

Notes

1. Stephen Scott and Kenneth Pellman, *Living without Electricity* (Intercourse, PA: Good Books, 1990).

2. "When fly closures for pants were introduced in the 1820s," writes Scott, "some considered them indecent. In 1830, the *Gentlemen's Magazine of Fashion* pronounced the fly 'an indelicate and disgusting fashion.' While the larger society eventually accepted this feature, many plain people did not." Among the plain people were the Old Order Amish. See Stephen Scott, *Why Do They Dress That Way?* (Intercourse, PA: Good Books, 1986), p. 114.

   Zellner was once given a workshirt and trousers by an ex-Amishman. Going to the bathroom requires a measure of planning. The trousers, flapped much like navy bell-bottoms, have seven buttons and snaps to undo. The gray shirt has wire hook-and-eye fasteners.

3. Scott, *Why Do They Dress That Way?* p. 86.

4. The Amish sometimes appear inconsistent in their prohibitions. Thus, wristwatches are forbidden whereas pocket watches are permitted. Sometimes there is a good reason for the seeming inconsistency, and the Amish are well aware of the explanation. At other times, the answer would likely be, "It has always been so."

5. Ibid., p. 6.

6. Ibid., p. 15.

7. For readers who appreciate a mystery, here is one with no immediate answer. The followers of Jacob Amman do not own cameras, and are dead set against having their pictures taken. Yet, on the basis of postcards, brochures, pamphlets, newspapers, magazines, and books, the Amish may well be the most photographed group in America!

8. For a discussion of Amish personality, see Hostetler, *Amish Society*, pp. 185–89, 333ff; and Donald Kraybill, *The Riddle of Amish Culture* (Baltimore: Johns Hopkins University Press, 1989), pp. 24–25.

9. Hostetler, *Amish Society*, p. 253.

10. Frank Allen, "Farm Folks Gather in Strasburg, Pa., against a Plague: Raising High the Roof Beams of Holmes Morton's Clinic Begins to Fulfill a Dream," *Wall Street Journal*, November 19, 1990, p. A1.

11. Jennifer Brown, "Amish Country Fertile Ground for Latest Gene Therapies," *Morning Call*, Allentown, PA, July 15, 1998, Sec A, p. 4.

12. Ibid.

13. In certain instances, Amish are required to make social security payments. An Amish person who works for a non-Amish employer will have social security automatically deducted from his or her paycheck. Also, an Amish employer who hires a non-Amish employee must pay the employee's social security tax. There are other examples. In no case, however, will an Amish person accept any of the benefits.

14. Donald C. Drake, "A Deadly Illness, a Choice for Amish," *Philadelphia Inquirer*, March 20, 1991.

15. "Rubella Breaks Out in Amish Communities," *New York Times*, March 26, 1991.

16. See Penny Armstrong and Sheryl Feldman, *A Midwife's Story* (New York: Arbor House, 1986). See also Carol Morello, "Embattled Midwife to the Amish," *Philadelphia Inquirer*, July 23, 1989.

17. Steven Ochs, "Amish, Mennonites Rally for Midwife Bill," *Allentown Morning Call*, March 13, 1990. In an interview with Pennsylvania House member Leonard Gruppo, Maurice Zellner determined that the medical profession, led by the Pennsylvania Midwives Association, fought to kill the bill. It died in committee. Under current law certified mid-wives must complete a course to practice outside of hospitals. According to Gruppo, most Amish midwives do not qualify under the law.

18. Larry Lewis, "The Reality of AIDS Touches Even the Amish: The Sect's Relative Isolation Cannot Shield It from the Pervasive Disease," *Philadelphia Inquirer*, April 12, 1992, p. B1.

19. Stephen Scott, *The Amish Wedding and Other Special Occasions of the Old Order Communities* (Intercourse, PA: Good Books, 1988), p. 103.

LABS

Internet Exercise

Religiosity in the United States

Introduction

One of the main features of the founding of the United States of America was the belief that freedom of religion should be guaranteed. Another characteristic that is relatively unique is the separation of religion and state within the country. These two traits create an incredible amount of religious diversity and tolerance in the United States. In fact, the United States is considered to be the most religiously diverse of all countries. Two key components to understanding religion in the United States are the measurement of religiosity and the secularization movement.

Religiosity refers to the level of attachment one holds for their religious beliefs. The way one displays their level of attachment to religion can vary considerably. For instance, does someone who claims to be highly religious have to attend service every week or every day? Does just being a member of a formal church constitute being religious? What about someone who does not attend formal religious services but prays on a daily basis? Questions about membership, attendance, and behaviors related to religion can result in various and conflicting answers. Therefore, it is important for researchers to clearly define the way they measure religious commitment and religiosity.

Secularization refers to the weakening of religious influence and the diminishing importance of religion in society. Modernization and scientific advances are the main contributors to secularization. Although the majority of Americans classify themselves within a religious denomination, attendance and participation rates within denominations have decreased over the years. Secularization also occurs when religious groups adapt to social changes and amend rules, requirements, and/or doctrine. For instance, it was once common for Catholic Mass to be performed only in Latin and only on Sundays. Such requirements have been abandoned for more flexibility but may have diluted the symbolic significance of the mass.

Idea in Use

There exists in the sociology of religion a debate about the relationship between religious diversity and religious participation. On the one hand, some believe that religious pluralism destabilizes religious vitality. It is thought that increased religious pluralism reduces the legitimacy of beliefs and thus produces a diminished amount of religious activity. On the other hand, some claim that religious pluralism is positively associated with religious vitality. Proponents of this claim suggest that competition between religious groups provides individuals with numerous options, thus increasing the quality and quantity of experiences. Mark Chaves and Philip Gorski attempt to resolve the debate by reviewing previous empirical work in their *Annual Review of Sociology* article "Religious Pluralism and Participation" (2001). They work through methodological issues and consider historical and comparative evidence. In the end, they conclude that there is no empirical support for the assertion that religious pluralism is positively related to religious participation.

Activity Instructions

In this exercise, you will use the internet to learn more about religious identification and participation in the United States.

1. The General Social Survey (GSS) is a nationally representative survey that asks respondents about a variety of issues. Questions of religion and religiosity have

been asked in nearly every year that the GSS has been performed. Go to http://sda.berkeley.edu:7502/cgi-bin/hsda?harcsda+gss04 where the cumulative data are stored for easy analysis. Open the codebook in an extra window and find the variables pertaining to religion (select the standard codebook and the sequential variable list, then scroll down to personal concerns and click on religion). You will need to refer to the codebook to understand the survey questions. In the window that you initially opened, choose the "Frequencies or Crosstabulation" option and hit start. For each analysis use "year" as the column variable, make sure column percent is selected, unselect color coding, and choose "No Chart" from the drop down menu in the Chart Options box.

- Use "relig" as your row column and run the table. Use the resulting table to describe trends (what is growing, shrinking, or staying the same over the years) and determine what has the highest religious preference.
- Return back to the previous window and use "Denom" as the row variable. What are the three largest Protestant denominations overall?
- Return back to the previous window. You will need to recode the "Attend" variable. To do this, use the following function for the row variable: attend(r:0;1-2;3-5;6-8;9). This recoding now makes 0 = never, 1–2 = rarely, 3–5 = often, 6–8 = regularly, and 9 = don't know/didn't ask. Report your findings.
- Finally, report on the trends for variables postlife, pray, neargod, and prayer that you find across years. To do this, just simply re-run the tables with each new variable in the row.
- Throughout your analysis, don't use the variable coding such as "relig" but rather refer to what the variable coding stands for (religious preference in this case). The codebook will be helpful with this.

2. Go to an online church directory called Church Angel at www.churchangel.com. Select "Find Your Church" and then navigate to the state and town/city that you live in. Report the count of all churches listed and indicate which denomination has the most churches. For instance, in Media, Pennsylvania there are 33 churches listed and Baptist has the most in the town (6 Baptist churches). Repeat the process of question 2 for Jewish synagogues in your city and state using http://www.mavensearch.com/synagogues/synagogues.asp. Are your findings in line with what you found in question 1 (specifically the results of relig and/or denom)?

3. Finally, go to the Map Gallery of Religion in the United States at http://www. valpo.edu/geomet/geo/courses/geo200/religion.html. Describe how religious adherents and how the number of church bodies differs across the United States. Where are the areas with high concentrations of adherents and how are the denominations dispersed across the country? Finally, select one specific denomination and discuss the patterns of membership across the country. Speculate on the reasons for your findings.

4. Turn in your findings and reports to your instructor as directed.

Individual Writing Exercise

Religion: Concepts and Functions

Introduction

Religion has been one of the most influential social institutions since the beginning of humankind. Emile Durkheim was one of the first sociologists to recognize the significance of religion for society. Durkheim defined religion as a set of beliefs and values that relate to sacred things. He maintained that all events consist of either the sacred or the profane. The *sacred* refers to elements that arouse feelings of awe, admiration, and respect, and transcend everyday life. The *profane* encompasses ordinary aspects of daily life. Different religions may view the same element as both sacred and profane. For instance, while Catholics hold that they receive the Body and Blood of Christ in the Communion wafer and Eucharist drink, Jews may see only bread and wine. Worshipers recognize the sacred by using *rituals*, or ceremonial behavior. Rituals are formal ways of demonstrating faith. Acts do not become rituals simply because they are regular routines, although repetition is one characteristic of rituals. Objects, language, prayers, and other elements that might otherwise seem profane, become sacred when utilized in a ritual. For instance, when Jewish boys become young teenagers they prepare for a Bar Mitzvah. In this ritual, the boy reads/chants from a sacred book (Torah), wears ceremonial clothes such as the tallith (prayer shawl) and yarmulke, and often lights candles. Those who observe the ceremony without knowing about the sacredness and purpose of the elements would have difficulty understanding the importance and significance of the ritual. Various rituals are used in all religions to mark rites of passages such as weddings and funerals.

Sociologists are concerned with religion's social dimension, rather than evaluating the truth or falsity of what the actual beliefs of the religion entail. A major focus of sociology, for example, are the several functions that religion performs within society. It provides a strong basis for social cohesion as people rally around common beliefs and share a similar world view. It also provides a sense of belonging and meaning for members of society. Finally, we can observe that religion has been a catalyst for much needed social change.

Idea in Use

There are many claims about the benefits of religious membership and spirituality for individuals. Neal Krause and Keith Wulff, however, investigated the potential negative consequences for people who do not have an active faith life. In their article "Religious Doubt and Health: Examining the Potential Dark Side of Religion" published in the *Sociology of Religion* in 2004, they test the hypotheses that 1) people who have more doubts about their religion and faith will report more health problems and experience more symptoms of depression than those who report no conflict of religious beliefs and that 2) individuals who occupy leadership positions within their church and experience doubt about their religious beliefs will be even less satisfied with their health and report more depressive symptoms than the individuals who report doubts about religious beliefs but hold no formal leadership positions within the church. Using the U.S. Congregational Life Survey, a nationally representative survey conducted in 2000, they found support for both of their research hypotheses. First, they found consistent evidence that religious doubt was significantly and positively related to respondent's reporting depressed affect and symptoms, as well as less satisfaction with their physical health. Secondly, they found that religious doubt does not affect all members of the congregation in the same way. Rather, they found that those individuals who reported doubts about their faith and were formal leaders within the church reported more severe depression and dissatisfaction than those people who did not hold such jobs. Krause and Wulff speculate that this is because those more involved have more to lose if their religious beliefs are questioned. They conclude that researchers should not only look at the potential benefits of religion but also the possible costs of religious involvement.

Activity Instructions

In this independent exercise, you will be exploring religions about which you are not closely familiar. You should take special note of the rituals used and the elements held sacred.

1. Identify a religious group that is very different from the one that you are already a member of, or know a lot about. You may want to consult the church or campus club that is affiliated with the church for information about worship times, appropriate dress, and any questions that you might have beforehand. Some possible choices include:

   - Attending another world religion church. For instance, if you are Jewish, attend a Muslim, Hindu, or Christian service.
   - Attend a church within your world religion that you are unfamiliar with. For example, if you are Greek Orthodox, visit a Methodist, Mennonite, or Baptist church.
   - Attend a church that is predominantly attended by members of another race. For instance, if you are white, attend a black church such as an African Methodist Episcopal (AME).

2. While you are at the service, take note of the rituals that are used. Also note if there is a book or hymnal used, the type of singing (solemn, spontaneous, etc.), who led the service, and the general atmosphere.

3. After the service, you may want to talk to some of the church members or leaders to clarify any observations. You may also want to further your learning about the rituals by investigating further. There are numerous informative websites that detail the world religions and specific denominations, as well as webpages created by local churches, temples, or synagogues.

4. Formalize your notes and write about your experience. Make sure to compare your experience with the new service to the religion that you have been involved with or know the most about. You must identify the religious group you observed as well as the group you are comparing it to. You must also provide specific details about the service and its rituals used.

5. Turn your paper in to your instructor as directed. You will be graded on your thoroughness, ritual identification, and the comparisons you make. Some religious groups may not have rituals that are as obvious or overt as others, and this will be taken into consideration in the grading.

Group Exercise

Types of Religious Organizations

Introduction

Sociologists identify three broad types of religious organizations. The defining characteristic of these three types is how well they are integrated into society. *Churches* are well integrated into society and often have an established history and well organized hierarchy of leadership. *Sects* are religious organizations that usually begin by dissociating from churches to maintain, in their view, a more "pure" form of faith. *Cults* are religious organizations that represent a fundamentally new and different belief system from existing religious organizations, and are often viewed negatively by mainstream society. Cults are less integrated into the religious establishment than are sects.

Churches are further divided by their level of inclusion within the nation-state. An *ecclesia* is a church that is formally incorporated within society and is recognized as the official religion of the nation/state. Membership is therefore determined by birth rather than a conscious desire to enter and abide in the faith. A church that is not officially linked with the political society is called a *denomination.* Denominations are typical in nations/states that recognize religious plurality and have separation of church and state. Oftentimes, members join the denomination out of a conscious and voluntary decision, although parental influences are often strong. The United States contains the most diverse number of religious denominations in the world. While not formally linked with government or political parties, denomination and groups within denominations often have some influence on politics.

Sects are relatively small religious organizations that have often splintered from larger religious groups because of an ideological divergence. Members are often recruited by proselytizers and accepted through conversion. Because of their "outsider" mentality and their refusal to accept differing beliefs, they are often very loyal and exhibit a strong enthusiasm for their faith. Often, sects have brief runs of existence, but there are several that have endured over many generations. For instance, the Pentecostalism is a sect that has endured for about a hundred years in the United States, and many suggest that this religious movement has matured into a denomination (see *Idea in Use).*

Cults are often controversial religious organizations that are viewed with distrust. Cults generally originate around a charismatic leader who promises an alternative and better way to live. These alternatives can be notorious for bizarre customs and extreme practices, such as mass suicide and brainwashing. However, such peculiar practices are not necessary to define a religious organization as a cult. Jehovah's Witnesses and Mormons are two examples of religious organizations that began as cults around charismatic religious leaders, and which have achieved a rather large following in the United States and around the world. As in sects, membership in the cult is voluntary and members are often recruited from among those who feel alienated from mainstream society. Because of the negative connotations associated with the word cult, many sociologists refer to them as new religious movements (NRM). Examples of some cults that have emerged notoriously throughout the past few decades include the Branch Davidians that followed David Koresh, Marshall Applewhite's Heaven's Gate, and Jim Jones' Peoples Temple.

Idea in Use

The process that moves a religious organization from sect to denomination can vary and force compromises for the organization. Paul Williamson and Ralph Hood analyze how the growth of the Church of God, now considered a Pentecostal denomination, moved from the label of sect in their 2004 *Review of Religious Research* article entitled "Differential Maintenance and Growth of Religious Organizations Based Upon High-Cost Behaviors: Serpent Handling Within the Church of God." Some of the unique features of the early sect were the use of tongues-speaking and the handling of serpents. However, as the sect grew in popularity and became recognized as a legitimate church by mainstream society in the late 1920s, the practice of serpent handling became prohibited within the Church of God. The church chose to reject the dangerous practice of serpent handling in favor of continuing the prosperity of group membership and acceptance into society. However, independent "renegade" Churches of God, mostly located in Appalachia, remain true to the original practices and beliefs such as serpent handling and thus maintain sectarian status apart from the larger Church of God denomination.

Activity Instructions

In small groups, you will discuss different types of religious organizations.

1. Have each person in your small group discuss what religious organization that they most identify with or are knowledgeable about. Each person should classify the organization as a denomination, sect, or cult and identify the characteristics of the organization that they used to classify the group. Discuss the similarities and differences of your answers. Why do you think that you found such patterns (HINT: think about the representativeness of your sample and where denominations, sects, and cults recruit members)?

2. Some have argued that the Church of Scientology is a cult that formed because of the charismatic leader L. Ron Hubbard. Go to the Scientology home page and learn more about this organization. It can be located at http://www.scientology.org/. Feel free to consult other sources of information about this group as well. Based on what you have learned about cults, sects, and churches discuss whether your small group classifies Scientology as a cult. What factors influenced your decision? Is there a certain number of people that must join or claim a religion as their own that takes it from a sect or cult to a church?

3. Prepare a brief summary of your discussion points and turn in as directed by your instructor.

Education

The Negotiated Order of the Classroom
Tim O'Keefe and Charles E. Faupel

Labs
Internet Exercise: Schools and Academic Standards
Individual Writing Exercise: Access to Higher Education
Group Exercise: School Choices

The Negotiated Order of the Classroom

On a hot September day, seventy-two students, most of whom did not know one another, met in a classroom for the manifest purpose of learning about sociology. Not unlike other organizational settings, however, the consensus which surrounds such generally articulated goals often masks divergent and even contradictory agendas of the various participating actors. It soon became apparent that there were a number of reasons why these seventy-two students were enrolled in Sociology 201. Some had taken a sociology course in high school and were apparently intrigued by the subject matter; others had prior exposure to sociology but were taking it as an interesting elective. Still others were enrolled in the course as potential majors. Most of the students, however, including myself, were probably enrolled in the course simply because it was part of their core curriculum requirements. Hence, while no one disputed that we were there to learn about sociology, this goal was differentially interpreted by the various participants in Sociology 201. For some, it meant performing satisfactorily on exams with a minimal level of effort. Others saw the course as an opportunity to raise their grade point average. There were also a handful of students who regarded the class a a forum to propagandize their religious, political, and ideological preferences. The professor too brought his own understanding of the purpose of Sociology 201 which was formally expressed in the syllabus, and more informally in the accompanying introduction to the course. That the professor's understanding of the purpose of Sociology 201 was not universally shared was manifest in the attrition of several students in the days following that first introductory session.

As the quarter progressed the uncertainty and ambiguity of the class gave way to rather predictable patterns of group life, not unlike many of the other groups which constituted the subject matter of the course. Even the informal exchanges between actors in the classroom became quite routinized. In short, Sociology 201 quickly evolved into a functioning social group, complete with social statuses and roles, norms, and corresponding sanctions. In addition, not unlike other social groups of comparable size, the class was clearly stratified with pronounced inequities existing, particularly between males and females. Before discussing this problematic feature, however, the structural and normative features of the class will be examined.

Actors and Their Roles

The only formal status distinction in the classroom was that of teacher and student. The "banking model" of education (Freire et al, 1970) depicts the teacher "curator" of the discipline, imparting the knowledge of the discipline to students through lecture, assigned readings, structured discussion, films, etc., and subsequently evaluating students' "withdrawals" from this fund of knowledge through periodic examinations. While this model was clearly expressed in the formal structure of Sociology 201, the status of the professor became less pronounced in the emerging social organization of the classroom. During times of heated debate over controversial issues, for example, the role of the professor radically shifted from that of lecturer to a much more subdued role of "moderator." Even in this negotiated role, however, the ultimate authority of the professor was clearly maintained. He stood while the rest of us remained seated. His position in the front of the classroom made him a focal point for most of the discussion which took place. His "professional" dress in contrast to the more casual dress of the students also set him apart from the rest of us. Finally, the professor effectively terminated such discussions at his discretion by retreating to his authoritative position "on stage" behind his lectern.

The status of "student" was a comparatively subordinate position to that of teacher. Students were not, however, an undifferentiated collectivity. A few of the students, for example, were especially active in class discussions while others did not participate at all. Related to this, I observed that most of the questions that were raised in class tended to come from a handful of students located in various strategic positions in the classroom. I also discovered shortly into the quarter that certain individuals were disproportionately targeted for questions, response, and commentary by the professor.

This differentiation was by no means a random or arbitrary process, and must be understood in the ecological context of the classroom. Sommer (1967) has observed, for example, that student participation varies considerably with the physical arrangement of the classroom as well as with the location of the student within that physical structure. The ecological character of our classroom made informal discussion with anyone but immediate neighbors most obtrusive. Consequently, there emerged several "pockets" of interaction as students had a few minutes to socialize before the arrival of the teacher and settling into the business of the hour. Friendships developed and a level of rapport was cultivated contributing to strong group ties among students within these pockets.

Importantly, these informal pockets of interaction which originated as pre-classtime socializing quickly became an integral part of the informal structure of the class. Moreover, they served an important academic function as illustrated by the following scenario which was repeated several times throughout the quarter: A student fails to understand a particular point in the lecture, and rather than interrupt the lecture to ask for clarification, the student confers with a fellow member of his or her interaction set. A flurry of verbal activity ensues as the group seeks to gain closure on this troublesome point. Failing to do so quickly attracts the attention of the professor who at this point is unsure how to interpret the confusion emanating from this section of the classroom. The attention of everyone is directed toward this group of students as the teacher interrupts his lecture with an obvious pause and gazes expectantly in their direction. In the embarrassing moments which follow one of the more articulate members of the group takes on the role of "questioner," and publicly poses the question. The teacher responds enthusiastically, mentally noting the bright young questioner and now defines the situation as an oasis of intelligence in the vast desert of bewilderment and confusion.

The status of "questioner" was clearly a vital status in the emergent social organization of the class, and the person occupying this position was elevated to a position of prominence in the emerging social hierarchy. In our class, three students emerged as "questioners" during the first two weeks of class from three distinct sections of the classroom as students in the three locales quickly came to rely on these questioners as the "official" spokesman for these emergent groups.

A second status to emerge in our class, which in some cases coincided with the questioner, was that of "keynoter." The keynoter was usually a gregarious individual who was willing to make comments when such opportunities were given. The teacher would carefully note such responses, and soon these individuals were being called upon quite frequently by the teacher for comment. Usually the professor did not call on them verbally, but would simply look expectantly in their direction.

The "keynoter" position played a critical function in maintaining the cohesiveness of the class. Not only was the keynoter someone who could be relied upon for commentary by the professor, but in so doing, elicited dialogue from other students. Many students in the class were hesitant to speak out on issues, particularly if doing so challenged statements made by the professor. I often observed, however, that these students were not at all hesitant to respond to commentary made by the keynoter. Dialogue was thus established, and not infrequently, literally dozens of hands would be raised wanting to contribute to the dialogue that was developing.

These dual statuses of "questioner" and "keynoter" were of paramount importance in the negotiated structure of the class. There was, however, a dark side to these positions as well. From time to time these individuals—particularly keynoters—abused their position by attempting to dominate the discussions that took place. When this occurred, other students reverted to a passive "onlooker" status, and found themselves simply observing a dialogue that was taking place between keynoter and teacher. While such a situation may be advantageous to the keynoter, and to the immediate goals of the teacher, it often created a climate of indifference and/or hostility within the classroom. This was evidenced, for example, by sanctions directed against those who talked excessively. Consequently, the questioner and keynoter often found themselves in the rather precarious position of being expected to contribute, but not "too much."

Sex in the Classroom

The foregoing analysis of the emergent social organization of the classroom portends what is perhaps the most pervasive theme to emerge in my observations in Sociology 201. The various statuses and roles negotiated in the classroom provided the basis for a clearly defined system of social stratification. That is to say, the process of negotiation was not an equilateral exchange.

With the exception of the obvious status differential between teacher and students, nowhere were the inequities in the classroom more pronounced than in the division between males and females. This stratification of the sexes is not unique to this class as evidenced by the growing concern in the literature regarding sexual inequality in the classroom. Hall and Sandler's probing study (1982) is probably the most comprehensive analysis to date of the detrimental character of the classroom environment on women. Numerous factors which sabotage the educational process for women are identified, ranging from overt sexual harassment on the part of professors, to the subtle nonverbal messages communicated by teachers, other students and women themselves which place females in a disadvantaged position in the classroom.

While there is much disagreement in the literature regarding the "chilly" effect of the classroom climate on women, I observed several of the grievances expressed by Hall and Sandler in Sociology 201. Particularly evident was the domination of class discussions by men. Not only did males dominate in terms of sheer number [and] of interactions, but the quality of the interactions that took place also reflected the differential status of men and women. Comments offered by males were straightforward, succinct, and "self-contained" (i.e., they did not encourage further elaboration or comment). In this way, male participation in the class was characterized by a great deal of self-assurance and even aggressiveness.

Females, by comparison, were considerably more hesitant in their manner of participation. Commentary offered by females was typically "open ended," appealing for affirmation by the professor or other students in the class. This open ended quality of female remarks was manifest in several ways. On a number of occasions, for example, I observed women prefacing their remarks with qualifying statements such as, "I don't know a whole lot about that but…" or "I can't be too sure, but it seems to me…" Often too, comments were offered in the form of a question, either with a slight rise in voice pitch at the end of a statement, or more directly by initiating a statement in the form of a question (e.g., "Don't you think that…?")

This style of participation on the part of females, which appealed to the authority of the teacher, clearly placed women in an inferior position in the class as compared to their male colleagues. Moreover, it served to further limit their effective participation in a number of ways. The teacher, for example, would frequently misinterpret their positional statement to be a question, and proceed to "tutor" them in a covertly condescending manner. Such a response on the part of the professor, it seems, can only be negatively experienced by the student. Male classmates also would often dampen the spirit of the female participation by responding to an irresolute statement in a chivalrous though often chauvinistic fashion.

These sex role dynamics are by no means limited to the college classroom. Indeed, both male and female students as well as the teacher brought with them a lifetime of socialization experiences which contributed to the sexual stratification in the classroom. Furthermore, the organizational features of the class itself provided a conducive context for the inequality I observed between the sexes. That our class was taught by a male may itself have contributed to the differential frequency and nature of student participation. A less obvious but nevertheless important structural characteristic of the class was the composition of the key leadership positions that emerged. All of the "questioners" and all but one of the "keynoters" in the class were males. Importantly, these positions carried with them a collective conferral of authority, which gave their incumbents a decided advantage in the verbal exchanges that took place. Moreover, because of the sex role socialization that students bring with them into the classroom, it might reasonably be argued that women are less likely to compete in these verbal exchanges than are men, resulting in a male dominated, sexually stratified class….

…I can still recall that warm September day that found all of us together as an aggregate of seventy-two students, strangers to each other and to the subject matter of Sociology 201. Within a short time we all learned about Marx and Weber, about culture and norms, socialization and deviance, with varying degrees of thoroughness and accuracy. Even more importantly, however, we grew familiar with one another, and out of this original aggregate of seventy-two individuals emerged a highly inter-active social group. This paper has attempted to highlight those features of the social organization of the classroom as they impact the educational process. Contrary to the rational bureaucratic "banking model," the observations reported here suggest that the classroom is a very dynamic locale, the nature of which is continually negotiated by the interacting participants. Invoking the perspective of the organizational the-ory of negotiated order as an alternative to the dominant "banking model," the social organization of the classroom is understood to be an emergent property of the *joint action* of actively participating individuals. Specifically, these observations highlight the negotiated character of the goals, norms, and structure of the class. Importantly, however, the social stratification of the classroom effectively limited the access of some participants—particularly females—to the negotiation process.

References

Freire, P., B. Glaser and A. L. Strauss, 1970. *Pedagogy of the Oppressed.* New York: Seabury Press.

Hall, Roberta M. and Bernice L. Sandler, 1982. "The classroom climate: a chilly one for women?" Project on the Status and Education for Women. Washington, D.C.: Association of American Colleges.

Sommer, Robert, 1967. "Classroom ecology." *The Journal of Applied Behavioral Science* 3:489–503.

LABS

Internet Exercise

Schools and Academic Standards

Introduction

Academic standards are expectations about what students should know and be able to do at a certain point in their educational career. These expectations are often clearly stated in public documents so that teachers, parents, and students are aware of the requirements to pass into the next grade. The standards in the United States can vary from state to state, as well as by school district, although there are minimum requirements that the Federal Government imposes. Benchmarks are usually determined for students in grades 4, 8, and 12.

There are advantages and drawbacks to academic standards. First, they are beneficial for students, teachers, and society in general as they gauge the educational progress and achievements, thus insuring jobs can be filled with capable and skilled workers. However, both tracking and testing biases can perpetuate social inequalities. *Tracking*, the process that assigns students to different educational trajectories can be racially and socially discriminatory. Research has shown that racial minorities and economically disadvantaged students are disproportionately placed in lower tracks. The lower tracks tend to prepare students for vocational jobs and non-college trajectories, and are characterized by rote memorization learning, inferior resources, and overcrowded conditions. Higher tracks place students on a college trajectory, are disproportionately white and wealthy, and are highly valued. Another drawback of an over-reliance on academic tests is that many tests are biased. The standardized tests used do not differ depending on the track level in which the student is placed, thus holding all students to a single standard while the learning objectives between tracks are drastically different. Additionally, critics claim that the standardized tests are created from the perspective of white, middle-class cultural experience. Therefore, students without these experiences will have an inherent disadvantage on the test.

Idea in Use

Grades given out at colleges and universities, especially at Ivy League schools and in particular fields, have come under scrutiny recently. Several studies, as well as news articles, have suggested that grade inflation has dramatically increased in the past couple decades. According to a report from the American Academy of Arts and Sciences, the percentage of students that received grades in the A range from Princeton University climbed from 30.7 percent in 1973 to 42.5 percent in 1997. A similar pattern was found at Harvard University. The reasons for grade inflation are debated, but many agree that it is not because today's students are smarter or more hard-working. Rather, as Henry Rosovsky and Matthew Hartley indicate in "Evaluation and the Academy: Are We Doing the Right Thing? Grade Inflation and Letters of Recommendation," SAT scores have declined and the number of students in remedial classes at all grade levels has increased. Much to the dismay of students, schools are taking steps to rectify grade inflation problems. At Columbia University and Dartmouth, transcripts include the number of students in the class as well as the average grade.

Activity Instructions

In this internet exercise you will be comparing the educational success at the state and national level and then determining how the United States ranks on global measures of academic standards.

1. The United States Department of Education provides a National Assessment of Educational Progress (NAEP) that tests the proficiency at various grade levels in multiple subjects. They publish their findings on their webpage, which you can find at http://nces.ed.gov/nationsreportcard/. Go to the state profiles and select your home state. Summarize the state's average scores for all subject areas tested and compare to the national average. Also be sure to include the percentage of students that test below the basic level. Use the latest year's findings and the highest grade level that data were collected from.

2. The same website also produces a data query from which you can find more detailed information. Go to: http://nces.ed.gov/nationsreportcard/nde/criteria.asp and choose:

   - Grade = 12
   - Subject = Mathematics and Science (will have to run separately)
   - National = Expand and select National
   - Variables = Gender and Public or Private Schools (to select both use the ctrl button and select with mouse)
   - Year = Most recent year only

   After you select the previous options, select the Go To Results button. You do not need to change any options in the next window. Report your findings and summarize the differences that you found.

3. Educational performance is also compared between countries. The Trends in International Mathematics and Science Study (TIMSS) analyzes students' achievement in math and science by country. Visit their site at http://nces.ed .gov/timss/ and click the TIMSS results icon. Use the tables that report the average mathematics scale scores and the average science scale scores for fourth graders and eighth graders (thus, you need to use four tables). For each table, report what the United States' score is and the international average score. Additionally, report which countries have the highest scores (indicate country, subject, grade, and score), the countries with the lowest scores (indicate country, subject, grade, and score), and the number of countries above and below the United States. Are any of the countries ranked higher than the United States a surprise to you? Why or why not?

4. There are many different variables that can affect student success in meeting academic standards. One that is often used is the student–teacher ratio. At the same National Center for Education Statistics homepage select the "Search for Colleges, Schools, and Libraries" button from the left side menu. Insert your state and city/town and select public and private schools. You will be comparing the high schools. If there are multiple high schools, select the ones that are closest to your residence (the neighborhood school you would likely have gone to). Do this for both the public and private institutions. Click on the school name and you will be presented with various statistics. You may have to click on the "More Information" or "District Information" buttons within the new window to get the needed statistics. Use this information to report the student–teacher ratio.

5. Finally, information is also available about the literacy of the United States compared to other countries. The Progress in International Reading Literacy Study

(PIRLS) scores fourth graders and evaluates the results based on demographical information. Go to http://nces.ed.gov/pubs2004/pirlspub/ and select the "How Different Groups Perform" and summarize the results that were found about sex, the control of school type, and the poverty level in public schools.

6. Turn in your assignment to your instructor as directed.

Individual Writing Exercise

Access to Higher Education

Introduction

It seems that every year college tuition and mandatory student fees increase. While tuition prices have risen, many states have cut back student financial aid and reduced state spending for public colleges and universities. The rising costs of higher education have prohibited the continuing education of many qualified applicants at the institutions of their choice and left others with major debt.

The National Center for Public Policy and Higher Education, a nonprofit agency, has investigated the affordability and access to higher education extensively. In a 2003 report entitled "College Affordability in Jeopardy," it was found that in every state, four year public educational systems increased their tuition and student fees, some drastically (e.g., Massachusetts had a 24% increase). Community colleges in all but two states also increased their tuition and mandatory fees. The increase in tuition has consequently resulted in more students borrowing more money. The Center's May 2002 report "Losing Group: A National Status Report on the Affordability of American Higher Education" indicated that students of all class backgrounds are obtaining more loans for more money to finance their educations. This resulted in over 60 percent of all graduating students finding themselves in debt.

While the situation of increasing tuition in higher education institutions is bleak, the cost of not furthering education may be more costly. It is widely documented that students with increased educational levels earn more money over a lifetime. Without a college education, job opportunities are limited, and immediate as well as lifetime earnings are affected. Sacrifice and curtailing unnecessary spending in order to go to college may be well worth it.

Idea in Use

Theoretically, if you are a superior, well rounded high school student you should be able to have a fair chance to enter the higher education institution of your choice. However, as Thomas Espenshade, Chang Chung, and Joan Walling report in their article "Admission Preferences for Minority Students, Athletes, and Legacies at Elite Universities" published in a 2004 edition of *Social Science Quarterly*, the playing field is not exactly equal. Using data from nearly 125,000 applicant records from ten selective schools, they found that preferences were given to students with high SAT scores (1500 or higher), black applicants, or recruited athletes. While not as dramatically preferred, Hispanic students and legacy students were given advantages during admission as well. For instance, the recruited athletes were nearly four times as likely to be accepted as were non-athletes. Legacy students had about three times the likelihood of being accepted than children without any parental or close relative alumni connection. The authors point out that while affirmative action is a hotly debated topic, preference is routinely given to many different types of applicants.

Activity Instructions

In this exercise, you will be learning about the costs of your college education. You will also be itemizing where your money goes and how it is spent.

1. First, provide a description of your college career so far. Write a brief summary of the colleges or universities you have attended and indicate what type of school it is (two-year, community, private, state, etc.). Also, list the services

that you use on a regular basis (computer labs or internet network, transportation, housing, food, college newspaper, etc.).

2. Now, determine how much tuition, room and board, and associated costs (student fees, computer charges, printing, books, etc.) you are required to pay each semester (over and above any financial aid support that you receive). You can find this information from your receipts, asking about the details at the admissions or bursar's office, or finding it online. If need be, estimate your costs such as textbooks and lab fees to the best of your ability. Once you have all the semester's costs determined, add them up to establish how much you are expected to pay over the entire time you are a student (also be sure to consider if you will incur additional costs such as graduation fees, or reduced costs if you move back in with your parents, etc.).

3. Find out what kinds of loans, grants, and scholarships your school offers. Choose three different financial assistantships to report on and write a brief summary (1–2 typed, double-spaced pages) of the qualifications for the aid, the application process, and approximately how much financial assistance it would provide.

4. Write 2–3 paragraphs justifying whether or not you think that you are receiving a good education for the money that you (or your parents) are spending.

5. Determine how much money per week you pay. Would missing three classes be worth the money you are losing? Justify.

6. Turn in your assignment to your instructor as directed.

Group Exercise

School Choices

Introduction

Schools function as a socializing agent, as an institution that transmits knowledge, and as a way to create social cohesion and order. Never before have there been so many schooling options. As the educational institution becomes more formally organized, its complexity also increases. The schooling decision for parents has become more difficult with options such as public, private, charter, magnet, and homeschooling becoming more common.

Overwhelmingly, the majority of school-age children attend their local public school. These schools receive public funds and promise a strict separation of church and state. The neighborhood school's reputation and performance is nearly always linked to its funding. Oftentimes, poorer neighborhoods do not receive as much financial backing per student as schools in more affluent districts. This, of course, affects teacher–student ratios and classroom size. When classroom size increases, the likelihood of students' "falling through the cracks," increased discipline problems and violence, and not enough individualized attention is more likely. The structure of public schools is now more varied than ever before. Many schools have a focus on the arts, the sciences, or vocational crafts. Magnet schools pull from a wide geographic area and students from various types of neighborhoods attend. Often, the magnet schools are centered on a specific discipline or on academically advanced students.

There is great diversity within private schools as well. Most private schools are operated by religious organizations, including and especially the Roman Catholic Church. Other private schools do not have a religious foundation and are highly specialized. These schools may have entrance exams, strict discipline codes, and are often less regulated academically than public schools. This is because tuition is paid for privately, rather than relying on taxpayers' money. The advantages of small class size, individualized attention, and a plethora of extracurricular activities are very appealing to families. However, the cost for such advantages is often very high.

Charter schools and homeschooling are relatively new concepts, which seek to bridge the gap between public and private schools. Charter schools are essentially non-religious privatized public schools. Generally, a state or school district will sponsor a charter school for a set period of time. Charter schools have more freedom with their academic requirements and school organization, but are held accountable to their sponsor. If they are successful at meeting academic and financial goals, the sponsor will typically extend the charter. Often, states or school districts will employ for-profit companies such as Edison Schools to run the charter schools. The rate of homeschooling in the United States has increased dramatically in the last decade. Estimates of homeschooling in 2003 suggest that about 1.1 million school-aged children are taught at home (National Center for Education Statistics), an increase of nearly 29 percent from 1999 when about 850,000 children were homeschooled. The requirements of the curriculum for homeschooled children vary by state and there is little follow-up to ensure progress of the student. Parents typically point to concerns about the school (e.g., drugs, violence, etc.) and dissatisfaction with the current educational opportunities for their children as reasons for switching to homeschooling. While the success and value of these new models are not fully known, there has been a growing trend of acceptance for new innovations in education.

Idea in Use

Ed Collom and Douglas Mitchell explore how much parents who homeschool identify as part of a social movement. In their 2005 *Sociological Spectrum* article, "Home Schooling as a Social Movement: Identifying the Determinants of Homeschoolers' Perceptions" they find that there are various indicators that create a more collective action identity. Using data from California, they determined that parents who were part of a homeschooling organization were more likely to identify as part of a social movement. Also, the level of participation in such an organization was significantly and positively related to a parents' identification with a social movement. Surprisingly, Collom and Mitchell found that neither social network ties nor demographic differences played a role in identity formation. They suggest that homeschooling is indeed an alternative social movement and that more research on future homeschooling and social movement is warranted.

Activity Instructions

In this group exercise, you will be debating the benefits and disadvantages of the differing types of school options that are currently available.

1. Each member of your group should indicate what kind of schools they have attended during the elementary and high school years (e.g., public, private, homeschooling, etc.). What is the most common answer? Also discuss the socio-demographic composition of your schooling. For example, what was the approximate percentage of whites, blacks, and other minorities in your school? How about social class—mostly upper, middle, working, lower, or mixed? Were there any issues or conflicts related to socio-demographic variables (busing, marked segregation within the school, etc.)?

2. Generate a list of the advantages and disadvantages of private and public schools.

3. Homeschooling is not an option for many parents, as they have to work to be financially stable. As a group, identify the characteristics that you feel a family that wants to homeschool must have in order to be successful.

4. Many homeschoolers are unable to participate in clubs, organizations, and sports teams because they have no affiliation with a school. Should homeschoolers be able to take advantage of all such benefits, resources, and services that the schools have to offer or should one of the consequences of homeschooling be that such opportunities are unavailable?

5. Turn in lists/opinion summaries to your instructor as directed.

Medicine

Millions for Viagra, Pennies for Diseases of the Poor
Ken Silverstein

Labs
Internet Exercise: HIV/AIDS: Locally and Globally
Individual Writing Exercise: Mass Media and Eating Disorders
Group Exercise: Social Construction of Sickness and Disease

Millions for Viagra, Pennies for Diseases of the Poor

Almost three times as many people, most of them in tropical countries of the Third World, die of preventable, curable diseases as die of AIDS. Malaria, tuberculosis, acute lower-respiratory infections—in 1998, these claimed 6.1 million lives. People died because the drugs to treat those illnesses are nonexistent or are no longer effective. They died because it doesn't pay to keep them alive.

Only 1 percent of all new medicines brought to market by multinational pharmaceutical companies between 1975 and 1997 were designed specifically to treat tropical diseases plaguing the Third World. In numbers, that means thirteen out of 1,223 medications. Only four of those thirteen resulted from research by the industry that was designed specifically to combat tropical ailments. The others, according to a study by the French group Doctors Without Borders, were either updated versions of existing drugs, products of military research, accidental discoveries made during veterinary research or, in one case, a medical breakthrough in China.

Certainly, the majority of the other 1,210 new drugs help relieve suffering and prevent premature death, but some of the hottest preparations, the ones that, as the *New York Times* put it, drug companies "can't seem to roll...out fast enough," have absolutely nothing to do with matters of life and death. They are what have come to be called lifestyle drugs—remedies that may one day free the world from the scourge of toenail fungus, obesity, baldness, face wrinkles, and impotence. The market for such drugs is worth billions of dollars a year and is one of the fastest-growing product lines in the industry.

The drug industry's calculus in apportioning its resources is cold-blooded, but there's no disputing that one old, fat, bald, fungus-ridden rich man who can't get it up counts for more than half a billion people who are vulnerable to malaria but too poor to buy the remedies they need.

Western interest in tropical diseases was historically linked to colonization and war, specifically the desire to protect settlers and soldiers. Yellow fever became a target of biomedical research only after it began interfering with European attempts to control parts of Africa. "So obvious was this deterrence…that it was celebrated in song and verse by people from Sudan to Senegal" Laurie Garrett recounts in her extraordinary book *The Coming Plague*. "Well into the 1980s schoolchildren in Ibo areas of Nigeria still sang the praises of mosquitoes and the diseases they gave to French and British colonialists."

U.S. military researchers have discovered virtually all important malaria drugs. Chloroquine was synthesized in 1941 after quinine, until then the primary drug to treat the disease, became scarce following Japan's occupation of Indonesia. The discovery of Mefloquine, the next advance, came about during the Vietnam War, in which malaria was second only to combat wounds in sending U.S. troops to the hospital. With the end of a ground-based U.S. military strategy came the end of innovation in malaria medicine.

The Pharmaceutical Research and Manufacturers of America (PhRMA) claimed in newspaper ads early this year that its goal is to "set every last disease on the path to extinction." Jeff Trewhitt, a PhRMA spokesman, says U.S. drug companies will spend $24 billion on research this year and that a number of firms are looking for cures for tropical diseases. Some companies also provide existing drugs free to poor countries, he says. "Our members are involved. There's not an absolute void."

The void is certainly at hand. Neither PhRMA nor individual firms will reveal how much money the companies spend on any given disease—that's proprietary information, they say—but on malaria alone, a recent survey of the twenty-four biggest drug companies found that not a single one maintains an in-house research program, and only two expressed even minimal interest in primary research on the disease. "The pipeline of available drugs is almost empty," says Dyann Wirth of the Harvard School of Public Health, who conducted the study. "It takes five to ten years to develop a new drug, so we could soon face [a strain of] malaria resistant to every drug in the world." A 1996 study presented in *Cahiers Sunte*, a French scientific journal, found that of forty-one important medicines used to treat major tropical diseases, none were discovered in the nineties and all but six were discovered before 1985.

Contributing to this trend is the wave of mergers that has swept the industry over the past decade. Merck alone now controls almost 10 percent of the world market. "The bigger they grow, the more they decide that their research should be focused on the most profitable diseases and conditions," one industry watcher says. "The only thing the companies think about on a daily basis is the price of their stocks; and announcing that you've discovered a drug [for a tropical disease] won't do much for your share price."

That comment came from a public health advocate, but it's essentially seconded by industry. "A corporation with stockholders can't stoke up a laboratory that will focus on Third World diseases, because it will go broke," says Roy Vagelos, the former head of Merck. "That's a social problem, and industry shouldn't be expected to solve it."

Drug companies, however, are hardly struggling to beat back the wolves of bankruptcy. The pharmaceutical sector racks up the largest legal profits of any industry, and it is expected to grow by an average of 16 to 18 percent over the next four years, about three times more than the average for the Fortune 500. Profits are especially high in the United States, which alone among First World nations does not control drug prices. As a result, prices here are about twice as high as they are in the European Union and nearly four times higher than in Japan.

"It's obvious that some of the industry's surplus profits could be going into research for tropical diseases," says a retired drug company executive, who wishes to remain anonymous. "Instead, it's going to stockholders." Also to promotion: In 1998, the industry unbuckled $10.8 billion on advertising. And to politics: In 1997, American drug companies spent $74.8 million to lobby the federal government, more than any other industry; last year they spent nearly $12 million on campaign contributions.

Just forty-five years ago, the discovery of new drugs and pesticides led the World Health Organization (WHO) to predict that malaria would soon be eradicated. By 1959, Garrett writes in *The Coming Plague*, the Harvard School of Public Health was so certain that the disease was passe that its curriculum didn't offer a single course on the subject.

Resistance to existing medicines—along with cutbacks in healthcare budgets, civil war, and the breakdown of the state—has led to a revival of malaria in Africa, Latin America, Southeast Asia and, most recently, Armenia and Tajikistan. The WHO describes the disease as a leading cause of global suffering and says that by "undermining the health and capacity to work of hundreds of *millions* of people, it is closely linked to poverty and contributes significantly to stunting social and economic development."

Total global expenditures for malaria research in 1993, including government programs, came to $84 million. That's paltry when you consider that one B-2 bomber costs $2 billion, the equivalent of what, at current levels, will be spent on all malaria research over twenty years. In that period, some 40 million Africans alone will die from the disease. In the United States, the Pentagon budgets $9 million per year for malaria programs, about one-fifth the amount it set aside this year to supply the troops with *Viagra*. For the drug companies, the meager purchasing power of malaria's victims leaves the disease off the radar screen. As Neil Sweig, an industry analyst at Southeast Research Partners, puts it wearily, "It's not worth the effort or the while of the large pharmaceutical companies to get involved in enormously expensive research to conquer the Anopheles mosquito."

The same companies that are indifferent to malaria are enormously troubled by the plight of dysfunctional First World pets. John Keeling, a spokesman for the Washington, DC–based Animal Health Institute, says the "companion animal" drug market is exploding, with U.S. sales for 1998 estimated at about $1 billion. On January 5, the FDA approved the use of Clomicalm, produced by Novams, to treat dogs that suffer from separation anxiety (warning signs: barking or whining, "excessive greeting," and chewing on furniture). "At Last, Hope For *Millions* of Suffering Canines Worldwide," reads the company's press release announcing the drug's rollout. "I can't emphasize enough how dogs are suffering and that their behavior is not tolerable to owners," says Guy Tebbitt, vice president for research and development for Novartis Animal Health.

Also on January 5 the FDA gave the thumbs up to Pfizer's Anipryl, the first drug approved for doggie Alzheimer's. Pfizer sells a canine pain reliever and arthritis treatment as well, and late last year it announced an R&D program for medications that help pets with anxiety and dementia.

Another big player in the companion-animal field is Heska, a biotechnology firm based in Colorado that strives to increase the "quality of life" for cats and dogs. Its products include medicines for allergies and anxiety, as well as an antibiotic that fights periodontal disease. The company's website features a "spokesdog" named Perio Pooch and, like old "shock" movies from high school driver's-ed classes, a photograph of a diseased doggie mouth to demonstrate what can happen if teeth and gums are not treated carefully. No one wants pets to be in pain, and Heska also makes drugs for animal cancer, but it is a measure of priorities that U.S. companies and their subsidiaries spend almost nothing on tropical diseases while, according to an industry source, they spend about half a billion dollars for R&D on animal health.

Although "companion animal" treatments are an extreme case—that half-billion-dollar figure covers "food animals" as well, and most veterinary drugs emerge from research on human medications—consider a few examples from the brave new world of human lifestyle drugs. Here, the pharmaceutical companies are scrambling to eradicate:

- *Impotence.* Pfizer invested vast sums to find a cure for what Bob Dole and other industry spokesmen delicately refer to as "erectile dysfunction." The company hit the jackpot with *Viagra*, which racked up more than $1 billion in sales in its first year on the market. Two other companies, Schering-Plough and Abbott Laboratories, are already rushing out competing drugs.
- *Baldness.* The top two drugs in the field, Merck's Propecia and Pharmacia & Upjohn's Rogaine (the latter sold over the counter), had combined sales of about $180 million in 1998. "Some lifestyle drugs are used for relatively serious problems, but even in the best cases we're talking about very different products from penicillin," says the retired drug company executive. "In cases like baldness therapy, we're not even talking about healthcare."
- *Toenail fungus.* With the slogan "Let your feet get naked!" as its battle cry, pharmaceutical giant Novartis recently unveiled a lavish advertising campaign for Lamisil, a drug that promises relief for sufferers of this unsightly malady. It's a hot one, the war against fungus, pitting Lamisil against Janssen Pharmaceutical's Sporanox and Pfizer's Diflucan for shares in a market estimated to be worth hundreds of *millions* of dollars a year.
- *Face wrinkles.* Allergan earned $90 million in 1997 from sales of its "miracle" drug Botox. Injected between the eyebrows at a cost of about $1,000 for three annual treatments, Botox makes crow's feet and wrinkles disappear. "Every $7\frac{1}{2}$ seconds someone is turning 50," a wrinkle expert told the *Dallas Morning News* in an article about Botox last year. "You're looking at this vast population that doesn't want frown lines."

Meanwhile, acute lower respiratory infections go untreated, claiming about 3.5 million victims per year, overwhelmingly children in poor nations. Such infections are third on the chart of the biggest killers in the world; the number of lives they take is almost half the total reaped by the number-one killer, heart disease, which usually strikes the elderly. "The development of new antibiotics," wrote drug company researcher A.J. Slater in a 1989 paper published in the *Royal Society of Tropical Medicine and Hygiene's Transactions,* "is very costly and their provision to Third World countries alone can never be financially rewarding."

In some cases, older medications thought to be unnecessary in the First World and commercially unviable in the Third have simply been pulled from the market. This created a crisis recently when TB re-emerged with a vengeance in U.S. inner cities, since not a single company was still manufacturing Streptomycin after mid-1991. The FDA set up a task force to deal with the situation, but it was two years before it prodded Pfizer back into the field.

In 1990 Marion Merrell Dow (which was bought by German giant Hoechst in 1995) announced that it would manufacture Ornidyl, the first new medicine in forty years that was effective in treating African sleeping sickness. Despite the benign sounding name, the disease leads to coma and death, and kills about 40,000 people a year. Unlike earlier remedies for sleeping sickness, Ornidyl had few side effects. In field trials, it saved the lives of more than 600 patients, most of whom were near death. Yet Ornidyl was pulled from production; apparently company bean-counters determined that saving lives offered no return.

Because AIDS also plagues the First World, it is the one disease ravaging Third World countries that is the object of substantial drug company research. In many

African countries, AIDS has wiped out a half-century of gains in child survival rates. In Botswana—a country that is not at war and has a relatively stable society—life expectancy rates fell by twenty years over a period of just five. In South Africa, the Health Ministry recently issued a report saying that 1,500 of the country's people are infected with HIV every day and predicting that the annual death rate will climb to 500,000 within the next decade.

Yet available treatments and research initiatives offer little hope for poor people. A year's supply of the highly recommended multidrug cocktail of three AIDS medicines costs about $15,000 a year. That's exorbitant in any part of the world, but prohibitive in countries like Uganda, where per capita income stands at $330. Moreover, different viral "families" of AIDS, with distinct immunological properties, appear in different parts of the world. About 85 percent of people with HIV live in the Third World, but industry research to develop an AIDS vaccine focuses only on the First World. "Without research dedicated to the specific viral strains that are prevalent in developing countries, vaccines for those countries will be very slow in coming," says Dr. Amir Attaran, an international expert who directs the Washington-based Malaria Project.

All the blame for the neglect of tropical diseases can't be laid at the feet of industry. Many Third World governments invest little in healthcare, and First World countries have slashed both foreign aid and domestic research programs. Meanwhile, the U.S. government aggressively champions the interests of the drug industry abroad, a stance that often undermines healthcare needs in developing countries.

In one case where a drug company put Third World health before profit—Merck's manufacture of Ivermectin—governmental inertia nearly scuttled the good deed. It was the early eighties, and a Pakistani researcher at Merck discovered that the drug, until then used only in veterinary medicine, performed miracles in combating river blindness disease. With one dose per year of Ivermectin, people were fully protected from river blindness, which is carried by flies and, at the time, threatened hundreds of *millions* of people in West Africa.

Merck soon found that it would be impossible to market Ivermectin profitably, so in an unprecedented action the company decided to provide it free of charge to the WHO. (Vagelos, then chairman of Merck, said the company was worried about taking the step, "as we feared it would discourage companies from doing research relevant to the Third World, since they might be expected to follow suit.") Even then, the program nearly failed. The WHO claimed it didn't have the money needed to cover distribution costs, and Vagelos was unable to win financial support from the Reagan Administration. A decade after Ivermectin's discovery, only 3 million of 120 million people at risk of river blindness had received the drug. During the past few years, the WHO, the World Bank, and private philanthropists have finally put up the money for the program, and it now appears that river blindness will become the second disease, after smallpox, to be eradicated.

Given the industry's profitability, it's clear that the companies could do far more. It's equally clear that they won't unless they are forced to. The success of ACT UP in pushing drug companies to respond to the AIDS crisis in America is emblematic of how crucial [and] also how difficult it is to get the industry to budge. In late 1997, a coalition of public health organizations approached a group of major drug companies, including Glaxo-Wellcome and Roche, and asked them to fund a project that would dedicate itself to developing new treatments for major tropical diseases. Although the companies would have been required to put up no more than $2 million a year, they walked away from the table. Since there's no organized pressure— either from the grassroots or from governments—they haven't come back. "There [were] a number of problems at the business level" Harvey Bale, director of the Geneva-based International Federation of Pharmaceutical Manufacturers' Association, told *Science* magazine. "The cost of the project is high for some companies."

While the industry's political clout currently insures against any radical government action, even minor reforms could go a long way. The retired drug company executive points to public hospitals, which historically were guaranteed relatively high profit margins but were obligated to provide free care to the poor in return. There's also the example of phone companies, which charge businesses higher rates in order to subsidize universal service. "Society has tolerated high profit levels up until now, but society has the right to expect something back," he says. "Right now, it's not getting it."

The U.S. government already lavishly subsidizes industry research and allows companies to market discoveries made by the National Institutes of Health and other federal agencies. "All the government needs to do is start attaching some strings," says the Malaria Project's Attaran. "If a company wants to market another billion-dollar blockbuster, fine, but in exchange it will have to push through a new malaria drug. It will cost them some money, but it's not going to bankrupt them."

Another type of "string" would be a "reasonable pricing" provision for drugs developed at federal laboratories. By way of explanation, Attaran recounted that the vaccine for hepatitis A was largely developed by researchers at the Walter Reed Army Institute. At the end of the day, the government gave the marketing rights to Smith-Kline Beecham and Merck. The current market for the vaccine, which sells for about $60 per person, is $300 million a year. The only thing Walter Reed's researchers got in exchange for their efforts was a plaque that hangs in their offices. "I'll say one thing for the companies," says Attaran. "They didn't skimp on the plaque; it's a nice one. But either the companies should have paid for part of the government's research, or they should have been required to sell the vaccine at a much lower price."

At the beginning of this year, Doctors Without Borders unveiled a campaign calling for increased access to drugs needed in Third World countries. The group is exploring ideas ranging from tax breaks for smaller firms engaged in research in the field, to creative use of international trade agreements, to increased donations of drugs from the multinational companies. Dr. Bernard Pecoul, an organizer of the campaign, says that different approaches are required for different diseases. In the case of those plaguing only the Southern Hemisphere—sleeping sickness, for example—market mechanisms won't work because there simply is no market to speak of. Hence, he suggests that if multinational firms are not willing to manufacture a given drug, they transfer the relevant technology to a Third World producer that is.

Drugs already exist for diseases that ravage the North as well as the South—AIDS and TB, for example—but they are often too expensive for people in the Third World. For twenty-five years, the WHO has used funding from member governments to purchase and distribute vaccines to poor countries; Pecoul proposes a similar model for drugs for tropical diseases. Another solution he points to: In the event of a major health emergency, state or private producers in the South would be allowed to produce generic versions of needed medications in exchange for a small royalty paid to the multinational license holder. "If we can't change the markets, we have to humanize them," Pecoul says. "Drugs save lives. They can't be treated as normal products."

LABS

Internet Exercise

HIV/AIDS: Locally and Globally

Introduction

One of the newest diseases to be identified also happens to be one of the most serious. The human immuno-deficiency virus (HIV), which causes acquired immune deficiency syndrome (AIDS) has accounted for close to 525,000 deaths of Americans since it was named in 1981 (Centers for Disease Control and Prevention 2003). At first, HIV/AIDS research did not receive much attention or funding because it was considered a disease that affected mainly homosexuals. Although homosexual sex is one of the predominant ways to contract the virus, it is clear now that there are numerous other ways of transmitting the disease.

Since its classification as a disease, the two leading ways that HIV/AIDS was transmitted was through homosexual male sex and intravenous drug use. In 2003, unprotected heterosexual sex became the second most prevalent method of contracting the disease, next to homosexual sex. Kissing, sneezing, saliva, tears, sweat, and other casual contact activities do not spread HIV/AIDS. There are cases in which infected blood is given through blood transfusion (although improved screening has lessened this risk) and through a pregnant woman to her child. However, the chances of infection through these methods are slim.

There are several racial groups that have been affected more severely than others. While whites do account for most HIV/AIDS cases, they also account for more of the nation's population. However, about half (49.6%) of all HIV cases in 2003 were attributed to African Americans. Men have always been more likely to contract the disease, but there has been a sharp increase in women with HIV/AIDS. Specifically, African American women have been disproportionately affected. Other categories that are increasingly becoming more prone to contracting the disease are Hispanics and children/adolescents.

HIV/AIDS is also a global epidemic, devastating parts of Africa. As of 2003, there were an estimated 38 million cases worldwide with a rate of 5.3 million new cases each year. In Africa, a common way of spreading the disease is through mother-child contact at birth and during breast feeding. In certain parts of Africa, particularly the sub-Saharan regions, the death rate due to AIDS is so high that there are 15 million AIDS orphans, who have lost one or both parents. The treatment, research, education, and funding for healthcare and prevention knowledge in many countries have not caught up to the epidemic and this has also undoubtedly contributed to the high mortality rates.

Idea in Use

Sesame Street introduced a new puppet to its South African viewers in 2002. The character, an orphan girl named Kami who is HIV positive, has received much attention from American conservatives despite no plans for such a character in the United States version. The Sesame Street Workshop executives contend that the character will make a positive difference in society by providing a strong role model with high self esteem. Current plot stories surrounding the new character teach youngsters what to do if someone gets cut, that shunning the Muppet is not necessary to avoid infection, and by supplying additional education about the disease. The show will not teach children how HIV is spread and will not reveal how the character contracted the virus.

According to the U.S. State Department, one in nine South Africans have HIV and about 40 percent of South African women of childbearing age have the disease. For more information about the program, see www.sesameworkshop.org/international/.

Activity Instructions

This internet lab will provide you with an overview of the national and global HIV/AIDS epidemic.

1. Many African countries have high concentrations of people living with HIV/AIDS and some of the highest infection rates in the world. Explore the site below to find the answers to the following questions. http://www.cnn.com/CNN/Programs/presents/index.aids.html

   - What is the worldwide total for people living with HIV/AIDS in 2000?
   - How many children under the age of 15 live with HIV/AIDS in 2000 in sub-Saharan Africa? In North America?
   - What is the percentage of women in sub-Saharan Africa living with HIV/AIDS? In Latin America? Worldwide?
   - What areas of the world experienced the greatest numbers of new HIV infections in 2000?

2. At the same site, take the quiz about AIDS and Africa. How many did you get correct? Were there any answers that surprised you?

3. Now head to the www.unaids.org website, a collaboration between the United Nations and the World Health Organization. This site has an incredible amount of information related to the global AIDS crisis. From the left side menu, select "Geographical Area" and then click on "By Country." Choose an Asian country and a European country to compare. When you reach the country's site, you can find the answers to the following questions from the first few pages of the linked fact sheet called the UN Epidemiological Fact Sheets on HIV/AIDS and Sexually Transmitted Infections. What countries did you choose? For each country, determine:

   - The number of citizens living with HIV/AIDS—report the total number and then break it down to adults and children
   - What method of transmission is most responsible for the spread of HIV/AIDS in the country
   - How the epidemiology of HIV infection has changed in the last ten years

4. State health data are presented at the Henry J. Kaiser Family Foundation webpage at www.statehealthfacts.org. Go to this site to answer the following questions. You will first compare all 50 states and then look at more detailed information for the state in which you reside.

   - What states have the highest rate of cumulative HIV/AIDS cases caused by male homosexual sex? By injection drug use? By heterosexual sex?
   - Where in the United States is the AIDS case rate per 100,000 population in 2003 the highest? The lowest?
   - For your state, what is the HIV death rate and how does it compare to the national average?
   - For your state, what is the estimated number of pediatric cases of people living with AIDS?
   - For your state, what is the gender breakdown of people living with AIDS? The race/ethnicity breakdown? How do these compare with the national percentages?

5. Turn in your answers to all the above questions to your instructor as directed.

Individual Writing Exercise

Mass Media and Eating Disorders

Introduction

Printed images have long influenced popular trends and ideals. In the past, body size was seen as a reflection of the amount of money one possessed. It was assumed that a larger person had enough money to have an overabundance of food. Artists painted portraits of women and men of varying sizes and depicted the average citizens. In the 1950s and 1960s, fuller shaped bodies were in vogue with Marilyn Monroe becoming the fashion icon. Further along the timeline of desired body shapes we find the waif-like model come into style in the early 1990s. Media representations in print and video still reflect only a narrow class of body types. For instance, the average model is 5'11" and weighs 117 pounds (classified as underweight by the Centers for Disease Control's Body Mass Index) and the average mannequin size displayed in stores is a size four. The ideal presented is very thin for women and very muscular for males. The images that are reproduced almost certainly play a role in the development of eating disorders. However, the extent to which the media has an effect on the body image of males and females is unknown and often debated.

Eating disorders, such as anorexia and bulimia, were once thought to only affect white, middle class, adolescent/early adult females in the United States. Repeated images of skinny women as always winning the guy, getting the job, and being well-liked, with an incredible dearth of overweight women achieving these same goals, were thought to contribute to the cultural argument of the development of such disorders. While the majority of those afflicted with eating disorders are predominantly white females, eating disorders have become increasingly more popular with other demographic categories. The emphasis by the media for men to have well sculpted bodies has spawned multiple new cases of under-eating and over-exercising. Men account for about 10 percent of all known cases of eating disorders. While traditionally, black Americans have been more accepting of fuller bodies, the increasing assimilation of African American women in advertisements, the media, and "white" suburbia, seems to have affected the eating habits of these women as well.

Certain subcultures are at a greater risk of developing anorexia and bulimia. Athletes such as gymnasts, figure skaters, ballerinas, cross-country runners, jockeys, and wrestlers have a higher preponderance of eating disorders. Identifying those at risk is very necessary to prevent serious health complications and even death. The deviant lifestyle of eating disorders can have a large support network. In recent years, there has been increasing attention to "pro-ana" and "pro-mia" websites where people share their tips and experiences with living with devastating eating disorders.

Idea in Use

While eating disorders are often thought of as a westernized and American disorder, cross-cultural studies have demonstrated that this is not always the case. Globalization may have had an unintended consequence of transmitting the thinness ideal for women to countries all over the world. In the 2004 *Deviant Behavior* article, "Exploring the Purging Behavior of Asian-Pacific Adolescents in Guam: Does Heavy Television Viewing Make a Difference?" Thomas Pinhey and Alton Okinaka investigate the empirical support for their hypothesis that Westernized television in Guam presents a restrictive image of body type for adolescents. Specifically, they suggest that the repetitive viewing of thin, tall, and athletic bodies would result in purging behaviors of adolescents who watched the most television. Using the Guam's

Youth Risk Behavior Survey, they found that males who were heavy television watchers were significantly more likely to exhibit purging behaviors. In addition, they found that overweight males were more likely to purge and females that perceived themselves as overweight were significantly more likely to purge than others. Their research emphasizes the importance of not solely focusing on female eating disorder behaviors.

Activity Instructions

You will be analyzing how various mass media outlets portray overweight males and females in this independent exercise.

1. During the week, as you watch television, pay special attention to the body size of characters in dramas, sitcoms, and even the news. Which shows could you find that presented heavy or overweight characters? How did they portray the characters (e.g., were they in the background, have a main role, etc.)? Were there any comments or jokes made about the person's size? If the "fat" characters were shown with food, was the food healthy or fattening? How does this compare to the "skinny" characters?

2. Also while watching television, analyze the commercials that you see for diets, supplements, and related diet products? Which gender is shown more? Do the results seem feasible or do the commercials seem to exaggerate results?

3. For the last task, look at some magazines and observe how body image is presented. Write down descriptions of underweight, normal-sized, and overweight images in advertisements. Explain what the models were selling, which size you saw the most of, and how they were presented (were the skinny models positioned in sexy poses, active, etc., while the overweight ones were sedentary?).

4. Create a log of the television shows and magazines that you used and submit this with a 2–3 page (typed, double-spaced) summary of your findings.

5. You will be graded on your creativity, insights, and descriptions. Turn in your assignment to your instructor as directed.

Group Exercise

Social Construction of Sickness and Disease

Introduction

At different points of time and place, sickness and disease can be constructed vastly differently. When a condition becomes defined as a sickness/disease that can be treated, the process is called medicalization. For instance, childbirth was once considered a natural phenomenon that required little to no assistance from physicians. Midwives were relied upon for support, not epidurals or other anesthetics. The natural event performed by women is now controlled and managed by medical staff, and arranged according to their time frames (e.g., inducements occurring mostly on Fridays). While childbirth is medicalized in the United States, practices such as an isolated birth is practiced by the !Kung San people of the Kalahari Desert, and is non-medicalized.

The symbolic interactionist perspective directly addresses the medicalization process and elaborates on the social construction of illness. Social interactionist ideas such as self-fulfilling prophecies and the Thomas Theorem can be used to help explain how people define their illness or health as real. For example, the placebo effect is a much documented phenomenon that relates how health improves when any type of treatment is given, even when the treatment is not expected to provide any benefits. Similarly, having a stigmatized disease can affect the treatment effects and the long-term prognosis. For instance, HIV is usually constructed as a disease with a death sentence, but in actuality many HIV-infected people are living long and prosperous lives.

A conflict perspective can also be used to evaluate illness and health. The legitimate medical profession stands to lose much status and profits when faced with competition or even with their own success. For instance, scientific and biomedical technology has produced many vaccines and treatments that have eradicated or reduced reliance on medicine. Therefore, the medical field can profit and maintain their control by medicalizing other disorders. By creating or defining conditions such as Internet addictions as an illness, they can preserve their influence. In addition, by characterizing alternative medicines such as acupuncture as illegitimate or fraudulent, they maintain their position of power.

Idea in Use

In a 2005 *Social Problems* article "From Quackery to "Complementary" Medicine: The American Medical Profession Confronts Alternative Theories" Terri Winnick essentially tests the conflict perspective and theorized suppression of alternative medicines as legitimate. Using a content analysis approach, Winnick evaluated five prominent medical journal's approach to unorthodox medicine. She found that the treatment of such approaches consisted of three distinct phases. From 1960 to the early 1970s, the journals condemned and derided any benefits or legitimacy of alternative therapies or medicine. The mid-1970s through the early 1980s was labeled the "reassessment phase," where authors questioned the legitimacy of unorthodox medicine but also were reviewing their own methods, as consumerism of alternative medicines increased in popularity. Finally, Winnick suggests that there was an integration phase in the 1990s. During this phase, physicians recognized that alternative medicine was here to stay, but suggested that it should only be a complementary component to the legitimate medical field and should be subject to the same scientific scrutiny as the orthodox methods.

Activity Instructions

In this group exercise, you will evaluate how American society constructs different conditions as sickness or disease.

1. There are many conditions that, over time, have been classified as diseases or illnesses. For the following list of conditions, discuss whether you feel that the condition is a disease. Also discuss whether you think that the illness is under the control of the individual to prevent or manage. Finally, debate whether insurance companies should supplement the management of the health conditions. Prompts are given for the first couple health conditions, but feel free to discuss any matter related to the defining and social construction of the health condition.

   - Alcoholism—is there a genetic disposition, is this a disease, should insurance companies pay for treatment and is there a statute of limitations of such payments (pay for three times in treatment but after the third relapse, pay no more, etc.).
   - Obesity—is this a disease/genetic predisposition/under the control of the individual, should insurance companies pay for gastric bypass or other procedures that help manage obesity, what should insurance pay for, etc.
   - Eating Disorders
   - Depression
   - ADD and ADHD
   - Gambling
   - Post-Traumatic Stress Syndrome

2. Approaches to healthcare and the methods of treating conditions may or may not be considered legitimate society. While there has been an increasing diversity of alternative medicines, such as acupuncture and herbal medicine, there is still resistance to treat the alternatives as anything more than supplementary help. For the following list of alternative medicines, have each person in your group research one or more of the approaches. Each person should present a short (1–2 minute report) describing the approach. Then, discuss these treatment approaches in your group and rank them in the order of acceptability. For the least acceptable method, identify what it would take for the method to become a legitimate, mainstream medical option. This would necessitate imagination and analysis of many different social institutions.

   - Acupuncture
   - Aromatherapy
   - Ayurveda
   - Chiropractic
   - Divine Healing
   - Herbal Medicine
   - Homeopathy
   - Hypnotherapy
   - Magnet Therapy
   - Naturopathic
   - Osteopathy

3. Turn in to your instructor as directed.

Population, Community, and Urbanization

16

Cornerville and Its People
William Foote Whyte

Labs
Internet Exercise: Demography
Individual Writing Exercise: Community Identity
Group Exercise: Urbanization

Cornerville and Its People

In the heart of "Eastern City" there is a slum district known as Cornerville, which is inhabited almost exclusively by Italian immigrants and their children. To the rest of the city it is a mysterious, dangerous, and depressing area. Cornerville is only a few minutes' walk from fashionable High Street, but the High Street inhabitant who takes that walk passes from the familiar to the unknown.

For years Cornerville has been known as a problem area, and, while we were at war with Italy, outsiders became increasingly concerned with that problem. They feared that the Italian slum dweller might be more devoted to fascism and Italy than to democracy and the United States. They have long felt that Cornerville was at odds with the rest of the community. They think of it as the home of racketeers and corrupt politicians, of poverty and crime, of subversive beliefs and activities.

Respectable people have access to a limited body of information upon Cornerville. They may learn that it is one of the most congested areas in the United States. It is one of the chief points of interest in any tour organized to show upper-class people the bad housing conditions in which lower-class people live. Through sight-seeing or statistics one may discover that bathtubs are rare, that children overrun the narrow and neglected streets, that the juvenile delinquency rate is high, that crime is prevalent among adults, and that a large proportion of the population was on home relief or W.P.A. during the depression.

In this view, Cornerville people appear as social work clients, as defendants in criminal cases, or as undifferentiated members of "the masses." There is one thing wrong with such a picture: no human beings are in it. Those who are concerned with Cornerville seek through a general survey to answer questions that require the most intimate knowledge of local life. The only way to gain such knowledge is to live in Cornerville and participate in the activities of its people. One who does that finds that the district reveals itself to him in an entirely different light. The buildings, streets, and alleys that formerly represented dilapidation and physical congestion recede to form a familiar background for the actors upon the Cornerville scene.

One may enter Cornerville already equipped with newspaper information upon some of its racketeers and politicians, but the newspaper presents a very specialized picture. If a racketeer commits murder, that is news. If he proceeds quietly with the daily routines of his business, that is not news. If the politician is indicted for accepting graft, that is news. If he goes about doing the usual personal favors for his constituents, that is not news. The newspaper concentrates upon the crisis—the spectacular event. In a crisis the "big shot" becomes public property. He is removed from the society in which he functions and is judged by standards different from those of his own group. This may be the most effective way to prosecute the lawbreaker. It is not a good way to understand him. For that purpose, the individual must be put back into his social setting and observed in his daily activities. In order to understand the spectacular event, it is necessary to see it in relation to the everyday pattern of life—for there is a pattern to Cornerville life. The middle-class person looks upon the slum district as a formidable mass of confusion, a social chaos. The insider finds in Cornerville a highly organized and integrated social system.

It follows, therefore, that no immediate and direct solution to the problems posed for Cornerville can be given. It is only when the structure of the society and its patterns of action have been worked out that particular questions can be answered. This requires an exploration of new territory. In order to see how the present organization grew up, we may review the history of the local Italian settlement. When this is done, it will be time to go in and meet the people in order to discover from them the nature of the society in which they live.

For the Cornerville of today, history began in the 1860s, when a small group of Genoese settled together on an alley in one corner of what was then an Irish district. The stream of Italian immigration expanded slowly in the seventies and eighties and grew to a great flood in the nineties and in the first decade of the new century. The North Italians were the first to arrive, but the great wave of immigration came from the south, particularly from the vicinity of Naples and from Sicily. By the time that the southern immigration was at its height, most of the early Genoese settlers had moved to other sections of Eastern City or to suburban towns.

As early as 1915 the racial composition of Cornerville was practically the same as it is today. All but a few Irish families had moved out. The Jews, who came in at the same time as the Italians, had also been superseded, though many of them retained Cornerville business interests, particularly in the retail dry-goods line.

The Italian settlers brought over with them not only their language and customs but also a large proportion of their fellow-townsmen. The immigrants attracted relatives and friends. People from the same town, *paesani*, settled together, formed mutual aid societies, and each year celebrated the *Festa* of their patron saint as they had in Italy. The *paesani* made up little communities within a community, and even today one can mark out sections of Cornerville according to the town of origin of the immigrants, although these lines are fading with the growth of the younger generation.

First-generation immigrant society was organized primarily around the family and secondarily along the lines of *paesani*. Ties between families were cemented by the establishment of godparent-godchild relationships. Relatives by blood and ceremonial ties, as well as friends of the family, were linked together in an intricate network of reciprocal obligations. The individual who suffered misfortune was aided by his relatives and friends, and, when he had re-established himself, he shared his good fortune with those who had helped him.

The general region from which the immigrant came was also important in the organization of Cornerville life. The North Italians, who had had greater economic and educational opportunities, always looked down upon the southerners, and the Sicilians occupied the lowest position of all. Since many North and Central Italians were able to establish themselves before the southerners arrived, these distinctions were accentuated in the period of settlement, and they have not yet completely died out.

As the American-born generation has grown to maturity, the pattern of Cornerville life has undergone far-reaching changes. The ties of loyalty to *paesani* do not bind the son as they do the father. Even the Italian family has been broken into two separate generations. The Italian-born are known to the younger generation as "greasers." The children are often strongly attached to their parents, and yet they look down upon them. A few of the older people hold respected positions, but on the whole they do not have the authority that is characteristic of the older generation in most societies.

The younger generation has built up its own society relatively independent of the influence of its elders. Within the ranks of the younger men there are two main divisions: corner boys and college boys. Corner boys are groups of men who center their social activities upon particular street corners, with their adjoining barbershops, lunchrooms, poolrooms, or clubrooms. They constitute the bottom level of society within their age group, and at the same time they make up the great majority of the young men of Cornerville. During the depression most of them were unemployed or had only irregular employment. Few had completed high school, and many of them had left school before finishing the eighth grade. The college boys are a small group of young men who have risen above the corner-boy level through higher education. As they try to make places for themselves as professional men, they are still moving socially upward.

In a society such as ours, in which it is possible for men to begin life at the bottom and move up, it is important to discover who the people are who are advancing and how they are doing it. This gives perspective upon Cornerville society, and, at the same time, it shows what the world outside Cornerville has to offer to local people. The stories of Doc and his corner-boy gang and of Chick and his college-boy club present the contrast between the two groups and explain the different careers of the individual members.

While Doc and his boys and Chick and his club members are representative of a large part of local society, they are all "little guys" in Cornerville. In order to understand them, it is necessary to discover who the "big shots" are and see how they function. In Cornerville the big shots are racketeers and politicians.

With the South Side and Welport, Cornerville makes up Eastern City's Fourth Ward. Until recently the ward was dominated by the Cleveland Club, an Irish Democratic political organization located on the South Side. When the Italians first settled in Cornerville and began displacing the Irish population, there were sharp clashes between the races. As the Irish moved out, the hostilities were transferred to the political arena. Italian politicians organized Cornerville to overthrow the Irish domination of the ward.

Illegal activities during the prohibition era centered around the liquor traffic. With repeal the racketeer built his career upon the control of gambling activities. Cornerville men have played prominent roles in this field, although their Irish and Jewish colleagues share in the direction of the Eastern City rackets.

The racket and political organizations extend from the bottom to the top of Cornerville society, mesh with one another, and integrate a large part of the life of the district. They provide a general framework for the understanding of the actions of both "little guys" and "big shots."

In this exploration of Cornerville we shall be little concerned with people in general. We shall encounter particular people and observe the particular things that they do. The general pattern of life is important, but it can be constructed only through observing the individuals whose actions make up that pattern.

The "little guys" will be first on the scene (Part I). We shall see how they organize the activities of their own groups, and then, to place those groups in the social structure, we shall move up and observe the "big shots." The description of the racket and political organizations (in Part II) will give a general picture, but we are still concerned with particular people. The question is: What makes a man a big shot and by what means is he able to dominate the little guys? To answer that question, let us watch Tony Cataldo. He is a prominent racketeer, and he is concerned, among other things, with controlling the corner boys. How does he go about it? And let us watch George Ravello, Cornerville's state senator, as he organizes his political campaign. He needs the support of the corner boys. How does he get it? We know in general that the heads of political and racket organizations in Cornerville co-operate with one another. But what is the nature of that co-operation, upon what is it based, and how is it established? In order to answer that question, let us look at the particular people again and see how they act in relation to one another in the various situations that confront them in their careers.

If we can get to know these people intimately and understand the relations between little guy and little guy, big shot and little guy, and big shot and big shot, then we know how Cornerville society is organized. On the basis of that knowledge it becomes possible to explain people's loyalties and the significance of political and racket activities.

LABS

Internet Exercise

Demography

Introduction

Demography is a branch of the social sciences that is interested in the study of human population. Demographers are interested in the size, distribution, composition, and migration patterns of humans, as well as the consequences of any changes in these areas. Fertility, death, and migration are the three central components to population change.

Fertility refers to the total incidents of childbearing and live births in a society's population. The fertility rates vary with culture; the law, religious beliefs, personal choice, norms, medical care, birth control and finances are all factors that influence fertility over time and place. Demographers use the *crude birth rate* to measure fertility and it reflects the number of live births per 1,000 people in a single year. More specific is the *total fertility rate (TFR)*. This refers to the mean number of children born to women during their reproductive years. For a society to replace itself, without any influence of migration, a TFR of 2.1 is required. Developed countries have lower TFRs than less developed countries, and many have TFRs below replacement level.

The total number of death incidents in a society is that population's *mortality* level. Factors that contribute to variations in fertility rates also are the elements that create differences in mortality rates. The *crude death rate* reflects the number of deaths that occur in a year, per every 1,000 people. The infant mortality rate is a more specific measure that describes the number of deaths among children under the age of one. The infant mortality rate is often used as a measure of health and well being of a population and can vary greatly between countries, as well as among populations within a single country.

Another important aspect of demography is migration. *Migration* refers to the transfer or flow of people into and out of a location. *Immigration* is the movement into a location, while *emigration* refers to the flow out of a location. The difference between immigration and emigration is called *net migration*. The measurement of this element is more problematic than other demographic factors. For instance, migration within a country is generally not recorded, people who move out of a location are generally not tracked, and immigrant populations are often transient and may or may not have entered a place legally.

A society's population is increased by fertility and immigration and decreased through mortality and emigration. The growth rate of a society is thus determined by subtracting the crude death rate from the crude birth rate, and then adding the net migration rate.

Idea in Use

Fears of overpopulation and reduced resources have prompted some countries to take population issues very seriously. In 1979, China enacted the "one-child rule." Chinese families are mandated by law to restrict their fertility to one child with penalties ranging from fines, forced abortions, and even sterilizations for those who do not abide. However, some provinces within the country are not strict enforcers of the one-child rule and many Chinese couples have two or more children without any penalty. Giovanna Merli and Herbert Smith found in their 2002 *Demography* article "Has the Chinese Family Planning Policy Been Successful in Changing Fertility Preferences?" that acceptance and obedience of the law is positively associated with the urbanization and development of the area, as well as the province's certainty of punishment. In rural provinces, women typically have more than one child and receive no punishment.

Activity Instructions

This internet exercise will test your understanding of global and national demography.

1. Go to the United States Census homepage (www.census.gov) and record the current United States and world populations. There are population clocks on the upper right hand side of the website.

2. Go to the International Programs Center on the census webpage. Find this site at www.census.gov/ipc/www/ and click on the International Data Base. Select "Online Access" and then "Display." There will be many options available on your screen. Select the Table "008: Vital Rates" and compare the United States with three other countries of your choice. Select the latest year available and the residence selection should highlight the total. Once you submit the query, record the crude birth rate, crude death rate, migration rate, rate of natural increase, and the growth rate.

3. Write 1–2 paragraphs analyzing the countries' rates and why they may be relatively high or low. Also discuss if the countries you selected had similar or dissimilar rates, and what you think may contribute to such patterns.

4. Now go to the United Nations Human Development Reports website at http://hdr.undp.org/ and click on "Statistics" and then "Get Data." Choose "Data by Indicator" and select "Fertility Rate, Total." Use the resulting table to answer the following questions:

   - From 2000–2005, which country/ies had the lowest TFR? The highest TFR?
   - How many countries have TFRs below the replacement level in the most recent time period?
   - What is the general trend between the time periods?
   - Describe the trends of TFR by income status of the country.

   Repeat the steps above for the infant mortality indicator. Answer the following questions:

   - For the most current year, which country/ies had the highest infant mortality rate? The lowest?
   - What is the general trend between time periods?
   - What region has the highest infant mortality rate?
   - Describe the trends of infant mortality rate by income status of the country.

5. Return to the Census website and record the current U.S. and world population counts. How have they changed since the beginning of this exercise?

6. Turn in your answers to your instructor as directed.

Individual Writing Exercise

Community Identity

Introduction

Community can refer to many things, but usually denotes a group of individuals that share a common identity. In the early 1920s, Ferdinand Tönnies described two types of communities that have differing levels of interaction and identity. *Gemeinschaft,* which generally is translated to mean community, describes a group with a strong, shared identity and personal social interaction. *Gesellschaft*, a term typically translated to mean association or society, is the term Tönnies used to describe a group with little intimate interaction and little sense of unity. Modern, industrialized cities where people interact with each other only when necessary, such as a retail clerk and customer, typify Gesellschaft.

Gemeinschaft is typical of pre-industrial cities and can be observed in tribal and village communities of today. Such societies are generally homogenous, with people sharing a similar culture, history, identity, and belief system. Reliance on one another for survival is necessary and collaboration is natural. As society industrializes, people become more divided in labor responsibilities and their unique talents are utilized. Reliance on one another to obtain necessary goods and services for survival becomes dependent on economic exchanges and brings diverse people together for short spurts of interaction. Tönnies saw the process of a place moving from Gemeinschaft to Gesellschaft as a process of modernization. Evaluating the environmental structure and organization of an area is often key to determining the solidarity and interaction level of its people.

Idea in Use

The prevalent use of computers and the internet has spawned the creation of virtual communities. The December 2002 issue of *City & Community* published an article entitled "Are Virtual Communities True Communities?: Examining the Environments and Elements of Community." This research evaluates the authenticity of cyberspace as a community. Robin Driskell and Larry Lyon find that while virtual communities do meet the two criteria (members with common ties and social interaction) to be defined as a community, the limitations of space and distance and the lack of place identification thwart it from becoming a true Gemeinschaft community. They conclude that while virtual communities have benefits, they do not include the holistic, emotional ties that a true community encompasses.

Activity Instructions

In this independent exercise you will reflect on the community/ies of which you have been a member and describe your current community environment.

1. Looking back over your life, reflect on the neighborhood/community that you most identify with and answer the following questions.

   - What does your neighborhood/community look like?
   - Discuss the major activities that took place.
   - How you would distinguish members of the community from "outsiders."
   - Did Gemeinschaft or Gesellschaft dominate?
   - Discuss anything else you think is important.

2. Now consider your current neighborhood/community. Describe what it looks like and how it differs or is similar to your growing-up neighborhood/community. Are there multiple "communities" that you identify with that might provide varying experiences of community? For instance, you may feel a Gemeinschaft type of relationship with your suitemates or sorority but experience Gesellschaft in relation to your college or university experience overall.

3. Gesellschaft generally typifies modern, industrialized places. Describe how you think life would be different if Gemeinschaft dominated. Be as specific as you can. Do you think it would be possible to return to Gemeinschaft existence after Gesellschaft has taken over for so long?

4. Finally, write a brief statement (1–3 paragraphs) about whether you think internet communities are true communities. Be sure to address whether Gemeinschaft is possible in such communities.

5. Turn in your reports to your instructor as directed.

Group Exercise

Urbanization

Introduction

Cities have been the center of business, economic, political, and social life in America since urbanization began to develop rapidly in the early 1800s. It is no wonder that many people choose to reside within cities to take advantage of all the opportunities that cities afford. The majority of the United States population lives within an urban area. The influx of residents within a city is called *urbanization*. The increase of factories within cities, the birth of the skyscraper and technological advancements, as well as improved transportation systems, aided the increasing concentration of people to cities. *Metropolis* was a term coined in the 1900s and means "mother city." A metropolis represents a large city that dominates the region. Since the mid 1950s, cities have experienced a transitory flow away from their center. The growth of the neighboring towns and suburbs lead to urban sprawl. *Megalopolis* is a term used to describe the unbroken stream of population concentrations that were created as a result of cities and associated sprawl that connects major cities. For instance, the Northeast area has a continuous region of large cities and populated suburbs from Boston, Massachusetts to Richmond, Virginia. Another new phenomenon is the creation of *edge cities*. Edge cities are locales near a large city that have strongly developed business centers but little residential areas. For instance, the Silicon Valley near the Bay Area of California and King of Prussia near Philadelphia are edge cities.

The study of the relationship between city structure and people is called *urban ecology*. There are several models of urban structures. Ernest Burgess and Robert Park evaluated the physical structure of Chicago and described the distribution of land use by *concentric zones*. The central zone is the downtown business center with skyscrapers and office buildings. An area populated with light manufacturing factories surrounds the downtown area. This is surrounded by layers of low class and then middle class residences. An exclusive area for the high-class residence surrounds the other residential areas. Finally a zone representing commuters from suburbs into the central city area encloses the entire circle. Burgess theorized that people competed for the desired land and as urban growth increased the zones would move further away from the downtown area. Sociologist Homer Hoyt refined the concentric zone theory with his idea of wedge-shaped *sectors*. The sectors still extend out as urban growth occurs but the areas are concentrated in triangle shapes. For instance, the rich may seek riverfront property, the factories may be centered near train tracks for easy shipping, and the ethnic enclaves may remain a singular community. The wedge sectors then allow for diverse but separated neighbors. Another popular model is the *multiple-nuclei* theory developed by Chauncy Harris and Edward Ullman. This model has several central points and certain types of housing and buildings cluster around the focal areas. For instance, there may be an entertainment area full of theaters, playhouses, etc., in addition to a financial district, retailing area, etc. Whatever the model, the importance of cities to the vitality of the country is evident.

Idea in Use

Edge cities are a relatively new concept described in the early 1990s, describing a pattern of "technoburbs" and other such places with a very high concentration of jobs in the United States that are removed from a central city, but remain a hub of office and retail activity. While edge cities have been a phenomenon located in the United States, many have questioned whether the process and creation of such sub-urb/city niches has or will occur in other parts of the world. Marco Bontje and Joachim Burdack attempt to tackle this question and argue that permutations of the American edge cities are slowly developing in Europe but have distinct differences from the edge cities of the United States. In their *Cities* article called "Edge Cities, European-Style: Examples from Paris and Randstad" the authors use case studies from Paris (Massy-Saclay and val d'Europe) and the Randstad (Schiphol airport area and the Amsterdam South axis) to track the emergence of these European edge-like cities. These areas are relatively new developments that occurred in the past few decades with a degree of specialization in industry. However, they found differences as well. In the United States, for example, private development firms generally spawned the phenomena while in the European cities government greatly intervened in the location and development of the hubs. They suggest that perhaps the European model is of 'city-edge' rather than 'Edge City' but propose that the area is emerging and more research is warranted.

Activity Instructions

Your group will be identifying a city to study and will evaluate its unique features and structures. This exercise will require some research activity investigating features of the city that you select, so you will want to meet initially to divide the labor.

1. As a group, identify a city that you would like to investigate. If you are familiar with or live near a major city, it may be easier to choose that one. What is the name of your city and the state that it is in?

2. Once you choose a city, identify its major components. For example, where are the retail areas, the manufacturing sectors, and the residential areas? Are residents segregated by class or race? Make sure to identify any large transportation routes that pass through, any major waterways, and any other important elements.

3. Briefly explain whether the city structure is composed of concentric zones, wedge sectors, or multiple nuclei. Also, report if suburban sprawl is evident.

4. Is the city part of a megalopolis? Is it known for a certain type of industry (for instance—Detroit and automobiles) that supports the city? In what area of the city would the majority of group members like to reside and why?

5. Finally, create a map of the group's selected city, outlining the areas of the city. Make sure to appropriately label the sectors, zones, or nuclei.

6. Turn in you assignment to you instructor as directed.

Environmental Sociology

The Historical Transformation of a Grassroots Environmental Group
Kelly D. Alley, Charles E. Faupel, and Conner Bailey

Labs
Internet Exercise: Distribution of Environmental Hazards
Individual Writing Exercise: Environmental Toxins
Group Exercise: Sustainable Development and Environment

The Historical Transformation of a Grassroots Environmental Group

This paper documents the historical transformation of a small environmental group in Alabama's Black belt soils region. This group, known as Alabamians for a Clean Environment (ACE), formed with the specific purpose of closing down the nation's largest hazardous waste landfill just outside the town of Emelle in Sumter County, Alabama. Although the group did not achieve this goal, the particular transformations ACE underwent bring together issues important to the understanding of environmental activism, social movements, and the politics of waste in America.

The Setting of Sumter County

Sumter County is located in western Alabama in the heart of the Black belt soils region, a corridor of land approximately seventy miles wide from Selma to the eastern counties of Mississippi. The Black belt was the center of Alabama's cotton plantation economy prior to the Civil War and Sumter County was the major population center in the state. During the 1830s, Sumter County hosted a population of nearly 30,000 and figured as a dynamic center of plantation culture. Nearly half of the

Reprinted with permission from "The Historical Transformation of a Grassroots Environmental Group" by Kelly D. Alley, Charles E. Faupel, and Conner Bailey in *Human Organization*, 1995, vol. 54, pp. 410–416. Copyright © Society for Applied Anthropology.

residents were slaves at that time and some plantations had over 1,000 slaves. Schools were established as the first railroads were built. In 1835, Livingston State Teacher's College (now Livingston University) opened its doors. After the Civil War, cotton continued to be produced through sharecropping arrangements, which kept the rural Black population in a condition of poverty and dependence.

The Civil Rights Act of 1964 brought few immediate changes to the racial hierarchy that had become institutionalized during the first half of the twentieth century. Towns in the county operated a segregated school system until 1969 when a federal judge ordered the desegregation of public schools. Within nine months of the court order, White residents in the county established Sumter Academy exclusively for White students. The Academy is still operating, thereby maintaining a racially segregated educational system.

Since the 1940s, the population of the county has steadily declined to less than 17,000, of which 70 percent are African American. The two largest population centers in the county are Livingston, the county seat (pop. 3,500), and York, the commercial center of the county (pop. 3,100) (CDCR 1991). With an unemployment rate fluctuating between 12 and 22 percent, Sumter County ranks near the bottom of counties in Alabama on per capita income. The per capita income in the county in 1991 was just over $9,800; this compared with $13,600 for the state and nearly $17,600 for the nation.

The first challenge to White minority control in the county occurred in the early 1970s when the training center for the Federation of Southern Cooperatives was transferred from Atlanta to Sumter County. The only Black secular organization in the county, the Federation coordinated local cooperatives of low resource (and primarily African American) farmers throughout the South. Bringing its members greater buying and selling power, this organization assumed a role in political affairs unprecedented in the county's history. A campaign to register Black voters for the 1976 election nearly led to the first election of Blacks to public office in that year. In the 1978 elections, two African Americans were elected for the first time to seats on the five member county board of education. White leaders attempted to strike back and undermine this process of empowerment by accusing the Federation of fiscal impropriety in what became known as the "Cotton Patch Conspiracy" (Bethell 1982). Although defendants were subsequently cleared of all charges, the shadow cast by the investigation adversely affected the Federation's subsequent funding.

Sumter County residents saw a short period of growth through the late 1960s and early 1970s, when industries looking for a cheap non-unionized labor force moved 'into the region. Failing to account for the cost of maintaining an infrastructure for industry while promoting cheap labor and low taxes, these companies perpetuated second-class citizenship in the region'. Relying on outdated technology, Southern workers struggled to eke out a living in the mills and timber industries until the mid-1970s, when industry began to leave the region. In Sumter County, by the early 1980s, several major employers which had moved in during the early 1970s were moving out again.

Hazardous Waste Moves into Sumter County

The hazardous waste industry arrived at the doorstep of the economically depressed period in the late 1970s. In 1977, a group of local and regional investors operating as Resource Industries, Inc. purchased a 300 acre tract of land near Emelle from a widow residing in Livingston. Earlier in 1974, the Environmental Protection Agency (EPA) had identified Sumter County as a possible site for a hazardous waste landfill (EPA 1974). Resource Industries, Inc. had beneficial political connections within the state. James Parsons, son-in-law of the Governor George Wallace, was a partner in the company. Resource Industries, Inc. received legal counsel from the mayor of Livingston who, as son of the Speaker of the Alabama House of Representatives, was one of the Governor's key political supporters in West Alabama. These political connections were instrumental in obtaining necessary operating permits from the Health Department to operate the site. In 1978, Resource Industries, Inc. sold its landfill permit to Chemical Waste Management, Inc. (Chem Waste) and through subsequent purchases, Chemical Waste Management expanded its Sumter County facility to 2,400 acres.

As truckloads of hazardous waste began rolling into the county, residents did not know what was happening behind the gates of the facility. Rumors spread that it was a brick factory, a limestone quarry, and a cement manufacturer. Even the engineer for the electric utility which serves the area and who connected the facility to the power lines was unaware that this was to become a hazardous waste landfill. Some believed a fertilizer plant was moving in. Another resident noticed Chemical Waste Management listed as a donor member to such county institutions as the Arts Council and inquired. When word began to leak out that a waste facility had moved into the county, residents were not aware of the nature of wastes to be treated and assumed it was a large solid waste landfill.

Resource Industries and Chemical Waste Management were reluctant to inform the public about the nature of their business, and they were not legally obligated to do so. The original permit, issued under the authorization of the Solid Waste Act of 1969, did not require the release of information to the public. Resource Industries convened a quiet meeting of local residents at Emelle after rumors began circulating, but it was not widely attended and did little to educate the public. Officials involved in the decision later argued that the public had been informed through the local press. Yet the two county papers did not report about the facility until 1981.

Gradually, local residents learned about the landfill operation through personal discoveries. One individual reported that, while fixing a flat tire at night on Highway 17, he observed lights and a great deal of activity at the site. This led him to ask questions. Another resident first learned of the facility when his daughter's boyfriend began working there. Still others observed trucks coming to and from the site, many of them late at night.

The siting of hazardous waste facilities has become an increasingly contentious issue during the past two decades, pitting community groups against industry and regulatory agencies. The waste industry is motivated by the desire to establish and obtain permits to operate treatment, storage, and disposal facilities which generate revenue and profits. State and federal regulatory agencies have different motivations but share a common goal with industry: to establish and permit facilities which can handle the nation's waste stream. The federal EPA and the various state agencies which are responsible for environmental protection are mandated under the Resource Conservation and Recovery Act (RCRA) to establish technical standards for solid and hazardous waste management, and to issue permits to those concerns which meet specified standards. Industry and regulatory agencies are locked in a symbiotic relationship that gives many outside observers, particularly those communities that have been selected as sites for hazardous waste facilities, the impression of an unholy alliance. Regulatory agencies do not own or operate waste facilities, but instead rely on industry to do so. The waste management industry, for its part, owes its very existence—was indeed created by—the increasingly stringent environmental standards of the past two decades. As regulations have become more precise and demanding, the number of firms with the technical and financial resources to participate in the waste management industry has declined. Industry spokespersons may complain about regulatory actions, but the waste industry depends on the regulatory agencies for its very existence.

When faced with the prospect of a major hazardous waste facility in the community, most residents will mobilize in opposition. However, in Sumter County, local residents did not have the opportunity to protest a proposed facility; rather they woke up to a full-scale operation. Moreover, the facility was supported by key local leaders, including locally elected officials whose county commission, school board, and municipal budgets were substantially enlarged by Chemical Waste Management's monthly payments of $5.00 in "user fees" for every ton of waste buried in Sumter County. Chemical Waste Management has paid approximately $20 million in user fees since 1978. Local governing bodies have become dependent on these fees, and both White and Black officials responsible for making budgets and maintaining staff have been reluctant to criticize the company's policies and procedures. Eventually, opposition to Chemical Waste Management came from outside of the local political establishment.

Grassroots Response to Hazardous Waste: The Formation of ACE

Shortly after Chemical Waste Management acquired the facility in 1978, a group of workers walked off the site complaining about unsafe working conditions. Organized by the Minority People's Council, a Black organization headed by a local activist, the walkout attracted the first local and regional media scrutiny that the Chemical Waste Management facility received. In response, Chemical Waste Management employed a full time community relations manager and began to encourage local residents, state officials, and other interested persons to tour the facility.

Shortly after the walkout, a few Emelle residents formed an organization called Sumter Countians Organized for the Protection of the Environment, or SCOPE. This was a largely White organization led by a tenured professor at Livingston University. SCOPE's aim was to insure more rigorous monitoring of the facility, greater public accountability, and free access to reliable information. It sponsored several community meetings featuring industry spokesmen and experts in the field in an attempt to provide a forum for the open exchange of information about the site. At first, local newspapers characterized SCOPE in rather derogatory terms but over time softened their characterization as SCOPE became aligned with arguments legitimating the necessity of the landfill.

In 1983, some residents, dissatisfied with SCOPE and the lack of critical examination of plant functions, established an organization called Alabamians for a Clean Environment, or ACE. A few White women formed the core of the group and, along with their husbands and other members, directed their efforts towards closing the Chemical Waste Management facility. Initially, ACE members received information from PEON (Protect the Environment of Noxubee County), a grassroots group from the adjacent county of Noxubee across the Mississippi-Alabama state line. PEON provided ACE with background material on Chemical Waste Management operations in other states. Some of ACE's first members were residents of Noxubee County who had opposed proposals for a waste site in their county. In one of ACE's first meetings, PEON members brought with them an "EPA whistleblower" who ignited their enthusiasm to oppose the Emelle facility.

Although core ACE members were not part of the traditional White power structure, they were employed home owners with some record of family service in the county. They were farmers, artists, professors, and teachers. But these members did not consider themselves members of the "establishment." Most distanced themselves from the civic and political life of Sumter County. Civic and political life, as they saw it, was shaped by a small White elite trying to maintain political power in the face of an increasingly successful process of Black political empowerment. Socially marginalized as well, core members of ACE endured threats, harassment, and social ostracism as they sought to mobilize opposition to the facility. Succumbing to the pressure, a few ACE members who held closer ties to the power structure limited their involvement in ACE over time and ultimately dropped their membership. From the outset ACE was discredited by representatives in the community with vested interests in the plant. One community leader characterized the organization as "a little local group" with limited influence. He commented, "As far as it having any effect, it's about like a mouse trying to stomp an elephant."

At one level, this characterization of ACE as a marginal player was apt. ACE was unable to initiate any substantive changes in Sumter County political affairs. Nor was it able to close down Chemical Waste Management operations. Moreover, its public appeal was limited. While ACE claimed a membership of more than 300, its core group comprised only about 10 people. ACE was particularly ineffective in reaching Sumter County's African American population, which makes up 70 percent of the county total. In a 1990 survey conducted among African American residents of Sumter County whose children received free or subsidized school meals, only 24 out of 366 respondents (6.6 percent) were able to name ACE as an environmental organization opposed to the hazardous waste landfill. Despite its marginal status as an organization, ACE was nevertheless effective in making knowledge about hazardous waste publicly accessible in Sumter County and in maintaining a voice of opposition in public meetings. Chemical Waste Management, the Alabama Department of Environmental Management (ADEM), and business and political elites who sought to promote the well-being of the hazardous waste industry had to respond publically when ACE made their presence known in hearings through hostile questioning. ACE members questioned the safety measures taken in the facility and the honesty of company representatives who claimed to be concerned with local community welfare. At a public hearing in Sumter County during November 1986, ACE's opposition to the issuing of a RCRA operating permit highlighted the risks of air pollution from the proposed incinerator and of groundwater contamination from landfill operations. ACE members and supporters also argued that Chemical Waste Management had a long history of environmental violations and could not be trusted to comply with safety and health standards. On occasion, ACE members planned and carried out guerrilla theater tactics, such as name calling and sign waving, to draw attention to their assessment of the public risks posed by the landfill. More importantly, ACE had access to highly visible and powerful actors to speak on their behalf. Don Siegelman, then Attorney General of the State of Alabama, appeared at the hearings on behalf of ACE to oppose the landfill along with Jimmy Evans, an ambitious attorney for the city of Montgomery who has since been elected Attorney General of Alabama. ACE also solicited the support of expert witnesses in Alabama and Tennessee who gave ACE's claims about the potential dangers of incineration greater credibility. These were invaluable resources which were mobilized in opposition to the incinerator, successfully resulting in the denial of a permit to Chemical Waste Management to burn hazardous waste in Sumter County. To local officials and Chemical Waste Management personnel, ACE's activities were little more than an annoyance. One sympathetic elected official remarked, "They [Chem Waste] have often reacted to ACE like it was a pesky fly you keep swatting around. [However], anytime you can get someone to keep reacting to you, then you're powerful."

Alliances with Translocal Networks

Gradually, core ACE members disengaged from local White discourse in Sumter County and forged an alliance with a key Black leader. This alliance was publically demonstrated in 1987, when ACE and a few Black residents of Sumter County supported by Greenpeace organized the "Toxic Trail of Tears" rally. This rally began with a public demonstration at the state capitol in Montgomery, followed by a funeral-like caravan procession which moved across the state to Livingston (Sumter County's county seat) and to the gates of the Chemical Waste Management facility. The "Toxic Trail of Tears" introduced issues of hazardous waste to minority groups in the state. It also made symbolic reference to the forced resettlement of Alabama's Creek Indians to Oklahoma during the 1830s, the decade in which county lines were drawn. Sumter County was the assembly point for the original trail of tears of the Creek Indians.

In the 1987 sequel, Native American and African American speakers were highlighted as they cited the disproportionate number of hazardous waste sites in minority communities. Civil rights songs and chants were intermingled with those familiar to the mainstream environmental movement in this early public charge of what was to become known as "environmental racism".

ACE's persistent voice and public activities caught the attention of national organizations such as Greenpeace, the Sierra Club, the Citizen's Clearinghouse for Hazardous Wastes, and the National Toxics Fund Campaign. These groups provided ACE a broader forum, a greater resource base, and access to technical expertise. They also provided information on the corporate reputation of Chemical Waste Management and other companies in the waste management industry, and shared insights on strategies for effectively opposing such companies. These larger organizations contributed legal advice, media publicity, and assistance in political lobbying. However, as "outsiders" these professionals were not confronted by the same forces of economic necessity and the well-oiled political machine promoting the local hazardous waste industry. Consequently, ACE's ability to translate these resources into strong local opposition was not realized.

ACE's opposition to the hazardous waste landfill came at a crucial time for the environmental movement. Through the early 1980s, the politics of the environment had been controlled by a small number of national environmental organizations known as the "Group of Ten." Membership in this group included the Environmental Defense Fund, Environmental Policy Institute, Friends of the Earth, Izaak Walton League of America, Natural Resources Defense Council, National Audubon Society, National Parks and Conservation Association, National Wildlife Federation, Sierra Club, and the Wilderness Society. These organizations were bureaucratically structured, technically competent, and proficient in raising money through direct mail campaigns. These organizations grew in size and influence during the early 1980s when the Reagan administration adopted an anti-environmentalist posture. Borrelli (1987) notes that membership in national environmental groups nearly doubled between 1980 and 1987. But as Hofrichter (1993:7) argues, these groups rarely provided a vision or perspective beyond narrowly defined legislative, judicial, and policy alternatives. They tended to focus their energies on litigation, political lobbying, and technical evaluation rather than on mass mobilization for protest marches and petition-signing. Increasingly, citizens in local communities faced with the risks of waste found these organizations unresponsive to their needs.

To project their intentions to wider audiences, ACE cultivated a relationship with one of the newspapers in the county which was sympathetic to its views. The other newspaper in the county not only refused to endorse ACE editorially (rather, they endorsed Chemical Waste Management) but as a matter of policy refused to print letters to the editor written by ACE members. In fact, in one of their editorials they accused ACE of using the editorial pages as a means of free advertisement. ACE members also encouraged national media agencies to report on the facility and the tensions in the county. ACE was featured in national media forums such as *Southern Living, Newsweek* and CBS's *48 Hours* as an active voice in the politics of waste in the South. *Southern Magazine* (Greene 1988) ran an article in which Sumter County was identified as the "nation's pay toilet." In the same article, a leader of ACE was cast as a suppressed marginal, "shunned in her own hometown." After the "Toxic Trail of Tears" protest, a column published in the *Montgomery Advertiser* (Benn 1987) carried the headline: "Sumter County Protest Brings Out '60s Escapees."

ACE was, however, allowed to define its own image in the national media. Two ACE members were involved in the production of a video for the music channel VH-1 in which they were featured riding down the highway in a convertible singing one of the many limericks they had written about Chemical Waste Management. The media coverage in general had the effect of casting ACE as a local voice of resistance, an image which invited television stations from as far away as Japan.

"The worst pollution is controlling people's minds," argued the husband of a former core ACE member in late 1993. Critically reflecting on power, knowledge, and the economy in Sumter County, the couple continues to feel isolated in their community. Their former contacts with outsiders helped push them farther to the margin of local culture. Rather than strengthen their local image, this national recognition transformed them into objects of curiosity at home. Several meetings with outsiders resulted in public spectacles. When the Japanese television crew came to town and set up lights and cameras in one member's home, the neighborhood was buzzing with curiosity. Many were curious about their activities while at the same time denouncing them.

While they courted the media, ACE members were suspicious of individuals who conveyed a deeper interest in their local work. Two of the authors here, Bailey and Faupel, were not considered "safe" outsiders for the first few years. ACE members were cautious because they had encountered negative experiences with other academics. A geologist who had approached them for information was later discovered to be associated with the Institute for Chemical Waste Management at the University of Alabama, an institute established through a grant from Chemical Waste Management. Other suspicions of phone tapping prevented ACE members from openly extending their network to unknown individuals inside and outside their community.

Meanwhile, individual members of ACE were recognized as able grassroots activists by government officials. In 1988, one member received the Alabama Volunteer of the Year award from the Governor of Alabama. Weeks later, she was one of a dozen persons from across the country honored by President Reagan for volunteer work. These awards brought her nationwide recognition and she became a featured speaker at conferences across the nation, including the widely publicized Southern Environmental Assembly of 1988 held in Atlanta, Georgia. She also served on the board of the National Toxics Campaign (NTC) based in Boston, Massachusetts from 1988 through 1992. During part of this period, she served as chair of the Board. Another ACE member and former president of the group was hired by the National Toxics Campaign to organize local communities in the southeastern region.

This state and national recognition, bestowed amidst local antagonism and apathy, was quite unexpected. One former president of ACE remarked that, prior to her involvement in the organization, she had never been involved in community issues. In her words, she was "nothing but a housewife and a Baptist Sunday School teacher." She had not envisioned that her role in ACE would lead to leadership responsibilities in other organizations such as the National Toxics Campaign.

The Dissolution of ACE

The national prominence of ACE and its key leaders ultimately sowed the seeds of the group's demise. By the early 1990s, less than 10 years after its formation, the organization dissolved. One couple centrally involved in the activities of the organization had marital difficulties; the partners separated and both moved away. Another couple exhausted by the frenetic pace of activities, chose to concentrate on raising their children. The two members mentioned earlier became involved with the National Toxics Campaign. One was hired as regional activist for the NTC while the other became a member of the Board. The key Black leader in Sumter County who joined with ACE in the struggle against Chemical Waste Management also became a NTC Board member before moving out of the state for other employment. In retrospect, one local leader acknowledged in 1993 that her move to the National Toxics Campaign "destroyed ACE." By the late 1980s, she had realized that the goal of closing the Chemical Waste Management facility was beyond their reach. However, she found that "sharing information" with others was a way to take what they had learned beyond Sumter County to other communities facing similar risks. When moving to a position as coordinator of grassroots environmental struggles on a national scale, this former ACE president felt some relief from threats by her own community members. An element of security was gained by the national media exposure they had received. No one could hurt them without a larger media-oriented public knowing about it.

Their association with the National Toxics Campaign led to the dissolution of ACE in part because their energies were turned towards national agendas. However, the final blow to the national support given to ACE came when the NTC Board made a decision to redirect organizational resources because of an internal financial crisis. One of the decisions taken by the Board, upon which sat an ACE member, was to terminate the position of the other ACE member, who had been working as community organizer for the NTC in Sumter County. The result was a deep division between two core ACE members, a division which has led them into separate career directions.

In 1992, these two core members turned their energies to refocus on home. One former ACE member assumed the position of Chair of the Water Authority of Sumter County, to bring her analysis of the impact of the waste industry to bear on the county's water supply. During the 1980s, a well had been drilled two miles north of the Emelle landfill to supply residents in the northern portion of Sumter County who were then served by a well in neighboring Pickens County. When the Pickens County well had to be shut down during 1993 for a three week period due to technical difficulties, the Sumter County Water Board had to decide whether or not to open up the Sumter County well near Emelle. Led by the former ACE member, then serving as Chair, the Water Authority held public meetings to discuss options. Based on public opposition to utilizing the new well, the Board voted not to make the connection, leaving several communities without water for a three week period. The Alabama Department of Environmental Management issued strong objections to this action, and began attempts to remove the Chair from the Board.

The other former ACE member, claiming she has gone "mainstream," returned to the homefront from nationwide networking to join the Board of the Historical Society in Sumter County. Looking towards generating new job opportunities for residents, she is writing grants for the Historical Society to develop projects in tourism to bring together White and Black members of the region in a display of southern culture. She continues to receive invitations from universities, churches, and conferences to speak on hazardous waste and community organizing issues as a representative of an organization she started in 1991—Southern Women Against Toxics. Without a funding base, she has created a loose network of activists from around the country who correspond on related issues.

Formerly ostracized by the residents of their communities, both women now claim that those who once called them enemies wave from their cars as they drive through town. They are invited to more teas and luncheons than they were in the 1980s. And particularly since Chemical Waste Management reduced its workforce from over 400 to approximately 250 due to a decline in the volume of waste handled at the facility, they have overheard more people speaking critically about the landfill. Today four of the former core members point out that some residents now thank them for their probing work. But in public discourse, residents continue to avoid criticism of Chemical Waste Management. Former ACE members argue today that most residents accept the waste industry as an important employer for the county.

Conclusion

The literature on environmentalism as a social movement suggests that a "movement" has developed along a predictable path towards institutionalization. This concept of movement has, in a rather presumptive manner, forced together processes which ought to be taken as distinctive historical transformations in various forms of collective action. The institutionalization of environmental groups such as the "Group of Ten" has alienated some grassroots organizers at the community level; yet translocal networks continue to be important vehicles for the expression of local voices in waste politics and for the mobilization of needed resources. An examination of ACE's agenda and activities in the context of the political economy of Sumter County conveys how an environmental group cultivated a marginal position in waste politics at the local level while forming alliances with national organizations. While sharing a commitment to their place of residence with others in their communities, ACE members acquired the status of "enigma." Discredited locally as "pesky flies" and "1960s escapees," these group members endured threats to their lives, homes, and family members. As marginals, ACE members challenged local power but did so with the ambiguous authority of being insiders yet "with" outsiders. Through the instability of shifting public denunciation and curiosity, they attempted to maintain their position as residents with a right to know about the implications and consequences of the local waste operation.

From this position of marginality, ACE members formed alliances with national grassroots network groups and media agencies to take their critical voice to the translocal level. Media attention gave Emelle a position in national environmental politics and ACE members used this sporadic coverage to denounce the reputation of Chemical Waste Management and publicize public health risks. From this, they developed a quiet local audience, a more active role in translocal networks of grassroots activism and the experience to move their knowledge in new directions beyond the homefront. As their careers developed, support from the National Toxics Campaign provided two ACE members the financial and organizational resources to move beyond the contingencies of local industry. But involvement in this organization drew their focus away from local activities and towards the national arena. The crisis within the National Toxics Campaign that led to the firing of one ACE member by the Board upon which sat another ACE member, was the final blow to ACE as a viable local organization.

The historical transformation of ACE as an organizational entity demonstrates that relationships between grassroots groups and national organizations do not push towards an increasingly inclusive and institutionalized "movement." Nor do strategies for resource mobilization focus exclusively on strengthening the group. In this case, a national networking group took the steam out of a local group by drafting one of its key leaders. Thus, the participation of group members in translocal networks had negative ramifications for ACE, demonstrated by the eventual dissolution of the group.

References Cited

Benn, Alvin, 1987. *Sumter County Protest Brings Out '60s Escapees. Montgomery Advertiser,* November 11, 1987.

Bethell, T.N. 1982 Sumter County Blues: The Ordeal of the Federation of Southern Cooperatives (Report to the National Committee in support of Community Based Organizations). Washington, DC: Center for Community Change.

Borrelli, Peter, 1987. Environmentalism at a crossroads. *The Amicus Journal* 9(3):24–37.

Center for Demographic and Cultural Research, 1991. *Alabama Population Data Sheet.* Montgomery: Auburn University.

Environmental Protection Agency (EPA), 1974. *Report to Congress: Disposal of Hazardous Wastes.* Office of Solid Waste Management Programs Publication No. SW-115. Washington, DC: U.S. Government Printing Office.

Greene, Johnny, The Poisoning. *Southern Magazine,* February, 1988. Pp. 26–29, 59–65.

Hofrichter, Richard, ed., 1993. *Toxic Struggles: The Theory and Practice of Environmental Justice.* Philadelphia: New Society Publishers.

LABS

Internet Exercise

Distribution of Environmental Hazards

Introduction

The distribution of environmental risks across the globe doesn't occur in a random manner. Rather, this distribution is unequal. The concentration of environmental hazards is highest for poor locations, for poor people in rich places, and also tends to disproportionately affect racial and ethnic minorities in the United States. In the United States, for example, the majority of the poor tend to live in cities and also tend to be black. It is in the cities, and specifically in poor black neighborhoods, where factories are located that release pollutants, where smog collects, and where the sitings of garbage dumps occur. The disproportionate impact of environmental hazards faced by racial and ethnic minorities is called environmental racism. Environmental racism can take many forms, from governmental policies and lack of enforcement, to living conditions that are typified by the pollution of noise, air, and water.

People in the lower social class often cannot afford an automobile or house. Rather, they tend to take public transportation and live in apartment buildings or smaller dwellings that take up considerably less land. People in the upper class typically commute to work and travel by automobile (families often have more than one) and have large houses that take up considerably more land and use more energy to heat, cool, and power. However, the people who are producing less waste and creating fewer environmental hazards are forced to deal with the waste of others on a daily basis and tend to develop more health problems as a result. Additionally, housing available around factories is typically low cost and therefore attractive to low-income families. Low-income rather than affluent neighborhoods are often the sites for new landfills, toxic waste sites, and other undesirable environmental hazards. In fact, in 1987, the United Church of Christ Commission for Racial Justice publication, *Toxic Wastes and Race* found that race was the number one predictor of the siting of toxic waste sites.

There is also an unequal distribution of environmental problems across the globe. Countries that produce the highest amounts of pollutants and deplete natural resources the quickest tend to distribute environmental risks elsewhere. Global warming is caused by industrialization and technological advances and is chiefly produced by rich, developed nations. However, the effects of global warming are experienced in poor countries that don't necessarily have the means to protect themselves from harm. El Niño, the cyclical ocean-atmosphere system, is caused by global warming and affects the entire world, creating massive amounts of rain in some areas and droughts in others. For less developed countries, the droughts can be extremely devastating as famine can result. Also, forest fires are more likely and can destroy settlements.

Idea in Use

There is little argument that a relationship exists between poverty and poor environmental conditions. However, speculation about the direction of the relationship exists. David Satterthwaite elaborates on the relationship by focusing on environmental degradation and the urban poor in Africa, Asia and Latin America. In a 2003 article published in the *Annals of the American Academy of Political and Social Science*, Satterthwaite finds no evidence of urban poverty causing environmental degradation.

Rather, he finds that the consumption patterns of the middle and upper classes contribute to the increasing environmental hazards faced by the urban poor. For instance, people with economic means use more and waste more nonrenewable resources (e.g., consumption of fossil fuels through use of automobiles) and use a higher amount of renewable but finite resources (e.g., occupying more space/land). However, Satterthwaite does find that environmental hazards are significant predictors of urban poverty. He concludes the article with suggestions for governmental and international agency interventions that can benefit both the urban poor and the environment.

Activity Instructions

In this exercise, you will use the internet to determine what kind of environmental risks your local community faces. Then you will move to examining how environmental hazards are distributed across the globe and the impact of such risks for the population.

1. Go to the Environmental Protection Agency's homepage at www.epa.gov and follow the link to the "Where You Live" section. Then click on "Search Your Community." You will be using the EnviroMapper. Input your zip code and hit submit. A map of your location should appear with several options. Make sure that the square options on the left-side menu are selected (from water dischargers to multi-activities). You may have to click to redraw map to see new results. Use this map to answer the following questions. You can also use the identify option to get detailed information about what business/school/etc. is contributing to this pollution.

   - What are the problems that the EPA has indicated are trouble spots in your zip code?
   - Which pollutant/condition is the most abundant?
   - Are there certain locations of the map that have a higher concentration of environmental problems? Why do you think that this is?

2. At the same site, click on the "Zoom by Geography" option underneath the map. Select your state and make sure the radio button of county is selected and then click on "Zoom to Chosen Geography." You will be sent to a page where you should select your county. Then follow the directions in question 1 and redraw the map. Now answer the above questions using the county data. Are you in a relatively "safe" zip code compared to the rest of your county?

3. Another site that has similar data but also provides information about unequal environmental hazard burdens is the Pollution Information Site called Scorecard, which can be found at www.scorecard.org. From the main page, select "Community Center" under Environmental Justice. Then select the hyperlink entitled "Locator for Unequal Burdens." Complete the following tasks two times for your state: once for race/ethnicity group and then for families below poverty.

   - There are four options to choose from (and you can select multiple burdens at once). Complete the exercise for each burden independently. Then repeat selecting all environmental burdens.
   - Report the number of counties affected by each burden and how it is unequally distributed across the groups.
   - Indicate if the county that you live in is listed in any of the disproportionately distributed hazards.
   - Create a table indicating your findings—the table should contain information about each group and environmental burden, the count and percentage of the state's counties affected (you will need to find how many counties

are in your state to calculate percent), and place a star next to the count to indicate when your home county is affected.

4. NOVA has produced interactive maps that show global distributions of factors relating to the environment. Go to the World in the Balance site at www.pbs.org/wgbh/nova/worldbalance/ and click on the "Earth in Peril" section under the interactive heading. You will then have to click the "Launch Interactive" hyperlink. Look at each map and compare the continents (you can omit Antarctica). Then head back to the original webpage and select the Global Trends Quiz. Take the Environmental Challenge. Write a 1–2 page (typed, double-spaced) report about how the continents differed and also report on how you did on the quiz and what kind of comparisons can be made across countries/continents.

5. Finally, go to the World Health Organization's webpage devoted to the Protection of the Human Environment at http://www.who.int/phe/. Click on the "PHE Health Topics" from the left menu and then select "Children's Environmental Health." Browse the webpage and associated pages to answer the following questions.

   - What percentage of the global burden of disease attributed to environmental risk factors do children under five experience?
   - How many children under the age of five die each year because of an environmentally related disease?
   - How much of malaria is caused by environmental problems and how many children died of malaria in 1998?
   - What factors does the website identify as making children particularly vulnerable to environmental hazards?

6. Turn in your exercise to your instructor as directed.

Individual Writing Exercise

Environmental Toxins

Introduction

There are various kinds of pollutants and toxins that contribute to environmental degradation and risk to health. While the technical, chemical and physical effects of these pollutants and toxins on the environment are not of central concern for sociologists, the effects and relationships among the individual, society, and the environment have grown increasingly important. A consumer culture that focuses on individual desires, efficiency, and convenience creates a lot of waste. This waste is not just in the form of material objects such as Styrofoam containers and disposable cameras, but extend to the consumption and/or contamination of nonrenewable natural resources, such as air and water.

In 2000, the United States produced 232 million tons of municipal solid waste (MSW), otherwise known as household trash. According to the Environmental Protection Agency's (EPA) website, in the year 2000, 69.9 million tons of waste were diverted from landfills and combustion because of recycling programs. While recycling and reusing programs have gained much public support, the trend of Americans has been to produce more MSW over time. Waste that is not recycled is disposed of either through combustion or landfilling. Combustion or incineration is used for about 14.5 percent of all waste and contributes to air pollution. Landfills treat about 55.3 percent of the trash in the United States but also have consequences such as polluted ground waters, that make neighboring land undesirable to live on, and a legacy of un-decomposed trash for future generations.

Water is limited in quantity and can be easily polluted. Numerous infectious diseases, such as cholera and dysentery, are caused by contaminated water. While the United States has relatively good water, contamination of water supplies varies greatly by location. In the United States, water is generally polluted through toxic waste and runoff of toxins from the land to the water (e.g., pesticides). Another source of water pollution is acid rain, which is harmful to plants and animals.

Air pollution is caused by many different factors. In developed countries, the level of industry, smokestacks, and exhaust from automobiles contributes the most to polluting the air, although environmental standards have now been instituted that has helped to eliminate these sources. In less developed countries, the burning of coal and wood for cooking and warmth create poor air quality.

There are many other environmental conditions in which social scientists are interested. Global warming, the declining biodiversity, and endangered species, as well as deforestation also have implications for human life.

Idea in Use

The federal government produces waste as well, including the potentially most harmful. Each year, 2,000 tons of nuclear reactor waste are produced and stored in steel casks inside concrete bunkers across the country. In 2002, the government approved Nevada's Yucca Mountain to be the centralized storing location for spent nuclear fuel and high-level radioactive waste. This decision was met with aggressive condemnation from environmentalists and Nevada state residents. Critics of the Yucca Mountain Project point to dangerous cross country transport of the nuclear waste through 43 states to Nevada, a centralized location that would be attractive to terrorists. They argue that accidents on the road and at the Mountain would have severe implications for the U.S. population. Moreover, they suggest that a lack of scientific data on storing radioactive nuclear waste should be a basis for re-evaluating plans and blocking the Yucca Mountain Project. The government is currently preparing the license to start building the storage center and expects to have the project up and running by 2010. It will then receive and store 77,000 metric tons of nuclear waste for 100 years. The container is expected to be 1,000 feet underground, about 90–100 miles northwest of Las Vegas. For more information about the project and the criticisms see the Yucca Mountain project site at www.ymp.gov and the Sierra Club at www.sierraclub.org/nuclearwaste/.

Activity Instructions

In this independent exercise, you will complete several tasks to determine how much you recognize and contribute to environmental problems.

1. For the next three days, keep a running log that records the following information:

   - The amount and type of garbage you throw out (food, plastic, paper, etc.) and the amount and type of your recyclables
   - How long you travel by any type of motorized vehicle—record also if you carpooled, took the bus, or otherwise considered air pollution
   - The amount of water you use—showers, brushing teeth, cooking, etc. (If it is too difficult to estimate the number of gallons, just keep track of the amount of time the faucet is turned on.)

2. Write 1–2 paragraphs about your consumption activities and your individual contribution to environmental problems. Do you think that your contribution plays a role in problems such as acid rain or smog?

3. Now think of a group that you belong to (e.g., this class, your dorm, etc.). Indicate what the group is, how many people make up the group, and then calculate the estimated amounts of pollutants that the entire group contributes weekly, monthly, and yearly, using your estimates as the average.

4. Turn in your assignment to your instructor as directed.

Group Exercise

Sustainable Development and Environment

Introduction

Sustainability is a term often applied to both development and environment. Sustainable development refers to ways in which society can continue to prosper, allowing population growth and industrialization in developed and less developed areas, without threatening the environment. Likewise, a sustainable environment refers to one in which the protection of the environment does not interfere with the continued development of society. While the ideas seem impossible to reconcile, policy makers and many others have identified routes to sustainability. The key to the sustainability, some experts indicate, is achieving an ecocentric perspective rather than an egocentric outlook. This means looking past our own time and space and recognizing that there is a large world of varying levels of development and that our actions are tied not only to the present, but influence the future as well.

One strategy for sustainability is conservation. Conservation requires the protection and preservation of our natural resources, energy, and the components of our ecosystem. This certainly requires a modification of our consumption practices. For instance, rather than each individual driving to work or school, a sustainability plan would suggest the use of public transit or carpooling. This not only reduces pollution, but also conserves gasoline. Conservation requires the responsible use of our precious materials, but also going without or living with less, thus reducing our waste.

The Environmental Protection Agency (EPA) has created a sustainability program called Smart Growth. The Smart Growth program is governed by ten principles. Such principles include the creation and utilization of mixed land uses, the strengthening and direct development of existing communities, and the creation of walkable communities. Similarly, the United Nations has a branch that deals with sustainability and has a more global perspective. The United Nations works with less developed countries in accommodating growth and development, with minimal environmental damage.

Population growth and sustainability are certainly linked issues. Unrestrained population growth taxes the environment. If the population is left uncontrolled, some project that natural resources will be depleted, the amount of land used for the cultivation of food will decrease and create food shortages for a growing population, and pollution will increase. The solution to rectifying population growth and the protection of the environment is very complex and riddled with moral questions.

Idea in Use

There are numerous initiatives that are proposed and undertaken in promoting sustainability. One tactic is the utilization of community gardens. John Ferris, Carol

Norman and Joe Sempik use a case study approach in their article "People, Land and Sustainability: Community Gardens and the Social Dimension of Sustainable Development." The purpose of the research was to investigate how community gardens work in the United States and evaluate the feasibility of implementing such a program in the United Kingdom. They identified many types of community gardens and created a typology based on the community gardens developed in the San Francisco Bay Area. Eight categories were identified and elaborated on, including leisure gardens, crime diversion gardens, and demonstration gardens. The authors suggest that community gardens not only help the environment, but also provide a community identity, and are a positive response to the degradation of lower income neighborhoods' social and living conditions. The authors conclude in this 2001 *Social Policy and Administration* article that community gardens would be a beneficial policy for United Kingdom communities.

Activity Instructions

This group exercise will evaluate to what extent you and your peers accept and embrace sustainable environment principles.

1. How many people in your group agree to the following:

   - Would be willing to go without air conditioning
   - Take the bus or carpool with others everyday
   - Create a compost pile of your garbage to use as fertilizer
   - Participate in community gardens and grow your own vegetables
   - Copy and print on both sides of the paper
   - Use less toxic, soy based inks for printers
   - Agree to pay an additional $25–50 fee each year in tuition so that your campus can implement more environmentally friendly policies
   - Support an initiative to tax items that are not environmentally friendly
   - Install a low-flow shower head
   - Support mandatory recycling (with fees applied to non-compliance)
   - Pay $5 a gallon in gasoline rather than drill oil in the Artic Refuge in Alaska
   - Accept a global mandate that restricts the number of children one can have to three
   - Pay more for more responsible energy (hydroenergy, solar powered electricity, hybrid cars)
   - Boycott your favorite restaurant/store because they over-package their products
   - Cap the amount of water a household can use depending on household size

2. Suppose your community has a legacy of unemployment and poverty but is situated in a pristine environment, with parks, fresh water, and clean air. Imagine that a corporation proposes a large manufacturing facility for your community. This corporation has a spotty environmental history with large smokestacks and the production of hazardous waste such as mercury. This plant would alleviate both the unemployment and poverty but at the same time would create environmental challenges. The only place for the large plant to be sited is the main community park, thus displacing animals and disturbing the ecosystem. Your community is desperate for development opportunities and needs to weigh the cost of the possible environmental risks. What would your group propose to do?

3. Turn in your group answers to your instructor as directed.

18

Social Change and Collective Behavior

How Will the Internet Change Society?
Conrad L. Kanagy and Donald B. Kraybill

Labs
Internet Exercise: Social Movements
Individual Writing Exercise: Collective Behavior
Group Exercise: Social Change

How Will the Internet Change Society?

The first Internet exchanges occurred in November 1969 under the authority of the U.S. Department of Defense. The Internet was born as ARPANET, a worldwide network of computers linking a few university scientists, military personnel, and computer experts. ARPANET's purpose was to enhance U.S. military prowess in the Cold War against communism. Initial communication was formal and official, some users worried that personal e-mail messages might violate U.S. postal laws. But by the mid-1980s, ARPANET was linked to other networks. The change created near chaos, a "full-scale Mardi Gras parade." By 1990 ARPANET had been shut down, and private companies were overseeing activity in cyberspace.[1]

To many college students today, the Internet is a taken-for-granted part of the objective social world, just like cable TV and Nintendo. They've grown up in a digital world. They've internalized expectations for high-speed communication on the Internet. They watch less television than their parents did, finding its old-fashioned pace too slow. They want technology they can interact with and control. The world has shrunk for these students; it lies at their fingertips.

Clearly, use of the Internet is changing our world. In fact, its effects might parallel the transformations brought about by the invention of the printing press. Both technologies expand exponentially the access of ordinary persons to information once held by experts and elites. Sociologists are beginning to develop a sociology of the Internet to study these social changes, and this subfield is likely to grow rapidly in the next several years.

Culture and the Internet

We already know a few things about the beliefs, norms, and values of Internet culture. For instance, social scientists have been debating for some time the reality of Internet communities, or virtual communities.[*2] Some have argued that such communities are little more than social networks, because they lack the typical characteristics of communities—things like residential proximity and economic dependence. However, digital technology has been pressing us to renovate some standard definitions, and the concept of community may be one of them. . . .

In the age of television, many bemoaned the loss of written text as a form of communication. Interestingly, text-based communication has returned on the Internet. The need for writing, reading, and critical expression are as great as, or greater than, ever. But electronic text is extemporaneous, transitory, and soon trashed, unlike the enduring works of Shakespeare and other classic writers.

A problem with text-based communication is the difficulty of expressing emotions and feelings. To counter this difficulty, many Internet users resort to "smileys," combinations of characters that symbolize emotional responses. (Examples . . . are presented in Figure 18.1.) Besides smileys, people communicating on the Internet are using some new forms of abbreviation and spelling, such as *jc* for "just curious," *bmf* for "biting my fingernails," *brb* for "be right back," *imho* for "in my humble opinion," and *lol* for "laughing out loud."

Internet norms, sometimes referred to as netiquette, are in the process of being defined.[3] Because of the rapid growth and fluidity of the Internet, ambiguity abounds about how people should behave in cyberspace. However, threats of censorship have hastened the development of some norms. Internet users are particularly concerned that outrageous behavior by some will prompt government agencies to censor the Internet. Certain legal norms probably will be defined eventually. In addition, subcultural groups will undoubtedly develop their own particular norms, just as subcultures do in the real world.

What are the values of Internet users that will shape these norms? Don Tapscott, in *Growing Up Digital*, identifies several themes that are important to this subculture.

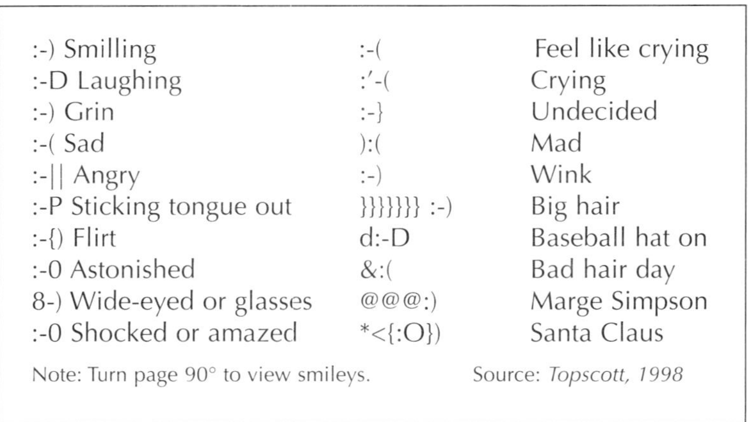

:-) Smilling	:-(	Feel like crying
:-D Laughing	:'-(	Crying
:-) Grin	:-}	Undecided
:-(Sad	):(	Mad
:-|| Angry	:-)	Wink
:-P Sticking tongue out	}}}}}}} :-)	Big hair
:-{) Flirt	d:-D	Baseball hat on
:-0 Astonished	&:(	Bad hair day
8-) Wide-eyed or glasses	@@@:)	Marge Simpson
:-0 Shocked or amazed	*<{:O})	Santa Claus

Note: Turn page 90° to view smileys.   Source: *Topscott, 1998*

Figure 18.1   Some "smileys" used in cyberspace to express feelings

*Eds. Note—Virtual communities are networks of relationships in which people identify with one another and share feelings for one another but don't share their physical selves or physical space. They share cyberselves and cyberspace.

For example, independence, free expression, and inclusion, which are core American values as well. These values are undoubtedly reinforced for Internet users by the freedom and diversity of Internet communication. Other cyberspace values, however, have been socially constructed and reinforced through electronic interaction.

- Openness characterizes Internet communication.
- Innovation created the Internet and continues to shape it.
- An investigative spirit is encouraged by the vast scope of the Internet wilderness.
- Immediacy is driven by the speed of Internet processing.
- Internet users, particularly the younger ones, are skeptical of corporate interests and the greed driving some efforts to shape Internet technology.
- Authenticity and trust are expected in the open environment of the Internet, where the cooperation of the parts (individuals) is needed to preserve the whole.[4]

Although several of these cyberculture values intersect with more traditional American values, others are relatively new and are likely to influence the cultural values of the larger society in years to come.

Social Structure and the Internet

The changes brought about by the Internet will accelerate as the number of youth who have been socialized into cyberculture grows. Some refer to this generation as the "net generation." These are the children of the baby boomers, the cohort born between 1945 and 1964, who now represent 29 percent of the U.S. population. The net generation, or "N-geners," born since 1977, comprise 30 percent of the U.S. population. The baby boomers represent the television generation, their children the digital generation. In their youth, many baby boomers sat staring at programs like "M*A*S*H," "The Brady Bunch," and "The Jeffersons." But N-geners controlled a host of interactive devices, such as Nintendo games and computers. For people who grew up with these technologies, their operation is second nature. The Internet will develop and become more influential as the people who grew up with it become a larger part of the population.

Two cohorts—baby boomers and N-geners—have unique intergenerational problems. In place of a generation gap, where the growing-up experiences of children and parents are simply different, we may have a "generation lap," as children outpace their parents in the race for technological knowledge. Young children often know much more than their parents about the computer. In one study by researchers at Carnegie Mellon University, children were the heaviest computer users in a large majority of families. Two-thirds of children in another survey said they are more proficient on the computer than their parents. In Finland, 5,000 N-geners teach computing to the country's teachers.[5] The "generation lap" turns typical patterns of socialization upside down: The parents, who typically teach their children, are now learning from them. As a result, children and youth have become the gatekeepers of technology and information for their families, teachers, and supervisors. This generational shift means that some entry-level employees will have greater skills and knowledge in some areas than their supervisors, managers, and administrators.

The new generation gap has four themes:

- Older people are anxious about the new technology being embraced by youth.
- Older people are uneasy about the new media, such as the Internet, which are part of everyday life among youth.
- Older media (newspapers, radio, television) are apprehensive about the newer media.
- The digital revolution, unlike previous revolutions, is not completely controlled by adults.[6]

Reconciliation between baby boomers and N-geners may lie in the willingness of N-geners to share their knowledge and the humility of baby boomers to receive it.

The digital revolution may create other structural fault lines as well. Some fear that computer technology will exacerbate the existing divide between rich and poor. In fact, only 7 percent of low-income households have a computer, while among those making more than $50,000 a year, 53 percent have a computer. Thus economic poverty leads to information poverty, which leads to even greater economic poverty. In addition, racial discrimination in society leads to racial discrimination in media and technology access.[7] Blacks are two-thirds less likely to have a computer than whites, and two-thirds of white students have used the Web as opposed to fewer than half of black students.[8] On the brighter side, the Internet has the potential to equalize without regard to race, sex, or economics. Students in poor, inner-city schools could have access equal to those in wealthy, suburban schools. The challenge for the government and for educators is to ensure such equality. Whether in the final analysis the Internet will increase or diminish social inequality remains to be seen.

Structural differences in technology use also occur in the global arena....Developed and developing countries differ substantially in their resources. Information technology will probably heighten those differences. In 1996, 66 percent of households connected to the Internet were in North America. Even developed countries in Western Europe fall behind the United States in Internet access and use. At the same time, the Internet has the potential to democratize political systems around the world, by giving everyone equal access to information, regardless of cultural or political boundaries. The Internet makes possible the development of a truly global culture, where children in Hong Kong can learn the same information as children in Papua New Guinea. They can also learn about each other.

Ritual and the Internet

Although some social divisions are sharpened by digital technology, the Internet levels the playing field for individuals communicating through e-mail, chat rooms, bulletin boards, and discussion lists. The only symbols of communication are written words; facial expressions, voice intonations, hand gestures, and physical appearance are gone. The context of each individual's social world—family life, occupation, income, residence—is minimized. Such decontextualization[*] is quite different from the high context of face-to-face interaction, where we can see the person. The decontextualized nature of Internet culture is the opposite of, say, Amish life, which is a high-context culture that values face-to-face interaction and knowledge of everyone in the community. In a high context culture, social actors know many background details of each other—home, habits, lifestyle, friends, and work. Conversation is embedded in this rich social context.

On the Internet, everyone is alike. The decontextualized space of the Internet brings a new openness in communication and weakens the features that often lead to discrimination and prejudice. People with disabilities, who usually face discrimination can interact without the scorn of prejudice. Age, beauty, size, body odor, color of hair and eyes, and facial hair lose their power. Labels, stereotypes, and stigmas disappear.

In Goffman's terms, on the Internet the frontstage is the same for everyone, without the typical props, signals, sounds, and appearances of social life. Individuals can create any frontstage that they wish. It may not be real, but who will ever know? Said one 14-year-old: "I'd have to say I'm very shy unless I know a person very well.

---

[*]Decontextualization is the loss of identifiable social landmarks in human interaction. In a decontextualized social world like the Internet, we don't have the contextual knowledge—the other person's facial expressions and gestures, a physical setting such as a home or office, and the other person's friends or family—that we usually use to interpret our interaction.

This doesn't happen though in cyberspace. On the Net, I am one of the most outgoing people I know. Probably why I spend so much time there."[9]

In general, we all have greater control over disclosure and our presentation of self on the Internet than in other social contexts. If we dislike someone, we can break off the communication without serious consequences, especially if we have kept our identity disguised. We'll likely never see the other person, and if we do, we won't recognize each other.

Relationships on the Internet are often disposable, fragile, and superficial. At the same time, however, they can be deeply intimate and personal, because so much contextual baggage is left behind. Some of the values of N-geners arise from these characteristics of ritual interaction on the internet.[10]

Decontextualized interaction on the Internet poses some interesting dilemmas, which some voice as concerns:

- Individuals can enter chat rooms or post messages on bulletin boards using multiple identities. Some deliberately create artificial identities to deceive unsuspecting individuals. On-line romances have occasionally resulted in fraud or homicide. Children can be manipulated and harmed by menacing adults.[11]
- Another danger is Internet addiction, sometimes called "netomania" or "onlineaholism." Some view this condition as a symptom of a psychiatric disorder; others see it as a disorder in its own right.[12] One analyst, Kimberly Young, has written a self-help guide called *Caught in the Net* to aid those who abandon family, friends, and work to be on-line. She believes up to 5 million Internet users may be addicted.[13] Examples of those with symptoms of Internet addiction include a 31-year-old man who spent more than 100 hours a week on-line, ignoring others and stopping only for sleep. In another case, a 21-year-old college student disappeared, only to be found in the computer lab hooked on seven consecutive days of on-line chat. Some individuals with Internet addiction have reported an average of five psychiatric disorders, including manic-depressive disorder, social phobia, bulimia or binge eating, impulse-control problems, and substance abuse.[14]
- Some experts fear that N-geners are losing their social skills. Others are concerned about the short attention span that N-geners may develop through overexposure to interactive communication. Some fear the Internet is stressing children and spreading them too thin. Others worry about the cruelty that children may experience on the Internet. Some argue that the opportunity to create one's own homepage leads to vanity—an artificially heightened self-esteem.[15]

All these issues raise a host of ethical questions for an Internet society. How much freedom should Internet users have? How much control should the government and other social institutions exert? Is it ethical to change one's identity on-line? When is on-line deception potentially harmful to individuals and society? Is Internet addiction harmful? Should we have Internet police to regulate activity in chat rooms and discussion groups? Should individuals be held accountable for everything they write on the Internet? How much further will the Internet renovate social relations?

Summary: Internet

Because the development of the Internet is relatively new, we can't really consider its renovation yet. But the recent development of the Internet provides a fascinating opportunity to watch a culture being constructed from scratch.

The construction of the Internet reflects to some extent the cultural norms and structural division of the larger society. The Internet has the potential, however, to make the same information available to everyone, regardless of race, class, education, occupation, or residence.

The rituals of interaction on the Internet are still being shaped. It is a decontextualized environment where we can minimize everyday prejudices by carefully controlling the presentation of self. We can remain relatively anonymous while still being intimate. We can create relationships with few obligations but with high levels of authenticity.

It remains to be seen whether the Internet will remain a communication medium of the middle and upper classes or whether, like television, it will override class lines and serve the masses.

Endnotes

1. Diamond, E., & Bates, S. (1995). The ancient history of the Internet, *American Heritage, 46*, 34–41.
2. Reingold, H. (1993). *Virtual communities: Homesteading on the electronic frontier.* New York: Harper Perennial, p. 5.
3. For an on-line description of netiquette, see <http://rs6000.adm.fau.edu/rinaldi/netiquette.html>. Another valuable resource, titled "A Primer on How to Work with the Usenet Community," is available through the news group news.announce.newusers, with the archive name usernet/primer/part1.
4. A substantial part of our discussion of the Internet is based on Tapscott, D. (1998). *Growing up digital.* New York: McGraw-Hill.
5. Tapscott, D. (1998). *Growing up digital.* New York: McGraw-Hill.
6. Ibid.
7. Ibid.
8. World White Web. (1998, April 27). *Time.*
9. Tapscott, D. (1998). *Growing up digital.* New York: McGraw-Hill.
10. Ibid.
11. Ibid.
12. Ibid.
13. Kiernan, V. (1998, May 29) Some scholars question research methods of expert on Internet addiction. *The Chronicle of Higher Education.*
14. Ritter, M. (1998, June 2). *Associated Press.*
15. Tapscott, D. (1998). *Growing up digital.* New York: McGraw-Hill.

References

Diamond, E., & Bates, S. (1995). *American Heritage, 4*, 34–41.
Reingold, H. *Virtual communities: Homesteading on the electronic frontier.* New York: Harper Perennial.
Tapscott, D. (1998). *Growing up digital: The rise of the net generation.* New York: McGraw-Hill.

LABS

Internet Exercise

Social Movements

Introduction

Social movements are special types of collective behavior that have certain characteristics that warrant their distinction from other forms of collective behavior. First, social movements are not formed in a haphazard, temporary, or spontaneous fashion. Rather, the purpose of a social movement is to exist for a relatively long period of time. Second, social movement participants expect a certain amount of significant and long lasting consequences of their work. They have a centralized goal, and that goal is often one that will dramatically change the society's attitudinal or behavioral climate. Finally, social movements are differentiated from other forms of collective behavior because of their well-organized, hierarchal organizational structure. It can be hard to identify all the actors within a social movement as it can encompass many global and local organizations and networks, as well as independent individuals.

There are various types of social movements that are often classified by who is expected to change (targeted individuals or everyone) and how much change is desired. Social movements can also differ in when they want the change to occur. Some movements demand immediate changes while others are more content with progressive, gradual changes. In addition, social movements can be either progressive or regressive in changing trends. There are five broad types of social movements: reformative, revolutionary, reactionary or resistance, redemptive or religious, and alternative movements. *Reformative social movements* aim for broad social change, but work to change society using strategies carried out within the existing system, and expect gradual change. Environmental, civil rights, and feminist movements are examples of reformative movements. *Revolutionary social movements* seek sweeping and immediate changes and typically work outside of the existing system. These movements may utilize illegal and violent tactics. For instance, the Irish Republican Army (IRA) and their quest for a unionized Ireland often resorted to violence and terrorism. *Reactionary*, often known as *resistance social movements*, seek to maintain or return to conditions that were in effect before social change. Oftentimes, militia groups are reactionary, resistance social movements. Other examples include the Ku Klux Klan and the pro-life movement. *Redemptive* or *religious social movements* target individuals for a significant change. Religious groups such as Hare Krishnas and right-wing Christian movements, as well as movements such as Alcoholics Anonymous are redemptive social movements. Finally, *alternative social movements* focus their change on specific and limited populations and expect slow and gradual changes. They are not especially threatening. For instance, a social movement that aims for better healthy choices in school cafeterias and other public places could be characterized as an alternative social movement.

Social movements are often described as having a life course or career. There are four general stages of social movements: emergence, coalescence, bureaucratization, and decline. The *emergent* phase of a social movement occurs when there is a general frustration or dissatisfaction that is shared in public. In this stage, leaders emerge and recognize that organization is essential. The *coalescence* stage is the primary organizational stage. In this phase, recruitment of members, identification of the primary and secondary goals, and determining the tactics and methods to achieving set goals are objectives. The *bureaucratization* stage occurs next and is characterized by a well-defined hierarchy and is more business-like, rather than confrontational. Finally, the *decline* phase occurs when either resources or interest fades or when they succeed in meeting their goals. Decline does not necessarily mean the disappearance of the social movement, but rather can simply mean a weakening or less vocal social movement.

Idea in Use

Rhoda Howard-Hassmann uses social movements literature to account for differing reparation responses for Japanese Americans and African Americans. In "Getting to Reparations: Japanese Americans and African Americans," Howard-Hassmann suggests that the framing of the claims-making and who is making the claims makes a difference in achieving reparations for past wrongs. The Japanese-American reparations movement was successful because the people directly affected were still alive, the perpetrators were easily identified, and the time period between the internment and reparations movements was relatively short (about 30 years). In addition, the Japanese-American reparations movement was well organized and had the support of several influential political leaders. Finally, the type and amount of reparations awarded to Japanese-Americans that were interned were considered reasonable by most. The African American reparations social movement has failed for several reasons, Howard-Hassmann proposes. First, the African American victims are so numerous, and many have already died, so that accurate identification is difficult. Additionally, there were many perpetrators who are also hard to identify. Also, the amount of time that has elapsed since past harms is too long making reparations claims-making too complex. Finally, the African American reparations social movement has failed to be legitimately and centrally organized and has few influential allies. In this 2004 *Social Forces* article, Howard-Hassmann outlines the differences in the social movements and suggests some methods for successful reparations claims-making.

Activity Instructions

This internet exercise is intended to give you freedom in your analysis of a selected social movement and tests your knowledge about the types and career of the social movement.

1. Chose one social movement to investigate. It can (but does not have to) be from the following list:

Women's	Environmental
Specific racial/ethnic	Gay Rights
Pro-life/pro-choice	Animal Rights
Right to die	Gun Control/Death Penalty/etc.

2. Visit at least two websites that pertain to your selected social movement.

3. What are they and what information do they present?

   - Are there many different organizations within the social movement that work together?
   - Are there any divisions within the social movement (i.e., do certain members favor one way to achieve the goal, while others favor another pathway)?
   - What are the central beliefs and aims of the social movement?

4. From your research above, you should be able to characterize the life-course of the social movement.

   - What stage is the social movement currently in?
   - How do you know this?

5. Turn in your write-up to your instructor as directed.

Individual Writing Exercise

Collective Behavior

Introduction

Collective behavior is a specific kind of behavior exhibited by multiple people at the same time. Collectivities, the assembly of people that make up collective behaviors, are distinct from groups. The main distinction is the amount of and intensity of bonds that unite people. In groups, bonds are important and mutually shared norms and values are typical. Collectivities on the other hand, refer to unions of people that share no defined bonds or values. Collectivities often form spontaneously and temporarily, and lack an organizational structure that is typical in groups. For instance, there are few if any leaders, and there is little or no hierarchal structure, within a collectivity. Collectivities come in two main forms: localized collectivity and dispersed collectivity.

A *localized collectivity* refers to a collectivity that involves face-to-face interaction with the participants in immediate proximity to one another when acting together. There are two chief types of localized collectivities: crowds and panics. A *crowd* forms when a large number of people temporarily gather together and are united by a common focal point. A unique component of crowds is that people can influence each other with their behaviors.

There are five main types of crowds: casual, conventional, expressive, acting, and protest. A *casual crowd* is the simplest form of a crowd and involves a spontaneous gathering around some event. There is very little interaction between people and there are no real norms to abide by. For instance, when people gather to watch a bar fight or an emergency crew taking care of a victim, a casual crowd often forms.

A *conventional crowd* is slightly more complex since the gathering is not spontaneous, but rather a planned event where institutionalized norms are abided. People at concerts, sporting events, and parades are examples of conventional crowds.

When people join together to share a common emotion, they form *expressive crowds*. Mardi Gras participants form a joyous expressive crowd while those who joined together after the passing of Pope John Paul II was characterized as a sad or sorrowful crowd.

The fourth type of crowd is an *acting crowd*. Such a crowd joins spontaneously to express intense emotion. The emotion is almost always one of anger and disgust. Often such crowds become unmanageable and form mobs and riots. A mob is an acting crowd that becomes violent in behavior. A mob is a fleeting situation that attacks a specific objective or target and then retreats. A riot is an acting crowd that acts out on a multitude of targets and is not decisively directed. There is typically a triggering event and then an ongoing response that characterize riots. Riots generally are unpredictable and can last several days. For instance, in the fall of 2005, youth in France joined together in rioting. The triggering event was the death of two boys that were running from the police; these riots were, more generally, a response of frustration due to poverty, unemployment, racial discrimination, and perceived lack of support from the Parisian government.

A final type of crowd is a *protest crowd* that forms to demonstrate disapproval or frustration with administrations, policies, or government. For instance, there are often protest crowds at presidential conventions and during wars.

The second type of localized collectivity is a panic. *Panic* occurs when a collectivity engages in competitive flight behavior, usually out of fear and anxiety, in reaction to real or perceived desperate situations. Often, the behavior within a panic can actually intensify and worsen the situation. *Hysteria* is a related concept and refers to a panic over an imagined or misinterpreted event.

Dispersed collectivities are collectivities that act and respond to a common stimulus or event that does not involve direct, face-to-face interaction. There are three main types of dispersed collectivities: rumor and gossip, fashion and fads, and public opinion.

Rumor refers to unverified information that may or may not be accurate and that is passed along from person to person informally. *Gossip* consists of rumors that relate to the personal and often intimate affairs of people.

Fashion refers to the current in-trend clothing and grooming styles, material preferences, and behaviors adopted by a plurality of people. Fashion is temporary and can be created by inspired marketers and entrepreneurs. *Fads* are even more temporary and are often slightly eccentric.

Public opinion is the response or point of view that a number of people express in relation to an event or issue over time. Public opinion is a general consensus and thus is not strictly unified. In addition, people change their attitudes about a subject over time and thus public opinion is also always changing.

Idea in Use

National newspapers are often used as a reference to construct databases such as collections of accounts of collective behavior events like riots. Daniel Myers and Beth Schaefer Caniglia set out to examine whether two national newspapers, the *New York Times* and the *Washington Post*, accurately and completely reported on civil disorders that occurred in the 1960s or whether there are selection effects in the coverage. In the 2004 *American Sociological Review* article "All the Rioting That's Fit to Print: Selection Effects in National Newspaper Coverage of Civil Disorders: 1968–1989" they compare the stories in the two national newspapers to local and regional newspaper accounts and found major differences. Less than half of the civil disorder events that were recorded by the local and regional newspapers made it into the two national newspapers. Items that made it into the national newspaper were more likely to occur near the city, creating an East Coast bias and were also more likely to be the most intense riots, those with the most participants and with more violence. In addition, the type of riot mattered. Street riots and riots at college campuses were more likely to be included in the newspapers than secondary school events. The authors then determined through multivariate analyses that the selection biases of the major national newspapers can produce markedly skewed results for civil disorders research. They suggest caution when relying on mass media sources since they can produce a "simplified" or "distorted" view of events.

Activity Instructions

This independent exercise will test your ability to differentiate different types of collective behaviors and will utilize fieldwork observations.

1. Select a crowd that you want to investigate and to which you have easy access. The larger the number of participants in the crowd, the better and more active your crowd will likely be. Some possibilities include: a sporting event, parade, protest, rally, musical, or theater performance.

   a. Take field notes that reflect your observations.
   b. Include:

      - Description of the main issue/event
      - How did the crowd demonstrate support for the common interest
      - What type of crowd it is
      - Were there sub-crowds, different responses in different areas, etc.
      - Demographic composition of crowd and sub-crowds
      - Description of the behaviors of the crowd after the main event is over

   c. From your field notes, write a summary of your findings. Make sure you provide specific examples of the crowd's activities. Also, be sure to provide details of the event—where it was held, the date and time, and any other methodologically important details.

2. Gossip, rumors, and urban legends often form the dominant component of entertainment reporting. In the span of a week, take notice of the items presented in shows such as *Inside Edition, Entertainment Tonight, E! News,* and in weekly entertainment magazines such as *US Weekly, People,* and *In Touch.* What are the dominant stories and how can they be categorized (are they gossip, rumors, urban legends, other)? Write a brief report about your findings and indicate whether you think that such "reporting" has consequences for the subjects.

3. Turn in your field notes and reports to your instructor as directed.

Group Exercise

Social Change

Introduction

Social change is a process that occurs in all places at all times and reflects transformations in culture, behaviors, and social institutions. The process can occur at varying paces for different locations and during different time periods. Social change is not always planned and is not necessarily an advancement or benefit. Also, there are varying levels of importance attributed to different social changes. For instance, the movement away from polyester suits and bell-bottoms is less vital to society than improvements in social inequalities.

There are numerous sources of social change, with four causes that are dominantly referenced: culture, demographic shifts, natural environment, and conflict. Invention, discovery, and diffusion are the three pathways that produce cultural social changes. Invention is the creation of a material object, idea, or process. Discovery is the uncovering or a new understanding of existing material and matter. Diffusion is a process that disseminates inventions and discoveries to other societies. Technology is a large component of cultural social change, especially in relation to invention and diffusion.

Another source of social change is demographic change. Population fluctuations such as changes in the size, composition, and distribution can have great effects for society. Suppose a place has a great increase in births and in-migration, while also improving healthcare so that people are living longer. This increase in people produces a demand for increased services, housing, jobs, and schools, which in turn, produce demands on the government and economy. Such a change in the size, composition, and distribution of the population can produce changes in the minority-majority divisions and a more multicultural society.

The natural environment can contribute to social change as well. Some events, such as hurricanes and earthquakes are out of the hands of humans, as we witnessed during the devastating 2005 hurricane season. Such disasters can promote and alter human behaviors, changes in policies, and governmental responses. For instance, Hurricane Katrina has certainly impacted New Orleans and the southeastern coast and has increased attention to disaster management, urban planning, and population displacement. There are some natural environment changes that are produced by humans over a slow period of time. The ozone depletion created by humankind was met with responses in the developed world, such as the United States banning the use of chlorofluorocarbons in aerosol cans and other products.

A final major source of social change is conflict, competition, and war. Karl Marx proposed that class conflict spurred the movement of societies, race/gender conflicts can produce movements that garner rights for underrepresented groups, and war can change the entire identity of a space (e.g., war in former Yugoslavian regions produced the separate countries of Serbia and Montenegro, Slovenia, Croatia, and Bosnia and Herzegovina). These sources of social change are certainly not exhaustive and work in conjunction with one another.

Idea in Use

Social change certainly is not limited to the above sources. Mass media have also been recognized as a potential source of social change. Jennifer Barber and William Axinn examined how mass media can shape individual behavior by changing attitudes and ideas. Their 2004 article "New Ideas and Fertility Limitation: The Role of Mass Media" published in the *Journal of Marriage and Family*, examines the exposure to mass media, ideas and attitudes toward fertility, and related behavioral changes in fertility for over 1,000 Nepalese couples. They found that both premarital and lifetime exposure to mass media are significantly related to higher rates of contraceptive use, and those exposed to the mass media have preferences for smaller families and weaker preferences for sons. Additionally, they found that the lifetime exposure to mass media was more influential than strictly a premarital exposure to mass media in the attitudes and behaviors related to fertility. While they are cautious in their causal modeling and do not preclude that other factors than mass media and attitudinal changes can precipitate behavioral changes, they do suggest that mass media can be a powerful agent of social change.

Activity Instructions

This group exercise will rely on your observations of social changes that have occurred in your lifetime.

1. Beloit College in Wisconsin publishes an annual Mindset List for faculty members to help them distinguish the generational differences of the typical student's life experiences. For instance, the Mindset List for the Class of 2008 has items such as:

   - Photographs have always been processed in an hour or less
   - They have always enjoyed the comfort of pleather
   - They were never tempted by smokeless cigarettes
   - They have always been comfortable with gay characters on television
   - There have always been night games at Wrigley Field
   - They have done most of their search for the right college online

   In your group, come up with your own list (at least ten items) of the current fads, trends, popular technologies, or events that you think have or will have an impact on social life. List the item and what changes that your group thinks it will bring about. For instance, you may want to list "wardrobe malfunction" and the increased censoring of television/radio. The items can be mundane or serious (how 9/11 impacted society, etc.).

2. *Time* magazine produces an annual list of the best inventions that were created each year. In your group, produce your own lists for the best inventions of all time in the following categories:

   - Health
   - On the Go
   - Household
   - Clothing
   - Miscellaneous

   Each category should have multiple entries of influential inventions. Decide within your group what the single, most influential, social changing invention of all time is.

3. Turn in your lists to your instructor as directed.